CW00569653

Gods in the city

Intercultural and interreligious dialogue at local level

Titles in the same series L&R - Local&Regional

Des dieux dans la ville
Le dialogue interculturel et interreligieux au niveau local
ISBN : 978-92-871-6380-6

50 years of local democracy in Europe
ISBN : 978-92-871-6385-1

50 ans de démocratie locale en Europe
ISBN : 978-92-871-6360-8

Gods in the city

Intercultural and interreligious dialogue at local level

Series L&R - Local&Regional

The opinions expressed in this work are the responsibility of the author(s) and do not necessarily reflect the opinions of the Council of Europe.

All rights reserved. No part of this publication may be translated, reproduced or transmitted, in any form or by any means, electronic (CD-Rom, Internet, etc.) or mechanical, including photocopying, recording or any information storage or retrieval system, without prior permission in writing from the Publishing Division, Communication Directorate (F-67075 Strasbourg or publishing@coe.int).

Edited by Council of Europe Publishing

http://book.coe.int

F-67075

ISBN 978-92-871-6384-4

© Council of Europe, December 2007

Printed in France by Ott Imprimeurs, Wasselone

Cover:
© photo credit Cliff Wassmann www.artseek.com -
Parthenon on the Acropolis, Athens (Greece)
Realised by OASE Studio

Preface: Halvdan Skard... 9

Introduction: Jacques Palard 13

Part one: The implications of intercultural
and interreligious dialogue 25

Introduction: Jacques Palard.. 26

Chapter 1: The management of cultural and religious diversity
and the promotion of interfaith and intercultural dialogue
by local authorities, by Jean-Marie Woerling 29

Chapter 2: Local Authorities and Intercultural Dialogue,
by Jean-François Husson and Julie Mahiels 49

Chapter 3: Strategies for strengthening interfaith dialogue,
by Philippe Gaudin 81

Part two: National situations and local strategies 89

Introduction: Jacques Palard.. 90

Chapter 4: Local authorities and interfaith dialogue in Spain,
by Flora Burchianti and Xabier Itçaina....................................... 99

Chapter 5: Local authorities and interfaith dialogue in Germany,
by Nikola Tietze.. 127

Chapter 6: Local authorities and interreligious dialogue
from a United Kingdom perspective - A missed opportunity,
by Anjum Anwar and Chris Chivers 147

Chapter 7: Interfaith developments in the United Kingdom,
by Brian Pearce... 183

Chapter 8: The relationship between national and local authorities
and religious communities in post-communist Russia,
by Agnieszka Moniak-Azzopardi.. 189

Conclusion: The twelve principles of intercultural
and interreligious dialogue for local authorities......................... 221

Preface

Halvdan Skard

President of the Congress of Local and Regional Authorities
of the Council of Europe

Political institutions, whether local, national or international, have the great responsibility of creating conditions for the effective exercise of democracy by closely involving citizens in decisions concerning them and giving them a part to play in the implementation of policy measures. As all political representatives know from their day-to-day experience, one of the main difficulties encountered when fulfilling this role lies in the wide range of, sometimes incompatible, choices and preferences expressed by the individuals and groups involved. Governance accordingly means attempting to manage diversity and complexity, not least the diversity and complexity of people's allegiances and identities. However, the aim is not to curtail diversity but, on the contrary, to wager on its inevitability and its positive aspects. Pluralism is indeed an essential facet of a society's creative capacity, constituting a source of enrichment and a key component of its heritage.

It has nowadays become clear that national and regional identities have a promising future since, in many respects, globalisation merely lends greater strength to them, and doubtless also reinforces their legitimacy and relevance. The same is true at a personal level. The need for self-assertion, to find one's bearings and to know one's identity, counters a trend which seems to be pushing people in the opposite direction, towards a standardisation of tastes and preferences. This need, or quest, for identity is sustained by the strong desire we all experience to give our lives a special, individual meaning, in keeping with our ethical choices and ideals.

When the member states invited the Council of Europe to devise an international instrument as a common framework for a co-ordinated approach to cultural diversity, the organisation asked itself how it could best promote and vitalise the founding principles of such diversity. It concluded that the European level was the most appropriate for an initiative of this kind. The outcome was the Council of Europe Declaration on Cultural Diversity, adopted by the Committee of Ministers in December 2000. The Council of Europe has since outlined its strategy for developing intercultural dialogue, which is set out in the Faro Declaration, adopted in October 2005 on the occasion of the 50th anniversary of the European Cultural Convention. This was an opportunity for the ministers responsible for cultural affairs to voice a joint political vision, deliberately placing cultural diversity on a par with the common heritage within the set of fundamental values destined to be shared and consolidated. Diversity implies recognition of others, which is in turn an invitation to engage in dialogue. Since it offers the best guarantees of outlawing intolerance and discrimination, intercultural dialogue is not just a means of expressing civic values, not least equality and equity, but also a powerful force for development.

When I presented my report on the state of the Congress of Local and Regional Authorities in May 2007, my aim was to draw attention to the chief objectives we must pursue and build upon: greater local and regional democracy, autonomous local and regional government, promotion of inter-regional and cross-border co-operation, stronger intercultural and inter-religious dialogue. Far from competing, or merely being juxtaposed, these objectives are interlinked and mutually enhancing. Each helps to make the others more relevant and meaningful. I wish to underline the symbolic significance and tangible importance of intercultural and interreligious dialogue, drawing attention to its merits and considerable strengths. It is no exaggeration to say that the quality of such dialogue is one of the most reliable measurements, and one of the surest indicators, of the vitality of local and regional democracy, the strength of inter-regional and cross-border co-operation and local and regional authorities' autonomy. Such dialogue is indeed synonymous with openness, trust, co-operation, mobilisation of social capital, working in partnership, mutual recognition and respect - in a nutshell with well-established social cohesion and acceptance of pluralism. It fosters positive debate and a spirit of sharing, with beneficial consequences for all spheres of local public policy: education, health care, sustainable development, town planning, culture, sport, inter-generational relations and so on.

Nonetheless, we must not be naive or ingenuous about these matters. As might be expected, a dialogue's importance is entirely commensurate with the stumbling blocks in its way and the mistrust it arouses, and today, more often than in the past, these difficulties and mistrust have their origin in or are inspired by beliefs or other forms of religious allegiance. Acknowledging this connection highlights the unique role played by religion in shaping personal and group identities at the individual and community levels. If religion today has a more decisive influence than before, the reason is doubtless the quest for life's meaning, already mentioned above, and the considerable muddling of traditional reference points. These upheavals are further intensified by greater mobility, due *inter alia* to migratory trends, by a heightened awareness of inter-ethnic relations, whether perceived as positive or negative, and by difficulties in socio-economic integration.

It is in fact this global picture of the concrete conditions for the exercise of democracy in pluralist societies that the Culture and Education Committee of the Congress of Local and Regional Authorities had in mind when it set out to promote intercultural and interreligious dialogue. I wish to take this opportunity to draw attention to the very fruitful, rewarding, constructive approach adopted here, as readers will be able to judge for themselves. This publication itself reflects one of the high points of the committee's action, in the form of a seminar held in the French town of Montchanin in November 2006 on a very topical theme, "Local authorities and religions: strategies for consolidating interreligious dialogue", and applying an innovative approach to the subject. It was in the wake of this event that the twelve principles of intercultural and interreligious dialogue for local authorities, as set out in full herein, were devised and developed.

I cannot overstate the significance of the local dimension to be given to the implementation of these recommendations. When it comes to breathing life into these principles and giving substance to the policy directions in which they point - knowledge and understanding of the local religious situation; mutual relations and knowledge between participants in the dialogue; the development of partnerships; appraisal of the action taken with a view to adjusting and fine-tuning it - is anyone better placed than local and regional authorities? I subscribe in full to the comments made in Lisbon in June 2007 by Pierre Corneloup[1] on the occasion of the colloquy "Promoting intercultural dialogue: issues and perspectives of the Council of Europe", at which he stated "We, in the Congress of Local and Regional Authorities, are convinced... that local authorities need to become aware of the growing part played by religions in processes whereby identities are forged, both individually and collectively." As Mayor of Montchanin and the Congress rapporteur on intercultural and interreligious dialogue, Mr. Corneloup knows what he is talking about. I also share his objective to "ensure that religions are perceived not as a problem but as an asset, the aim being to involve them in the democratic management of pluralism." Lastly, I also believe that this is a field where it is necessary to avoid both indifference and interference and to strive to ensure that interculturalism can replace multiculturalism, and an interreligious society a multi-religious one. Interreligious dialogue is a fundamental, founding aspect of intercultural dialogue, and it is also a forum for interaction built on reason, not faith, encompassing both the private and the public spheres.

Local authorities have a twofold role here: running experiments on their home ground and exchanging ideas and experience. Running experiments entails creating, initiating and inventing spaces and opportunities for gatherings capable of portraying the other, if not as a possible partner, at least as a fellow citizen, and the other's culture or religion as a breeding ground of values and ideals. Exchanging ideas between local authorities is a form of cross-fertilisation process, aimed at identifying and testing "good practices" that have proved their worth elsewhere. The Congress of Local and Regional Authorities is clearly the body par excellence to hold such an exchange of views. As everyone knows, from the standpoint of relations between states and religions, Europe is a complex mosaic, and the Congress's role is hence to devise and promote a model which feeds on the positive aspects of all the different arrangements in place. This is perhaps idealistic, but can something great be achieved without a dose of idealism?

---

1   Pierre Corneloup, Mayor of Montchanin, Vice-President of the General Council of Saône-and-Loire, France, Member of the Congress.

Introduction

Jacques Palard[*]

[*]   Director of Research at CNRS, SPIRIT, Institute of Political Science, Bordeaux, France

At least three questions immediately emerge from the 2006 conference on the theme *Local Authorities and Religions: strategies to consolidate interreligious dialogue*, which was organised in the French town of Montchanin at the suggestion of the Committee on Culture and Education of the Council of Europe's Congress of Local and Regional Authorities. Are belief systems and religious forces having sufficient socio-political impact to warrant such an initiative? Is it pertinent to hold pan-European discussions on this subject? And lastly, is defining activities geared to developing interreligious dialogue in the framework of local societies and institutions primarily a practical objective, or does it actually also fit in with the researchers' interests, constituting a legitimate field for analysis from their point of view? The answer to all these questions is a definite "yes".

Danièle Hervieu-Léger is justified in thinking that the reason for the ambiguity in Western, and particularly European societies as regards religion is that the movement that led to emancipation from the traditional religious universe and turned them into secular societies derived much of its energy from the Jewish and Christian humus of their modes of worship[2]. The governments of these societies are today facing a polytheism of values and a pluralism of cultural identities which are based, more clearly than previously, on religious beliefs and/or affiliations which are veritable hotbeds of identity references and bonds. The process of ethnic differentiation, which obviously varies from one country or territorial community to another, plays a conspicuous role in the emergence of a new context, a new configuration: by providing minorities with strength and visibility and encouraging them to adopt protective and representative strategies, international population flows are helping give religious diversity an unprecedented scope and new challenges. This scope, these challenges are further enlivened, or exacerbated, by acts of extreme violence, the perpetrators of which, most of them operating along the fringes of the national state structures, lay claim to a justification and foundation which are usually religion-based.

In Europe and beyond, these phenomena help produce local, national and international networks which operate as forums for expression and vehicles for action. Vigorously interacting with the systems of social representation, they promote change in the conditions for exercising religious activities (worship, social assistance, etc.) at the local level: figuratively speaking, "God changes in the city" to the extent that the religious panorama changes, and "God changes the city" in that the quantitative and qualitative development of the religious panorama transforms the conditions for managing social relations and even the organisation of the political system. In many European countries

---

2   Danièle Hervieu-Léger, *La religion des Européens : modernité, religion, sécularisation*, in Grace Davie and Danièle Hervieu-Léger (ed.), *Identités religieuses en Europe*, Paris, La Découverte, 1996, p. 15.

and local communities, for instance, the increasing presence of Islam and the challenges accompanying its development in terms of acculturation, organisation of worship and attempts to find public forums for expression, constitute a focal point lending renewed prominence to the question of the triangular relations between religion, civil society and the political system, an issue which is relevant not only to Islam but also other religions.

Having considered the background to the preparation and organisation of the conference, this introductory section will attempt to describe the specific challenges of the Islamic dimension of religious differentiation.

1. The approach adopted by the Congress of Local and Regional Authorities

1a. The objective

The changes going on before our very eyes are particularly noticeable because most countries are seeing two more or less parallel trends: on one hand, decentralisation is reinforcing local authority powers, and on the other local religious communities are being (re)affirmed and sometimes gaining in autonomy. This dual trend is in itself an exceptional circumstance that is inducing observers and politicians to look into the potential relationships between the local political and religious authorities which are responsible for the same area. They are also conducive to a comparative analysis homing in, on the observable similarities and differences in national *and* local practices, attempting to answer the following questions: in view of the special (legally established) conceptions of relations between religion and politics, and given the transformation of the urban landscape and the competences of local institutions, etc., how is interreligious dialogue being built up and institutionalised? What role is played here by local authority representatives, and above all what extra roles could they take on in the future? The political issues at stake are particularly important in that the religious component, whether explicit or implicit, of urban conflicts throws down a real challenge to the holders of public power: within their particular field of action, the latter must first of all understand how and why some of their active fellow citizens base their identities and action strategies on their religious belonging and beliefs, how and why this belonging, these beliefs provide those who hold them with a response to their quest for meaning and also the wherewithal for creating a repertory of actions deemed to be relevant and effective.

It was precisely in order to clarify and answer these questions that the Committee on Culture and Education of the Council of Europe's Congress of Local and Regional Authorities organised the Montchanin Conference in November 2006. This work was epitomised the growing realisation of the aforementioned changes, which would seem to call for a change of practical paradigm. It is as if the process of secularising and "demystifying" the world, which was long considered general and inevitable, has been superseded by an equal and opposite process of desecularisation and remystification[3], based *inter alia* on reconsideration of the "social need for the religious".

1b. Implementation

The Congress members who initiated this debate considered that it should be made part of a comparative analysis of a number of European countries. So how were these countries to be chosen? In his interpretation of the results of a 1980s European survey on values, the French sociologist Jean Stoetzel divided up the then EEC countries into four religious types: a mainly catholic area (Spain, Italy and Ireland), a mainly protestant area (Great Britain and Denmark), a mixed area (Germany) and a "secular" area (including Belgium, France and Holland, which shared the fact of over a quarter of their populations claiming to be "without religion"). Since the general configuration had not fundamentally changed, the organisers opted for one country from each of these religious types, i.e. Spain, the United Kingdom, Germany and France. Russia, which mainly comprises Orthodox Christians, was also covered. These surveys constitute the second section of this work, and are put into comparative perspective, so to speak, by the transverse or transnational reports in the first section.

What about the angle from which these different projects were designed and carried out? The main focus was in fact their purpose, namely to elucidate the debates and exchanges among participants in the Montchanin conference, starting with the representatives of the Congress of Local and Regional Authorities. Accordingly, these studies and reports, rather than meeting purely academic criteria, are component parts of a research-action primarily geared to preparing guidelines and recommendations to be submitted to local political leaders by the Council of Europe. We might clarify the spirit of this approach by outlining some items in the discussions of the Committee on Culture and Education in February 2006 geared to highlighting "best practices". These items, in italics below, were turned into questions and proposals for joint analysis, and sent out to the originators of the surveys, particularly national ones, as part of a common analytical grid:

- *"taking account of traditions in institutional organisation in the receiving country in the religious field"*:

---

3   See Peter L. Berger (ed.), *Le réenchantement du monde*, Paris, Fayard, 2001.

- how do the "majority" and "minority" cultures interact?

- How should we design and implement the negotiation or elaboration of "common reasons" or "common references" conducive to initiating and developing a process of mutual recognition and a feeling of shared national and local belonging?

- *"the local authorities are on the frontline in taking account of religious activities, e.g. where places of worship are concerned"*:

  - what does the expression "frontline" actually mean?

  - How are we to build up a negotiated institutional position that is neither indifferent nor interfering?

- *"Structuring dialogue involves a number of principles conducive to use as a leitmotif for elected representatives and cultural and religious associations and communities wishing to engage in dialogue: the equality principle, the Council of Europe's action against discrimination [...], the principle of freedoms, [...] promotion of "dialogue instruments" guaranteeing the principle of reciprocity, interaction and exchange, of the "advisory council" type"*.

  - Can these fundamental principles be used as criteria for assessing the action taken by local authorities in the field of intercultural and interreligious dialogue?

  - If so, for each of these principles (equality, freedom, reciprocity, exchange, etc), what operational indicators can be pinpointed to assess the structuring of the dialogue, covering both the procedure and the results?

1c. Thematic focus and methodological conditions for the approach used

The authors of the various surveys were in no way working in a vacuum, with their analyses just coming "out of the blue". A multitude of projects have been conducted in this field in recent years, covering not only relations between religion and politics in general but also, more specifically, the position of religion in the public sphere. Nevertheless, in the collective work which they published recently on comparative study of religion as a subject of public policy, Pauline Côté and T. Jeremy Gunn noted the relative novelty of this perspective, with its undeniable breadth of scope: "In a development which would have been unthinkable a few years ago, the religion issue is now on the public agenda of Western governments for good. We now have parliamentary committees, governmental reports and laws on sects and the wearing of religious symbols, not to mention terrorism and security, which are treated as new challenges arising out of the diversity of religious manifestations and the unprecedented problems allegedly caused by their coexistence"[4]. These two North American academics concentrate particularly on "improvisation and the difficulties of institutionalising religious diversity in connection both with the unsuitability of the existing instruments and conceptions and with the political problems arising out of new religious dividing lines and segments in a universe which is supposed to be pluralist and secular"[5]. There can be no clearer statement or justification of the debate that has been launched on this new public policy field, whether at national or local level.

In this connection, the discussions that have developed in the Committee on Culture and Education of the Council of Europe's Congress of Local and Regional Authorities are animated by an "intuitive" conviction: local authorities are best placed to promote intercultural and interreligious dialogue. Their proximity to the citizens and their close acquaintance with all the local players enable them to assess local cultural and religious diversity and instigate consultation and dialogue with representatives of the religious denominations and local residents in order to provide an equitable response to the different groups' concerns and demands. Besides, the issue at stake may not be a mere wish to pacify relations between religious groups: more positively, it could also help people to consider difference as a resource, an asset, making religious diversity a priority dimension of intercultural dialogue based on shared values, rather than just a problem[6]. In this field too, the local level is a central challenge.

This no doubt involves seeking prior agreement on a conception of religion capable of underpinning such dialogue. It might legitimately be said that the latter can only be initiated where the discussion partners are free of any obligation to engage in an apologetic defence of specific beliefs, which would make the latter non-negotiable absolute truths, or ideological justifications (a conception which we might call "substantialist" since it refers to the actual substance of the beliefs in question). This leaves room for a "functional" or "organizational" dimension in religious beliefs and denominations, which, on the contrary, is conducive to negotiation and compromise on controversial subjects: relations with school authorities, intergenerational conflicts, relations

---

4   Pauline Côté and T. Jeremy Gunn, (eds.), Presentation in *The New Religious Question. State Regulation or State Interference?*, Brussels, IPE – Peter Lang (coll. God, Humans and Religions), 2006, p. 13.

5   Ibid., pp. 14 and 15.

6   This is in fact the Council of Europe's current approach, as exemplified by the process of preparing the *White Paper on Intercultural Dialogue*: the 19th of October 2006 version of the working paper takes deliberate account of the "religious dimension of intercultural dialogue": "In the international debate, intercultural and interreligious dialogue are sometimes seen as two separate, though interrelated issues; whereas others, like the Council of Europe, stress that religious beliefs and traditions – like agnostic, atheist or secularist convictions – are one dimension of culture" (p. 8).

between the sexes, relations between immigrant groups, management of the calendar of religious festivals, etc. In her study of the situation in Germany, Nikola Tietze considers that the success of what she calls the "Hamburg approach", i.e. the special "microclimate" prevailing in the Federal Land of Hamburg in terms of interreligious relations, stems from the efforts of all concerned, on both the Muslim side and that of the public and academic authorities, to prevent religion from getting bogged down in cultural, political and ideological thinking. Consequently, the partners involved in negotiating the inclusion of Muslims in the institutional system, are managing to treat Islam as a system of beliefs, a theology conceptually equal to those of Christianity. In other words they strive to leave identity politics outside when they meet up for discussion on Muslim participation in the established system. This opens the door to what French Canadians call an "accommodement raisonnable" (a reasonable agreement).

Interreligious dialogue therefore, requires the religious and public authority representatives to follow an ethics of openness, recognition and respect for otherness. This is a close relationship which combines practices, justifications of practices, conceptions of truth and forms of authority and power[7], and which helps deal with any deadlock emerging. Mgr Albert Rouet, the Catholic Bishop of Poitiers (France) counters any overly self-sufficient, self-congratulatory position by, unusually, advocating a kind of Christianity which admits to "fragility": "I would like a Church which dares show its fragility. Unfortunately the Church sometimes gives the impression that it needs nothing and that men have nothing to give it. I would like a human-sized Church which does not conceal its fragility, ignorance and occasional perplexity"[8].

2. The challenges of the Islamic dimension of religious differentiation

One of the main facts to be considered, in order to grasp the peculiar issues arising out of the Muslim component of the whole fabric of religion, is the undeniable reversal of the balance of power and the influence of the international dimension. It should be stressed that two of the countries

---

7   Jacques Lagroye, *La vérité dans l'Eglise catholique. Contestations et restauration d'un régime d'autorité*, Paris, Belin, 2006, p. 9.

8   Albert Rouet, *La chance d'un christianisme fragile*, Paris, Bayard, 2001, p. 57. In the 1980s, Michel de Certeau developed a similar argument: *We must accept our weakness, abandon the ridiculous, hypocritical masks of an ecclesiastical power which is no more. Perhaps theory and practice become Christian when the strength of lucidity and competence allows us to risk exposing ourselves to the outside world, accepting the stranger's arrival, the grace to make room for (i.e. to believe in) the Other* (*La faiblesse de croire*, Paris, Seuil, 1987, pp. 313 and 314).

covered by national surveys, Spain and the United Kingdom, have suffered Islamist-inspired terrorist attacks which took a particularly heavy toll: the Madrid attacks on 11th March 2004 (191 dead and some 1,500 injured), and the London attacks of 7th July 2005 (56 dead and some 700 injured).

Nikola Tietze's survey of the situation in Germany, highlights the creation of Muslim communities and the attrition of the majority catholic and protestant religious identities as the prime results of the increasing numbers of religious references and the newly diversified religious landscape confronting German local authorities[9]. Over the past 25 years, therefore, the public authorities have been facing a twofold evolution. On one hand, new religious needs have emerged in the Islamic field, challenging the established rules on relations between the political and religious spheres; and on the other, the structures and organisation of the Christian Churches have weakened, transforming the status of such provisions of public religious policy (*Religionspolitik*) as denominational teaching in state schools. The creation of Muslim communities in Germany is thus the result of a non-linear process. As might be expected, the three phases highlighted by N. Tietze also apply to a good number of other countries:

- the first phase involved the recruitment, in the 1960s, of workers "from countries with Muslim populations, particularly Turkey and, to a lesser extent, former Yugoslavia and Morocco. Nevertheless, the large number of individuals of Muslim religion who then arrived in urban areas with labour-intensive industries, raised no political problems in terms of religion". Although the workers and their families who followed them did form a specific social group with specific problems, their identification with Islam did not require any particular political measures. On the contrary, the concessions made by entrepreneurs and government departments vis-à-vis the religious practice of these Muslims, who were mainly Turkish nationals, guaranteed social stability in the workers' residences and the workplace. To the public authorities and economic operators, Islam was a component of a culture alien to the Federal Republic of Germany – so alien, in fact, that they thought they could overlook it[10]. N. Tietze describes this initial period, significantly, as one of an "accommodating attitude and interested indifference to Muslim practices", but also, and this explains the whole situation, "conceptual exclusion of foreign workers from the Nation-State and from community

---

9   In 2005, 31% of the population were members of one of the regional Lutheran Churches (*Landeskirchen*), 32% members of the Catholic Church and 0.1% adherents of Judaism. The Muslim population of Germany is estimated at 3.8%.

10   The German word *Gastarbeiter* ("guest worker"), which was applied to foreign workers until the 1980s, reflected the conviction that they would return home at some stage.

and political life in the urban centres". National allegiance to the country of origin was more important than the religious dimension of identity;

- the second phase began with new action to promote family reunion following the official termination of the policy of recruiting labour abroad. "Foreign" workers thus became "immigrants". The high profile of Islam in the urban environment went hand-in-hand with the settlement of families of Muslim culture and religion. This meant that Islam acquired the status of a "cultural differentiation marker" leading to the creation of Islamic areas, which fomented many neighbourhood disputes and prompted the public authorities to take action to settle these problems. This development was particularly sensitive because it was reinforced and highlighted by the increasing influence of political Islam in international relations;

- the third phase began in the 1990s, with the emergence of educational issues for immigrant children and demands for rights within the German legal and institutional system: the Nationality Code adopted in 1999 partly replaced *jus sanguinis* with *jus solis*, thus bringing Muslim community organisations closer into the national social system. This legal change was accompanied by a novel perception of the issues of institutionalising Islam as a precondition for regulating intercultural and interreligious relations. It also reflected the importance of the role of the rule of law and the judicial authorities in the diversification of the religious landscape.

Islam is a minority religion in Spain, but there too, it originated in immigration from countries where it holds majority status or indeed has a virtual monopoly on the religious sphere. Demands for inclusion in the public space and for visibility and stability must be seen in relation to a veritable break-up point in the representational and worldview system, which break-up point can bring in new demands and strategies for negotiation. The number of Muslims in the country is estimated at between 500,000 and 1 million, most of them Moroccan immigrants, although there are also Algerians, Pakistanis and Spanish converts. F. Burchianti and I. Itçaina note that the complexity of the political regulations on religion stems in particular from the very nature of the religions in question, which do not draw the same line between the sacred and the profane as Christianity. Quoting Dominique Schnapper, they stress that Islam, like Judaism, is simultaneously a morality, a culture, a way of life and a history. The fact is that Islam has become much more visible in the public space over the last few years; it is an increasingly important issue for political regulation *"from below"*. The vitality of the Muslim communities, despite their longstanding presence, particularly in southern Spain, is mainly due to the involvement of Spanish converts. The main conflicts have had the effect of spotlighting the need for the public authorities to promote dialogue and develop policies to stabilise both the practice of the Muslim religion and the immigrant communities themselves; this was the reaction, for instance, after the riots in El Ejido in Andalusia in February 2000, when agricultural day labourers, mostly of Moroccan origin, were attacked, and even more so after the Madrid terrorist attacks.

In their comparative study of national and local situations in Europe, Jean-François Husson and Julie Mahiels note that in France "the obligation to direct the bodies of deceased Muslims toward Mecca led to the creation of *de facto* "Muslim plots" in municipal cemeteries, even though mayors are legally prohibited from discriminating on the basis of the dead person's beliefs or religion". In this case, however, the local authorities managed to show flexibility in meeting expectations while still safeguarding neutrality in the cemeteries. The "Machelon Report" submitted to the French Minister of the Interior and Spatial Planning in September 2006 also stressed this margin of manoeuvre, which is all about listening and showing pragmatism: "The law prohibits the creation of "denominational plots" to the extent that the latter would force the mayor to ponder the religious affiliation of the deceased in exercising his policing powers, notably when allocating burial plots. Yet the text does not prevent the mayor from taking account of the deceased person's wish to be buried at a particular place. Therefore, *de facto* grouping of graves as the sum total of a number of individual decisions is not prohibited by the law"[11].

The words of the Mayor of Mulhouse, Chair of the Association of Mayors of Major French Cities, is redolent of a change of attitude and an approach consisting of both listening and mediating: "We cannot overlook a major fact which has emerged over the last thirty years or so: nowadays, most religious requests come from religions which were virtually non-existent in France in 1905 (particularly Islam). It is on the basis of this totally new situation that my fellow Mayors of major cities and myself have for several years now been implementing a policy of recognising Islam and facilitating its practice. This need for recognition is expressed in a variety of ways, from the building of places of worship, respect for customs, identification of valid religious spokespersons and action to promote the teaching of religion"[12]. Plans to build mosques reveal tensions and objections which have to be managed and settled: once local people hear of such a plan they regularly launch petitions,

---

11 Report by the Legal think-tank on relations between religious denominations and the public authorities, chaired by Professor Jean-Pierre Machelon, 20th September 2006.

12 Jean-Marie Bockel, *Grande villes et gestion territoriale des cultes. Entre volonté politique et pragmatisme* (Major cities and territorial management of religious denominations. Between political will and pragmatism), *Pouvoirs locaux* n° 69, 2006, p. 121.

ask the municipality to pre-empt the plot of land in question and demand that building permission be withheld. In such cases the mayor has to assuage concerns and prove his/her ability to explain the fact that their worries are unfounded.

More broadly, the challenge of Islam necessitates reconsideration of the relations between "majority" and "minority" religions in a context where religions traditionally in the majority are declining rapidly. Germany, Spain and France clearly illustrate this situation: the Muslim communities have grown up in step with the decline in the substance and power of the Christian Churches, even though those in a position of authority are still animated by a denominational rationale which might be said to have an undeniable force of inertia. N. Tietze says that this being the case, non-Christian religions are becoming "the Other", considered as minorities *vis-à-vis* the national culture, which is defined by the Christian, Western reference. And so in Germany, despite the reform of the Nationality Code, Muslims are considered as *Ausländer,* Turkish foreigners. The outcome is that the conception of state neutrality is now contradicted by the *de facto* position of the Christian/ Western culture. In other words, the conception of "majority" and "minority" cannot be a matter solely of a numerical balance of power.

In their British analysis, Anjum Anwar and Chris Chivers also provide a clear illustration of this apropos of "Anglican assimilationism". They consider that a religion assimilated into the heart of the State can induce civil servants and elected representatives to lose their need to address the religion issue because they think they have every reason to believe that "it is already there". This leads to a kind of marginalisation of religion in the minds of local authorities even where, as in such municipalities as Blackburn with Darwen in which they conducted their public interreligious dialogue activities, some 20% of people are Muslims.

Religious denominations are not only providers of rites or social and other services. Their primary role is to promote the socialisation of their members and to help form their individual, collective, social and territorial identities. They are also a vehicle both for the construction of the *anima loci* (the soul of a place) and local awareness (nowadays, for instance, there are specific Marseille or London slants on Islam, on Judaeo-Christian relations, etc.) and for connecting up before/after and elsewhere, time and the international sphere. To that extent they forge their members' collective imagination, train them in symbolic thinking and provide some of their cultural references and ideological representations. This means that they ensure the religious regulation of things political, even indirectly and unintentionally.

Obviously, there are still some uncertainties surrounding the implementation of this new local public policy as regards motivations and the scope and effects of the action taken. These uncertainties bear witness to the vagueness of some of the aims and the fact that public and/or collective measures are not always accepted by the social operators in question. This brings us back to the questions put by Anne-Sophie Lamine, which we might use for our future-oriented inquiries: "Is religious plurality recognised? Are we determined to secure stability in urban neighbourhoods? Are we prepared to grant recognition to the Maghrebi or Jewish communities? Is Islam being confused with Maghrebi culture? Alongside the obvious and necessary benefit of recognition, plurality and cultural and religious otherness, there is also the risk of over-ethnicising social problems, leading us to underestimate or even forget the actual underlying causes"[13].

---

13 Anne-Sophie Lamine, *Quand les villes font appel aux religions. Laïcité et novelles prises en compte de la pluralité religieuse* (When municipalities call on religions. Secularism and new approaches to religious plurality), *Les Annales de la recherche urbaine*, n° 96, 2004, p. 156.

Part one

The implication of intercultural and interreligious dialogue

Introduction: Jacques Palard[14]

At the beginning of their study on UK local authorities and interreligious dialogue, which can be found in part two of this publication, Anjum Anwar and Chris Chivers take as their starting point the position adopted by Samuel P. Huntington in *"The Clash of Civilizations and the Remaking of World Order"*, which they strongly criticise. Arguing in favour of a multiple-identity approach, they consider that Huntington is in fact concerned with a battle between world-views originating from what is perceived, in their contention wrongly, as a fundamental clash of religious beliefs: "... the particular single-identity characteristic upon which Huntington draws is the paradigm of faith. Why this single-identity characteristic and not any other? ... One can of course navigate the world with greater ease if one deploys such reductionist tools." In their opinion, the Huntingtonian viewpoint and paradigm are not merely over-simplifications, they are also and above all "dangerous" since they strongly influence local elected representatives' and local public officials' attitudes towards religious communities, despite the fact that conflicts and divisions are fed by many other identity sources, not just religion. Anwar and Chivers add that this viewpoint "also fuels a perception – common, in our experience, among so many in local government – that religion is part of the problem not the solution." They maintain that this all-pervading clash-of-civilisations rhetoric at the macro level has significant implications at the micro level, since it validates and deepens narrow-minded human prejudice.

Starting from the local level as a basis for analysing the newly reconstituted religious scene does not involve taking a sideways or secondary approach. Franck Frégosi rightly points out that it is firstly at the local level of the towns, municipalities and, possibly, the *départements* and regions of France that the primary issues of regulation of the religious sphere arise[15]. In this field too, the local level is now of vital importance, since it is the diversity of local politico-religious configurations that inspires new forms of recognition and action. The typology of frameworks for the local regulation of religious pluralism proposed by this author should therefore also be given our endorsement: methods of perceiving and apprehending pluralism along with identification of the players able to assume a mediating role in conflict situations; methods of integrating religious groups into local society and, lastly, methods of effective recognition of religious pluralism in and by local government policy. Claire de Galembert, who has made a comparative study of the Muslim religion in

---

14   Director of Research at CNRS, SPIRIT, Institute of Political Science, Bordeaux, France

15   Franck Frégosi, «*Introduction. Les régulations locales du pluralisme religieux : éléments de problématique*», in Franck Frégosi and Jean-Paul Willaime, «*Le religieux dans la commune. Les régulations locales du pluralisme religieux en France*», Geneva, Labor et Fides, 2001, p. 17.

Germany and France, also regards the local level as the most propitious for inventing new public policy approaches[16].

Local authorities' focus on establishing relations with religions - which is admittedly more common than the desire to foster genuine interreligious dialogue - stems from concerns linked to the conditions in which social ties are forged, to the political regulation frameworks and to the forms taken by a deliberately pragmatic, willingly experimental approach. In a publication brought out by the French government's strategic planning agency, the Commissariat général du Plan, Cécile Jolly stresses the importance of rediscovering "religion's citizenship dimension", which she regards as "a source of meaning and a template for social relations", especially in socially disadvantaged areas[17]. She points out that this approach and this reform are "bottom-up" in nature, since it is at the local level that their input is today most clearly identifiable. At that level the religious aspects and others aspects of community life are more closely interconnected. On the basis of her work in a number of urban locations, Anne-Sophie Lamine also draws attention to the fact that religion has truly become part of the public sphere and points out that this has led to a reorganisation of secularism: "Although [the] term multiculturalism brings to mind the fear of identity-based isolationism, it can also mean recognition of plural, civic identities. Cities where different kinds of forums for exchanges between religions are organised: intercommunity and intercultural structures aimed at improved knowledge and understanding of religion."[18] She bases her arguments on the examples of Marseille-Espérance, an inter-community structure set up in 1900 by the city's then socialist mayor, Roubaix-Espérance, which has the legal status of a non-profit association and the Centre civique d'études du fait religieux (Civic Centre for Religious Studies) in Montreuil, established by the mayor of this municipality on the outskirts of Paris.

Jean-Marie Woehrling's contribution underlines the importance, for both those active in the field and researchers, of distinguishing between "old" and "new" cultural minorities. This distinction is useful in pinpointing possible rivalries and also in using traditional minorities' past experience to develop a form of expertise regarding protection, the strengthening of social ties

---

16   Claire de Galembert, «La gestion publique de l'Islam vue du "local". Des acteurs en quête de repères» in «Pouvoirs locaux» No. 69, 2006, pp. 71-77; «L'islam des acteurs publics territoriaux : entre incertitude et ressource d'autorité politique» in «Les Cahiers de la sécurité» No. 62, 2006, pp. 33-53.

17   Cécile Jolly, «Religions et intégration sociale», Paris, Cahier du Plan No. 8, July 2005, p. 21.

18   Anne-Sophie Lamine, «Quand les villes font appel aux religions. Laïcité et nouvelles prises en compte de la pluralité religieuse» in «Les Annales de la recherche urbaine» No. 96, October 2004 (Urbanité et liens religieux), p. 149. Also see the same author's «La cohabitation des dieux. Pluralité religieuse et laïcité», Paris, Presses universitaires de France, 2004: A.-S. Lamine takes the view that "in all cases, whether at local or national level, relations between religions (no matter who initiates them and be they regular or ad hoc) contribute to the recognition of minority religions and their accreditation in the public sphere." (p. 101).

and mediation tools and, perhaps even more, the legitimacy of cultural and religious diversity. Mutual recognition is then founded on the principle of a "virtuous circle" born of interaction between loyalty and generosity, of giving on both sides: "The more loyal the minority, the more generous the majority, and vice versa: the community is concerned that the minority should be in a comfortable position, but the minority is concerned about the community's interests." The difficulty lies in the possible contradiction between the desire for openness and the desire to safeguard cultural specificity, of which minority groups are tacitly aware. The local authority is faced with a similar dilemma, pitting social cohesion against recognition of pluralism and public order against freedom of expression. This goes to show the importance of relationships of trust developed and tested over time, which are destined to become stabilised via a negotiated, "soft" institutionalisation process, which may take the form of a local interreligious council.

The overviews presented by Jean-François Husson and Julie Mahiels in the first part of their contribution give an idea of the great diversity of national - and local - situations in Europe; they give form and substance to the concept of a "mosaic". In their presentation of the specific issues, they stress how much is at stake in enhanced knowledge of the different religious and philosophical communities so as to improve co-habitation and achieve greater mutual understanding. The "Observatoire des relations administratives entre les cultes, les organisations laïques et l'État" (ORACLE) allows them to have a very broad view of both the diversity of the issues raised and the various players' responses or attempted responses to these issues. They highlight the fact that the UK government has established a Faith Communities Consultative Council, aimed at encouraging inter-faith activities through regional conferences and support for local initiatives; this body's success can be gauged from the growing involvement of faith communities in local social and urban regeneration projects.

The cases cited as examples of local government involvement in interreligious dialogue possibly have their foundation in what Philippe Gaudin terms "intelligent secularism", which, as he explains in his contribution to this work, can come about only through better mutual understanding and in which religious education and collective action in the social and cultural spheres have a significant role to play. It is not irrelevant to reiterate his proposed definition of French secularism here: "Secularism is a great political idea according to which nothing should undermine the unity of the people, particularly any form of clericalism that would offer a small section of that people different rights and duties. Moreover, it is an ideal that must always be pursued since no people can become really worthy of the sovereignty it must exercise unless it forms an educated nation that is fully self-aware."

Chapter 1

The management of cultural and religious diversity and the promotion of interfaith and intercultural dialogue by local authorities

Jean-Marie Woehrling[*]

[*]   President of the Local Laws Institute of Alsace-Moselle

Introduction

The Chamber of Local Authorities has been asked to address the question of the role of local authorities in promoting intercultural and interfaith dialogue. Interfaith and intercultural dialogue are concepts that are much used, but often in such a way that there are no practical implications of use to local authorities[19]. Despite their popularity, these concepts fall far short of establishing a workable model for the management of European cultural diversity, reflecting instead the mere realisation of how increasingly difficult it is to manage the complex and sometimes conflict-ridden relationships between different cultural groups.

These difficulties are mirrored in the problems encountered by local authorities when managing cultural and religious diversity. There are plentiful examples of local projects, but they are difficult to transpose elsewhere and only some can be sources of practical recommendations. With a view to clarifying the options open to the Chamber of Local Authorities in this area, this note will attempt to set out some general pointers on how to approach the issues raised.

1. Complex situations

The term "cultural and religious diversity" might create the mistaken impression that distinct cultural and religious features are expressed in a uniform manner that can be analysed using uniform methods. In truth, the term covers highly disparate situations, whose fundamental differences need to be identified straight away, as the "management" of the various categories of cultural or religious group raises very different questions.

1a. Long-standing and new cultural minorities

Many European regions are inhabited by population groups linked by a specific culture, which have lived in the area for a very long time (they are often the original inhabitants). Most often they are distinguished by specific linguistic features but they may also have other distinctive characteristics stemming, for example, from their history and religion. They are sometimes called "national minorities" (because their members have the nationality of the ruling state or because they feel they have a national identity) but they

---

19 See, for example, Declaration of 20th October 2003 on intercultural dialogue and conflict prevention adopted by the European Ministers of Culture (Council of Europe DGIV/CULT/PREV(2004), 16th February 2004); colloquy on intercultural dialogue held by the European Commission's DG on Education and Culture as part of the Jean Monnet Programme, 20th and 21st March 2002.

generally do not have social integration problems, although they may demand special status in order to be able to manage their own cultural distinctiveness or sometimes to gain political autonomy. Even if they are scattered, there are often also areas in which they are relatively concentrated or even form the majority of the local population.

In most European countries, other population groups deriving from more recent waves of immigration have grown up alongside these traditional minorities. Most of them have major social problems (linked with unemployment, integration and living standards) and some still have their own distinct national identity and display cultural characteristics which are perceived as foreign. Sometimes these new minorities are concentrated in certain districts, but more often than not they are spread throughout the country. Particular problems affect the younger members of these populations (for example, failure to integrate and delinquency).

These two different types of minority pose quite different problems. Whereas in many countries the situation of the long-standing minorities is tending to resolve itself, either because they are dying out or because their special status is being recognised, the difficulties posed by the new minorities are considered to be growing, at least as far as some groups are concerned. In point of fact, cultural diversity attracts the authorities' attention precisely because there is a growing problem with the management of some communities of immigrant origin.

Management is complicated where these two types of minority coexist. It is not uncommon for the political authorities or the *de facto* situation (especially demographic circumstances) to set them off in competition against each other. Sometimes, however, the presence of traditional minorities can provide useful experience, which can help when it comes to dealing with new minorities.

At any rate, the difference between the two is important[20] as it is unusual to be able to deal in the same way with the two sets of circumstances[21]. There are few minorities with intermediate characteristics[22].

---

20 This is why the Council of Europe's two treaties in this field (the European Charter for Regional or Minority Languages and the Framework Convention for the Protection of National Minorities) make a clear distinction between the two types of minority.

21 The distinction is often presented as an unjustified form of discrimination, but this is simply an intellectual misunderstanding, stemming from the fact that the two phenomena, though different, are combined under the same heading of "minorities".

22 This is the case, in particular, with the Roma.

1b. Cultural minorities and religious minorities

In many respects religious ideas are articulated in a similar way to cultural characteristics (through traditions, cultural references, behaviour, values, etc.). It may be tempting to conclude on the basis of a sociological approach that religion is just another form of culture. However, a distinction does have to be made between these two different social phenomena.

The main reasons for this are legal and political. In Europe, religious convictions are afforded special treatment, characterised by particular protection in terms of human rights. There is also a specific obligation for public authorities to show restraint in this area. The principle that the authorities must act impartially with regard to religious convictions is generally accepted. By contrast, in the cultural sphere, interference by the authorities is regarded as not only legitimate but necessary. Cultural policies, which are also pursued at local level, are universal. Protecting national or regional languages and cultures is regarded as a public duty. However, individual cultural rights are often afforded legal protection only when they are granted special status.

Furthermore, as far as content is concerned, religious and cultural manifestations occur in relatively distinct contexts. Purely cultural demands are generally less rigid and direct than religious demands. This difference sometimes fades where those making ethnic or cultural demands rely on religious traditions to give their claims more weight[23]. In such cases, religious traditions are used to express an ethnic or political affiliation. Moreover, in many cases, religious convictions have turned into cultural traditions, which have more or less lost their spiritual dimension. However, it is important to make a proper distinction when dealing with these situations.

2. Managing cultural diversity – the underlying issues

The authorities, and the local authorities in particular, have two aims, which seem in many respects to be incompatible, namely preserving cultural diversity and strengthening social ties.

2a. Preserving cultural diversity

The "monolithic" or "unitarian" concepts of the community that used to prevail, are now increasingly giving way to the belief that cultural pluralism is a development that is both inevitable and beneficial. This view is based on two ideas:

---

23   In some respects, the case of those who wish to wear the Islamic headscarf can be seen as a situation of this type.

- *The idea of the right to cultural difference*

> Groups with distinctive cultural characteristics must be able to preserve them and indeed enhance them. In particular, the view is taken that people belonging to national minorities must be able to maintain and develop their culture and preserve the essential elements of their identity, and must not be assimilated against their will[24].

- *The idea that cultural diversity is an asset for the entire population*

> Cultural diversity enables each individual culture to become aware of what makes it different and to benefit from what other cultures have to offer. Communities can take advantage of a diverse range of cultural amenities. Conversely, processes of cultural levelling linked to globalisation are regarded as impoverishing culture. It is therefore the local authorities' task to maintain and promote cultural diversity locally by offering the different groups living in the area, the opportunity to develop their culture and their identity[25].

2b. Strengthening social ties

One fundamental question with which our modern European societies are faced is that of "social cohesion", in other words the existence within society of structural elements which give its members the feeling that they are part of a community. Social ties are particularly important at local level, because this is where people have tangible experience of situations that strengthen or weaken such ties. The local authorities - regardless, incidentally, of their formal legal powers - are confronted with the essential task of making the local population a mutually supportive local community.

This task is broadening in scope and becoming more difficult as European countries are having to adapt to a number of changes that are altering the context in which it can be carried out:

- growing diversity among populations: as a result of population movements, ethnic, cultural, religious and linguistic groups are diversifying; because of changes in mentality and the role of the media, while the social aspirations, lifestyles and religious and philosophical beliefs of the majority are dissipating;

- at the same time, traditional structural frameworks (such as church,

---

24   Article 5 of the Framework Convention for the Protection of National Minorities.

25   Some "traditional" minorities are dying out because the features that make them different (religion, traditions, etc.) are not being passed on from generation to generation. This decline calls for measures to support minorities from society as a whole.

family, school, the army, trade unions and political parties) are becoming weaker, or finding it more difficult to function. The new economic context, high geographical mobility and increasing emphasis on individuals are undermining social cohesion;

- at the same time, there is a lack of any analytical or conceptual reference frame enabling the population and their leaders to understand and control current developments and decide how to go about addressing the issue of unity in a multicultural society.

Accordingly, there is considerable conflict between ideas that favour the promotion of cultural pluralism and those concerned more with cultural cohesion. The debate on "multiculturalism" is an illustration of this.

Social cohesion based on a set of joint cultural references is of particular concern to population groups with an immigrant background, which are at risk of social exclusion because of their precarious economic situation.

3. The uncertainties surrounding intercultural and interfaith dialogue

There can be no doubt about the importance of fostering dialogue with and between cultural and religious groups. However, the notion of dialogue covers a number of different things.

3a. Dialogue between local authorities and particular groups

It is a particularly good idea for local authorities to establish contact with religious groups in their geographical area for the following reasons:

- these groups form part of the local community and cannot be ignored. They can help to strengthen social ties and cohesion in the community at large[26];

- these groups must not be left on the margins of the wider community, otherwise they may be tempted to move away from it. To establish successful links with people whom it is difficult to approach, it is often a good idea to go through the intermediary of a group to which they belong;

- these links are essential in order to determine these groups' needs and establish with them to what extent these can be catered for;

---

26 Most religious groups have an altruistic side. Local authorities can capitalise on this readiness to serve others, particularly by encouraging groups to pursue aims that transcend the group concerned.

- it is only by having a full range of contacts with all the groups in the community that local authorities are able to play their role as impartial bodies endeavouring to take equal account of the interests of all their inhabitants.

It is important that, as part of their general policy, local authorities promote such dialogue and acknowledge the existence and the legitimacy of cultural and religious diversity within the local community.

3b. Dialogue between particular groups

Dialogue between different groups is also a means of enhancing knowledge and mutual understanding. It makes it easier to accept the specific cultural traits of communities of immigrant origin and to dispel misunderstanding, fear and hostility. Well-organised intercultural contacts enable groups both to discover their own identity and to take an open-minded approach to the distinctive features of other groups. Intercultural exchange is a guarantee that groups will pay attention to one another and that each will show due regard for the wider community's collective interests. However, it has to be borne in mind that true intercultural dialogue means more than simply exchanging information and satisfying mutual curiosity.

Neither must intercultural dialogue be confused with the kind of intercultural "blending" that takes place as part of a process of globalisation, which appears on the face of it to foster diversity but ultimately mixes everything up together and ends up standardising everything. Dialogue entails taking differences seriously but resisting the temptations of sectarianism.

3c. The demands of intercultural and interfaith dialogue

Many intercultural encounters do not give rise to genuine dialogue but to "juxtaposed monologues", in which each party simply tries to explain how it sees things. True dialogue is an exchange, in which people are prepared to rethink their ideas in the light of what they hear from others, and it can therefore change the views and values of those involved.

Yet certain groups, particularly religious ones, have no desire for true dialogue resulting in this kind of change:

- above all they want to stay the way they are and not be exposed to outside influences[27];

---

27   All groups have a legitimate desire for integrity, continuity and the preservation of their identity but this should always be combined with a wish to be part of society as a whole.

- they consider their values to be superior to those of the wider community and those of other groups;

- they wish to assert their rights without having to accommodate the rights claimed by other groups.

Intercultural and interfaith dialogue therefore implies adopting open-minded and flexible views, which are not accepted by all cultures. It also means creating a climate of trust for minorities. For them to be willing to engage in intercultural dialogue, they need to be reassured that they will not be assimilated into an amorphous blend of beliefs and cultures. Intercultural dialogue is not cultural "cross-breeding".

3d. Intercultural dialogue and social problems

In many regions attention is focused on communities of immigrant origin. These are giving rise to increasing concern, particularly those from a Muslim background. Several problems affect these population groups:

- economic problems (such as financial insecurity, lack of vocational training and discrimination in employment);

- rapid population growth (large families, family reunion, etc.);

- the formation of ghettos (people willingly, or are forced to, become concentrated in the same neighbourhoods);

- difficulties in integrating among the younger generations (under-achievement at school, unacceptable behaviour or delinquency);

- growing religious demands, whereas the rest of the population seems often to be turning away from religious worship.

For these reasons, intercultural and interfaith dialogue often seems to boil down to ensuring the best possible integration of these communities, which is a debatable approach as it makes dialogue less meaningful and may even make for stigmatisation of a particular community.

In conclusion, if local authorities are to be effective in promoting intercultural and interfaith dialogue, they must begin by establishing their own identities and creating a feeling of belonging and togetherness among their members. This means that, as well as making all the legitimate distinctions necessary, they must *identify common interests*[28].

---

28 Many different terms are used for this concept, including the general interest, the common good and common values; see section 4.3.a. below.

4. Analytical tools

The situation in which groups with separate identities actually live within a population has to be considered within an analytical framework through which action can be managed. Only brief reference will be made here to the kind of analytical framework that is based on a monolithic concept of society, according to which the aim is to make separate cultures disappear by assimilating them into the dominant culture, and dialogue with particular groups is only a means of dissolving them. There is little point in going into the arguments against this approach; suffice it to say that it no longer reflects the actual situation in European societies.

The concepts proposed for addressing cultural and religious diversity are those of minority, recognition and common values. These ideas warrant some explanation:

4a. Law on minorities

Many cultural groups can be regarded as minorities within the meaning used by instruments for the legal protection of minorities[29]. Local authorities must therefore address the question of the protection that must be afforded to minorities by law. However, in many respects this is not enough:

- the management of cultural and religious diversity by local authorities goes beyond what is governed by legislation, which is often imprecise and incomplete;

- some cultural and religious aspects are not covered by the concept of minority because, for example, they also concern majorities or situations which do not relate to specific groups;

- this approach must be combined with another, namely that of promoting the interests of the community as a whole and relations among its various components.

For the authorities, while it is important for specific cultural or religious groups to be protected, it is just as important for them to become well-integrated in the broader framework of the society to which they belong.

---

29 A smaller group than the majority, with distinctive characteristics of a cultural, religious or linguistic nature which they wish to conserve.

4b. Means of achieving mutual recognition

The proper integration of minorities is based on the principle of a virtuous circle of loyalty and generosity, or "give and take". The majority[30] recognises the minority and gives it advantages and, in return, the minority recognises the majority and abides by the rules that it lays down. The more loyal the minority is, the more generous the majority will be, and vice versa. The community is anxious to ensure that the minority is in a comfortable position but the minority is concerned about the interests of the community[31].

The principle of the virtuous circle requires much more than the mere granting of minimum rights to the minority and the minority's compliance with the law. There needs to be mutual recognition, implying an all-encompassing[32] concept of society. The two sides (majority and minority) must regard the minority as part of the community in the best sense of the term. For this virtuous circle involving the minority and the majority to be a success, there needs to be a balance, which is never stable, between distinguishing and sharing:

- the minority wishes to preserve its distinctive features;

- but it also wants interaction with the community and other minorities.

Intercultural and interfaith dialogue is therefore an important test of whether the delicate balance between the majority and the minority has been preserved. These are issues of concern to society as a whole, at national and European level. However, it is only at local government level that the fine tuning of these basic principles can be carried out. It is only at local government level that individuals can experience the fact that there is a wider community to which they all belong and whose cohesion affects the interests of all individuals and of all the smaller communities which derive their legitimacy from this framework.

4c. The question of common values

Many local officials believe that for cultural and religious groups to be integrated into the wider community and for intercultural and interfaith dialogue to be possible, it is necessary to have a core of common values. The idea would appear to make good sense, but it is not always easy to apply in practice.

---

30 A more appropriate expression is the "wider community" but the simpler term "majority" has been used because, as far as minority groups are concerned, relations are generally considered to be with the majority. Often, the interests of the community are actually those of the majority.

31 Otherwise, a vicious circle of provocation and repression is created, resulting in mutual rejection and a breakdown of relations between the community and the minority.

32 A preferable term to the word "unitary".

a) Definition of common values

The common values considered to be crucial to European societies are generally as follows:

- acceptance by all individual groups that they belong to the wider community (the membership principle);

- recognition that everyone is free to join a particular group or not (the principle of autonomy);

- recognition that all members of society are fundamentally equal (principle of non-discrimination).

However, these values are not necessarily accepted by every group. Some groups consider themselves to be distinct, separate communities. Furthermore, some groups believe that it is reasonable to deter their members from leaving them. Lastly, some groups have a specific view of social roles (particularly the roles of men and women), which may undermine true equality among their members. These views are not totally absurd, because minority groups can ensure their survival and preserve their identity only by exercising a degree of disengagement from the wider community and displaying attachment to their identity.

More generally, it must be said that although the values of freedom and autonomy may be perceived to be universal, this is not actually so. Alongside ideas of society based on integration (universalist and individualist models based on abstract values), there are separative, culture-based notions (the idea that society should be organised around specific beliefs and cultures whose survival takes precedence over group members' freedoms).

It has to be said that the principle of religious and philosophical impartiality which holds sway in most of our societies relates only to impartiality vis-à-vis ideas and philosophies that fit in with common values and not to a form of general impartiality applying to all ideas of whatever kind.

b) Attitude towards groups that reject common values

What attitude should be adopted towards groups that refuse to subscribe to common values? (Some groups may formally bow to the rules but nonetheless consider them illegitimate as far as they are concerned, ask for exemptions or try to overthrow them). The authorities' decision can be a difficult one:

- adopting too lenient a stance may compromise the wider community's collective interests and undermine social cohesion;

- adopting a punitive stance is at odds with the wider community's liberal, pluralist principles.

They are obliged therefore to adopt a more complex position:

- some forms of behaviour have to be punished (for example, violence inflicted by groups on their members to make them obey the group's rules);

- non-punitive, incentive-based attitudes may encourage "separatist" factions to subscribe to the values of the wider community (financial or material aid can be made conditional on this);

- different options in the sphere of values may be allowed if these options do not pose a threat to law and order and the group concerned agrees to engage in dialogue.

It is particularly when the latter two strategies are pursued that intercultural and interfaith dialogue can prove very useful. However, the complexity of the process must not be underestimated.

5. Guiding principles for local authorities faced with religious or cultural requests

Local authorities are faced with an increasingly diverse range of requests and queries from religious and cultural groups. It can be difficult for them to decide how to deal with these, bearing in mind considerations of cost, complexity, equality and the need to safeguard the cohesion and the common interests of the entire community. Here are some examples of requests that may be made by particular groups:

- authorisation to open a place of worship;

- organisation of teaching in a foreign language;

- catering for cultural and religious traditions in school meals or public canteens;

- special bathing times reserved for women in public swimming pools;

- authorisation to wear traditional or religious clothing at school or in buildings providing public services;

- establishment of areas for different religions in cemeteries;

- access for particular groups to the local media (radio and television programmes);

- ritual slaughter of animals, particularly on major feast days;

- religious teaching in schools;

- acknowledgement of traditional religious festivals specific to certain groups;

- adaptation of hospital services to take account of religious or cultural traditions.

To make the right choices, local authorities must bear certain principles in mind.

5a. The principle of religious freedom

This principle entails not only tolerance of religious convictions but also a duty to take positive steps to establish the conditions necessary for the effective exercise of religious freedom. One of the main implications of this is that the authorities must do everything within their power to enable religious groups to live out their beliefs in satisfactory conditions, to have appropriate premises, to manifest their beliefs and to pass them on. The extent of this duty may be interpreted differently, according to national traditions and legislation.

5b. The principle of religious impartiality

According to this principle, the authorities must distance themselves from religious beliefs by refraining from taking any positive or negative views in matters of faith. However, interpretations of this principle will vary according to country. In fact, no authority can be totally impartial, for the following reasons:

- it may be compelled to adopt a negative approach to religious groups considered to pose a threat to law and order (although, often, the extent of the threat is difficult to gauge objectively);

- it may be necessary for it to take affirmative action to support religious freedom. Furthermore, an authority may have legitimate interests in common with certain religious groups. These may be cultural interests, where religious culture and state culture overlap (for example, many religious monuments are also cultural monuments symbolising a region). They may also be social interests, where a religious group does work to promote social integration and can help to solve social problems in this way.

The principle of impartiality does not therefore rule out varying attitudes on the part of local authorities towards different religious groups. However, they must be objectively and reasonably justified.

5c. The principle of freedom of expression

At all events, the local authorities' management of cultural diversity must be in keeping with the legal framework of fundamental freedoms. It must therefore observe the principles of:

- freedom of expression and of communication;

- freedom of assembly and of association.

The proper exercise of these freedoms rules out restrictions, unless they are justified by serious law-and-order considerations, and implies positive steps to make it possible to put them into practice. The local authorities therefore, have a duty to adopt appropriate measures in their own field of legal competence to facilitate, for example, media access for all cultural groups.

5d. The principle of strict compliance with the law

The local authorities must, of course, apply the law, which may include precise rules on the rights and duties of cultural and religious groups. Even where a legal rule is contested, it must be applied faithfully for, particularly where there are differences of interpretation, it provides an objective common reference point. However the law is not always clear. It can contain incompatible provisions. There is nothing inherently wrong in this, as the rule that the law must be complied with does mean applying a simple list of instructions; it involves a process fuelled by collective thought and debate.

5e. The principle of proportionality

When requests by cultural or religious groups are processed, it is reasonable to take account both of the scope of the measure being asked for and of its cost (in financial, social or other terms) for the community. If the measure would incur little or no cost or trouble, there is no reason to refuse; if it would cause serious inconvenience, the group has to show that, as far as it is concerned, it fulfils an essential or very important need. This rule of proportionality is reflected in the concept of "reasonable accommodation" developed by the case-law of some countries in the area of religious practices. Even where a request cannot be justified by a right, it deserves to be taken into account if it reflects a serious concern and can be accommodated without too much difficulty.

Whatever the circumstances, refusing on principle to accede to a request by a religious or cultural group which would not cause any significant inconvenience is unreasonable.

5f. The principle of transparency

Whatever attitude local authorities take to requests from cultural or religious groups, they must give reasons, that is to say they must clearly and honestly explain their stance, particularly if they make use of "discretionary powers" when dealing with such requests. This rule can be exacting and difficult to follow, but it is the key to frank and open debate.

5g. The principle of non-discrimination

This principle is acknowledged by all European countries but it is particularly tricky to put into practice. Firstly, equality does not mean the uniform application of the same measure to all situations, but adjusting a rule to particular situations so that there are equal opportunities for cultural or religious development for all. Secondly, differences in treatment may be justified by public-interest considerations. Non-discrimination does not therefore imply identical treatment, but efforts to check that special measures are appropriate and justified.

True equality can therefore entail specific positive measures in favour of certain cultural or religious groups. This is the case wherever it is considered appropriate to cater for a particular cultural characteristic (for example, by making adjustments to the school education system so that the language, culture and history of a particular community can be passed on).

6. Guidelines for action

It is difficult to establish general guidelines in view of the diversity of local situations. However, some suggestions can be made.

1)   A good means of determining whether a specific measure in favour of a minority is appropriate or not may be to look at its integrating effect. A measure that fosters the integration of a minority group into the wider community is, on the face of it, a useful measure, even if it means making an exception to the general rule. For example, should Sikhs who wish to join the Canadian Mounted Police be allowed to wear their turbans instead of the hat which is normally worn with the uniform? The Canadian authorities' answer to this was "yes" because it made it easier for Sikhs to have access to public-service jobs. Conversely, if the result of the measure being requested is to sideline or isolate a community, a much more guarded approach is required.

2)   Measures likely to destabilise a minority group must be opposed because there is a danger that they will radicalise the group and make it intolerant. On the other hand, measures that enable it to take better

advantage of collective institutions and advance its interests fairly are likely to strengthen its confidence in these institutions and help it to accept further integration without fear of losing its identity.

3)   Special arrangements for minorities must, wherever possible, be made as part of a deal, in which the minority group is given certain advantages in return for committing itself to measures benefiting the wider community or measures conducive to its integration in that community. For example, measures may be taken by the local authorities to promote knowledge of the language of a country of origin while, at the same time, representatives of the minority group in question commit themselves to efforts to improve knowledge of the language most widely spoken in the country or region. This is a way of giving tangible form to the principle of mutual recognition of the minority and the wider community. In the same vein, it may be advisable to make use of formal agreements between local authorities and particular groups to put their mutual undertakings on an official footing.

4)   There is also the option of inviting the different cultural or religious minorities to take part in drawing up a "common charter of values" for the wider community, which:

- establishes the common interests and aims of the community as a whole;

- sets out mutually agreed forms of conduct that are desirable in relations between cultural and religious groups in a spirit of tolerance and mutual respect;

- makes provision for participation in dialogue and mediation bodies.

5)   As far as the award of financial aid and grants is concerned, it is best for there to be a general framework laying down the conditions for local authority contributions to cultural and religious groups so that an objective, impartial approach can be guaranteed.

6)   Among the "techniques" that have proved effective in improving the integration of traditional minorities into the wider community, a particularly useful one is the establishment of representative bodies able to express the group's needs constructively, act as consultative bodies, engage in dialogue with the authorities and assume responsibilities towards the community at large[33].

---

33   See, in particular, the handbook on local consultative bodies for foreign residents, ISBN 987-92-871-5455-2. See also the Convention on the Participation of Foreigners in Public Life at Local Level (ETS No. 144).

7. Some basic measures

The first stages in the process of establishing dialogue between cultural and religious groups and the local authorities will be the same no matter how much the situations differ.

7a. Provide the "tools" needed to find out about and communicate with the various cultural and religious groups in the area

This implies two fundamental measures:

- a survey and full analysis of the situation of each local authority with regard to the religious and cultural diversity on its territory (looking at factors such as the different groups, their characteristics, their expectations and the abilities of persons in positions of responsibility in the groups, and analysing the situation to determine the main problems encountered, the solutions that might be envisaged and the resources needed for the purpose);

- organisation of the local authority's administrative departments in such a way that there are people within these departments with responsibility for this activity and the appropriate skills and resources.

7b. Create a climate of trust between the local authority and the groups concerned

Local government officials must show their readiness to engage in dialogue by contacting the groups in their area. They must begin by identifying the group leaders and creating conditions conducive to good communication with them, then discuss the situation of the group and its desires with them.

7c. Set up a system for listening to the needs of these groups and providing advice, information and assistance with projects

In this context, it might, for example, be possible to prepare a joint publication presenting the groups concerned. At this stage, it may be a good idea to specify exactly who will be in charge. Very often, success will depend on having people capable of playing the role of "intercultural mediator", to whom the task of supervising dialogue can be assigned[34]. It is also worth summing up local authority measures in a local intercultural co-operation

---

34   See, for example, the dialogue between Jews and Muslims organised in the Baarsjes district of Amsterdam under the guidance of Erwin Brugmans and Mustafa Laboui.

programme, which can offer an overall blueprint for local government action in this area.

7d. Hold intercultural and interfaith meetings

These enable groups to meet, introduce themselves to one another and launch joint activities. Meetings can also be a first step towards establishing a more formal framework for interfaith co-operation.

7e. Set up a local interfaith council

Any such body should be set up unhurriedly. It is necessary to take a number of precautions:

- ensure that the faiths invited to take part in this broadly reflect the actual local situation as regards religion;

- ensure that those representing the faiths concerned are truly representative;

- give the body a status that is truly independent of the local authority setting it up;

- see to it that religious groups recognise themselves in this body and consider themselves to be properly represented, in the light of the weight given to each belief;

- establish a climate of trust so that participants in this body are willing to work constructively with the authorities;

- propose activities for the body that match the concerns of all the groups represented on it.

These are all conditions which it is difficult to satisfy. It may be prudent to begin by organising the interfaith council on an informal basis and to put it on an official footing only gradually, as it gains experience. Among the tasks that might be assigned to such a council are:

- giving the local authority its opinion on the management of religious and cultural diversity;

- examining requests from the various groups;

- adopting common principles and rules of good conduct with regard to the expression of religious and cultural diversity.

Conclusion

Cultural diversity is a term currently on everyone's lips. However, some superficial forms of diversity actually undermine the protection of genuine diversity. We must beware of contributing to the routine use of this term to designate forms of globalised cultural communication and consumption. The fact that we can all decide freely with which values we wish to identify is a step forward, but there is a danger that this freedom will result, under the label of cultural diversity, in a mishmash of trends, which, although they have different ingredients, will become increasingly uniform worldwide. To avoid this, we need to approach the management of cultural heritage with rigour and a concern for authenticity. Local authorities are in an ideal position to do this.

Chapter 2

Local Authorities and Intercultural Dialogue

Jean-François Husson[*] and Julie Mahiels[**]

[*]   Secretary General of the Interuniversity Centre for Permanent Training, Charleroi, Belgium

[**]   Scientific Adviser at CIFoP.

Introduction

The first part of this report sought to set out the role of the various levels of government with respect to religion in the countries under review.

The second part deals with a series of specific issues that fall more directly within the jurisdiction of local authorities, and presents a series of situations.

This is an interim version that does not claim to be exhaustive and can be supplemented by further research on our part and by the ideas, suggestions and information provided by participants and the Council of Europe. At this stage, most of the examples are from Belgium and France; the scope will be broadened in the final report.

A series of questions dealt with below is introduced by emphasising a number of risks and issues. This is quite brief at the moment but will be added to later.

Various sources have been used, since local practices in this field are little documented. Some documents are quoted to illustrate certain points or for information.

1. Context

Faced with the challenges presented by an increasingly multicultural and multireligious society, it is above all local authorities that are confronted with the expectations of citizens, whether or not they are members of philosophical or religious communities. Responses to those expectations sometimes vary widely in different countries and depend above all on how the first disputes between Churches and States were resolved in their day. The importance of this factor was again underlined recently in Great Britain where, in the framework of the performance objectives set for local authorities, "Councils will also be given responsibilities to ensure community cohesion. The document insists that all councils should address concerns about migration and cultural and religious differences"[35].

At the same time, religious groupings have placed great emphasis on their presence in the community, as is shown by initiatives such as the International Congress for the New Evangelisation, Brussels-Toussaint (November 2006, following previous congresses in Vienna, Paris and Lisbon) and the ideas collected in works such as "Spiritualities in the City" (Great Britain).

---

35   "Town halls set targets on local problems", *The Times*, 24th October 2006.

2. Specific issues

2a. Fostering greater knowledge of the various communities

Issues:

- greater knowledge of the various religious and philosophical communities improves social relationships and helps to improve mutual understanding;

- the target audience may be the general public; it should in particular address those in senior public and voluntary sector positions who are most in contact with people from the religious and philosophical communities concerned.

Risks / points requiring care:

- perception of proselytising; need for balance; risk of making a hierarchy of beliefs;

- what limits should there be as to the religious and philosophical communities to be presented (cf. the issue of sects, in particular).

Instructive experiences

In Brussels (Belgium), the exhibition "God, Directions for Use", mounted by the Musée de l'Europe in October-November 2006, a look at the world's major religions[36].

Extract from a newspaper article: '*"The intention of the ASBL Musée de l'Europe was clearly not to make a hierarchy of religions, much less to question the 'truth' they convey"*, explained Benoît Remiche, who, with Elie Barnavi, created the exhibition. *"By giving an idea both of the universal aspects and of the particularities of the world's religions, we have placed them in the context of everyday life. So the exhibition is not about theology or the history of religions in the strict sense, but about how the faithful live out their beliefs in their ordinary everyday lives. For the same reason, it is not a religious art exhibition, although objects that give meaning to believers' lives are displayed"*.'[37]

Perpignan (France): Spirituality in the City Programme

---

36 Presentation of the exhibition (in French and Dutch): http://www.expo-dieux.be

37 *La Libre Belgique*, 28-29th October 2006, http://www.lalibre.be/article.phtml?id=5&subid=106&art_id=311001

"Perpigan's experience of the Spirituality in the City Programme over the last 15 years has become a reference for what the will for dialogue can do to bring about genuine social cohesion. One of the key elements Perpignan has given us is the conviction that the various religious faiths do not have a monopoly on spirituality, but that it is shared by agnostics and people who describe themselves as atheists."[38] [39]

Another interesting example is the *Guide on Religion and Belief in the MOD and Armed Forces*, which sets out the different religions, their main characteristics, festivals, etc, and was produced by the British armed forces. It could be used at local level.

Others initiatives have aimed to make the different religions known through visits to their places of worship. For example, in Charleroi (Belgium), the Groupement d'Action Inter-Religieux (GRAIR), with the city council's support, organises a visit to several places of worship every year (in 2006, Catholic, Protestant, Orthodox, Jewish and Moslem), followed by a conference at which the participating religions are invited to debate various issues.

Similar initiatives have been taken in other cities (particularly in Arlon on the initiative of Mouvement Ouvrier Chrétien).

Generally speaking, this also raises the question of the information municipalities may distribute on the religious groups in their areas. For example, a number of Belgian municipalities mention on their sites the recognised religious communities, as well as other, unrecognised communities. In France, too, where "The Republic shall not recognise, fund or subsidise any religion", many municipalities provide information on the various religious communities in their territories.

2b. Fostering intercultural dialogue at local level and with the authorities

Issues:

- to make the various philosophical and religious beliefs better known in order to foster greater mutual understanding (-> general public);

- fostering contact between representatives of the various communities in the municipality, town and province in order to avoid tension and develop joint projects;

---

38   Extract from *Laïcité, spiritualités dans la cité*, p. 4

39   Expo Bible de Perpignan (http://www.mairie-perpignan.fr/pdf/fra.pdf)

Risks / points requiring care:

- perception that they are being taken over that might create difficulties for some community leaders;

- how representative certain groups are in reality.

Instructive experiences

This type of <u>dialogue</u> can take place in the framework of contacts between religions in order to enhance mutual understanding; in some cases the authorities may take the initiative. Some Belgian examples:

- In 1997 representatives of the Moslem, Buddhist, Jewish and Christian communities of Antwerp formed a Working Group for Interreligious Dialogue in order to promote mutual respect in society "through the liberating force of the religions".

- In Liège, Benedictines from the Abbaye de la Paix Notre-Dame, Moslem Families of Liège, and Sant-Egidio organise occasional meetings between the Christian and Moslem communities.

- In the Brussels-Capital region, a committee for intercultural dialogue has been established on the initiative of Mr Chabert, a regional minister[40].

This may also involve bringing together the representatives of the local religious communities to <u>take stock of municipal questions</u> (for example, in the case of public funding, on available budgets, priorities for public works, etc). For example, in Liège (Belgium) in the late 1990s the deputy mayor with responsibility for religions used to meet with local religious communities every year to take stock of current issues; other cities and municipalities have also organised such meetings on a regular basis. Examples, also from Belgium, are the mayor or his/her representative being involved in maintaining the fabric of Catholic churches and the governor or his/her representative sitting on the board of the provincial moral assistance body (though there is no public representation on the bodies of other religions)[41].

Similarly, the British Government has set up the Faith Communities Consultative Council (FCCC) a forum that brings together members of various religious communities (Christian, Hindu, Jewish, Moslem and Sikh) and encourages interreligious activities through regional conferences and

---

40   http://www.hoopvolbrussel.be

41   In September 2005 the French Interior Minister, Nicolas Sarkozy, called for local elected representatives to be present in the associations managing Moslem religious associations (see http://www.maire-info.com/article. asp?param=6087&PARAM2=PLUS).

support for local initiatives. (The FCCC has taken over the work the Inner Cities Religious Council had been doing since 1992.)

Based on the observation that religious communities have substantial resources, both human and material, the FCCC's aim is to work with government on local renewal, social integration and any other issues that might require its assistance, and thus serve as an intermediary between religious communities and government on local issues.

The FCCC's success can be measured by religious communities' ever-increasing involvement in local renewal projects, especially in the New Deals for Communities. These were launched in 1998 and are partnership projects between local communities and government that aim to tackle the many problems afflicting the poorest local communities. A recent report highlighted the factors that may encourage or limit religious community involvement in these projects, while a brief practical guide on how to involve communities in the various activities was published in 2004.

Many local authorities have used this model to set up their own local intercultural committees on which people from different religions can meet and work together for a more peaceful society. An example of this is Kirklees Council's Huddersfield Inter Faith Council[42].

2c. Cemeteries

Issues:

- to enable everyone to be buried in compliance with their beliefs;

- problem of converts' burials – no possibility of return to country of origin.

Risks / points requiring care:

- health issues;

- communalism;

- vandalism aimed especially at specific plots or cemeteries.

In most countries local authorities are responsible for managing cemeteries. It is therefore municipalities that receive requests for specific plots for Moslems and special forms of burial. Cremation gives rise to similar issues that will not be dealt with at this stage.

---

42   http://www.kirklees.gov.uk/community/localorgs/orgdetails.asp?OrgID=3356

The first request confronting municipalities is for <u>specific plots</u>, something that may present a problem in countries strictly applying the principle of neutrality. Geneva, for example, is the last Swiss canton not to have plots, imposing a strict principle of neutrality. The Jewish and Moslem communities of Geneva are now working together to change this legislation dating from 1876. Up to now, the Jewish community has been burying its dead in a cemetery on French soil, but with an entrance and car park in Switzerland[43] .

In France, the requirement that the bodies of the dead should face Mecca has led to the creation of *de facto* "Moslem plots", despite the legal prohibition on mayors establishing distinctions based on the beliefs or religion of the dead. The local authorities have shown themselves to be flexible in the face of this problem and two Interior Ministry memoranda have endorsed the practice, provided the neutrality of cemeteries is preserved and it is simply a facility offered, rather than an obligation[44].

The recent Machelon Report noted that "the lack of confessional plots would seem to be the major reason for the expatriation of about 80% of Moslem dead" in France. Given this dilemma and the existence of *de facto* plots, the report suggests a number of solutions, including amending legislation to allow the extension of some existing "private" confessional cemeteries, rather than continue such "privatisation of public space"[45].

Other countries accede more readily to religious communities' requests. In 2003 Austria was the first European country to open a Buddhist plot in Vienna's Central Cemetery. The new Moslem cemetery in the Liesing district of Vienna was still under construction in May 2006. In April of that year it suffered an arson attack. Despite the fire, the cemetery should be operational by late 2006. A great deal has also been done in the United Kingdom to accede to such requests[46].

Several Belgian municipalities have Moslem plots. Funeral and burial arrangements have been in the jurisdiction of the Regions since the Act of 13th of July 2001, which came into force on the 1st January 2002. Also to be noted is the recent inauguration of a multifaith cemetery in the Brussels region in 2002, thus taking into account the changing composition of Belgian society.

---

43 World Jewish Congress, 13th of October 2006, *Religious minorities in Geneva lobbying for own cemeteries*, http://www.worldjewishcongress.org

44 Higher Council for Integration report, *Islam in the Republic*, November 2000, p. 43.

45 Report of the Committee on Legal Examination of the Relations between Religions and the Authorities, 20th September 2006 p. 60 ff, known as the Machelon Report after its Chair, Jean-Pierre Machelon.

46 Altay Manço, "Good cities, good practices: systematisation of theoretical and methodological framework for local actions designed to combat religious discrimination" in *Migration Letters, Recognition of Islam in European Municipalities*, A. Manço and S. Amorantis (eds.), Vol. 2, No.3, December 2005, p. 193.

The second problem that may arise is compliance with a <u>particular rite</u>, such as direct burial of the body in the earth (conflicting with to the public health requirement to use a coffin), prohibition on burial (given the temporary nature of concessions) or orientation of the body towards Mecca.

Four Belgian cemeteries at present allow compliance with Moslem rites. In this respect, the City of Ghent has made a very interesting agreement with the local Moslem community: burial in a coffin in a special plot where graves are orientated towards Mecca and in a temporary concession that can be renewed by the deceased's descendents[47].

The Turkish and Moroccan Moslem communities in the Netherlands still repatriate most of their dead to their countries of origin. The problem of burial according to special religious rites does not arise as acutely as in other countries. For example, only about 70 burials of Moslems are recorded in Rotterdam each year, most of them of converts. Nevertheless, the legislation on funerals and graves was amended in 1991 to allow religious requirements to be respected. For example, it is possible to bury the deceased directly in the earth (although one study suggests that the practice is not followed and that instead the coffin is placed in a wooden "funerary chamber")[48]. According to the information at our disposal, there is no Moslem cemetery, mainly for financial reasons, although some major cities have Moslem plots in their cemeteries.

In Sweden, where parishes and parish associations are responsible for managing most cemeteries, ten Moslem cemeteries have been established and placed under the responsibility of the municipalities in which they are situated. There is no restriction on compliance with particular religious rites.

2d. Funding religious activities

Issues:

- funding religions and secular organisations can be understood as "positive secularism", the authorities considering moral and religious assistance to be a service to the population;

- generally speaking, funding also enables the groupings funded to have a degree of transparency, even a degree of supervision.

---

47 Meryem Kanmaz and Sami Zemni, "Religious discriminations and public policies: Muslim burial areas in Ghent", in *Migration letters, Recognition of Islam in European municipalities*, ed. A. Manço and S. Amoranitis, Vol. 2. No. 3, December 2005, p. 271.

48 N. LANDMAN, *Dutch responses to Muslim religious practices*, Presentation for the Fachtagung der Katholische Akademie / Friedrich-Ebert-Stiftung, Muslime in Europa — ein Ländervergleich 9–10 februari 2001, http://www.euro-islam.info/pages/landmandutch.html

Risks / points requiring care:

- funding criteria must be absolutely objective;

- and what about local authorities' agreement or opinion with respect to recognising local religious establishments and their budgets?

General survey

In some countries (Belgium, Alsace-Moselle, etc.) local authorities provide recognised local religious communities with various forms of funding: they cover the deficits of religious establishments, pay for the maintenance and upkeep of places of worship, etc. In many cases they have a statutory duty to do so.

Recognition of local communities usually involves:

- recognition of a religion; this is generally within the jurisdiction of central government (or the Land) and will not therefore be discussed further;

- recognition of local communities (parishes, etc).

It is usually a higher authority that determines recognition criteria for local communities. As an example, the criteria used in Belgium are as follows:

- for the Catholic religion, one parish per 600 inhabitants[49]; for "minority" religions, 200 to 250 followers[50]; secular services are organised on a territorial basis; this very old federal administrative precedent is still applied in the Walloon Region[51], pending the adoption of specific provisions;

- in Flanders, quantitative criteria have been set aside in favour of integration in local life, use of the Dutch language and compliance with the European Convention on Human Rights;

- in Brussels-Capital, recognition of mosques also takes into account security considerations with respect to places of worship.

In such cases the opinion of the local authorities concerned may be desirable (particularly if funding is being given).

In other countries (e.g. Germany) local authorities also give funding to local religious communities, but this is often optional, i.e. left to the discretion

---

49   Although the last time a parish was recognised on this basis seems to have been in the mid-1970s.

50   It is left to the representative body of the religion to assess this figure, however, since compliance with respect for private life makes it unthinkable that a list of followers be communicated to the authorities.

51   The decisions taken by the Walloon Government in October 2005 concerning Islamic communities provide for organisational modalities but not for recognition criteria.

of the authority, which is responsible for identifying beneficiaries, the nature of financial support, etc.

In another group of countries local authorities do not fund religious communities at all (e.g. France, where it is illegal to do so; Great Britain). There are, however a number of forms of indirect financial support, which may concern:

- funding social and charitable activities (see below);

- funding places of worship (see below);

- discretionary subsidies.

2e. Funding social and charitable activities

Issues:
- Social and charitable activities organised by religious groupings very often supplement local public services.

Risks / points requiring care:
- risk of proselytising (recruitment through social assistance);

- risk of communalism (assistance to community members only);

- indirect funding of religious activities.

General survey

In some countries, independently of funding religious activities, the social and charitable activities conducted by religious groupings at local level may be funded.

In countries that do not fund religious activities, this type of funding is often:

- either the result of a wish to encourage the voluntary sector as a provider of social and charitable services (Great Britain);

- or a means of funding associations under the pretext of "culture", although they are primarily "religious" (the case in France); here, however, it should be recalled that the administrative court of Montpellier (France) overturned a decision that the city should fund a mosque, presented as the construction of a "multi-purpose community meeting hall", whose purpose was in fact Moslem worship[52].

---

52   http://www.maire-info.com/article.asp?param=7417&PARAM2=PLUS

2f. Buildings – taxation

Issues:

- Should places of worship receive special treatment with respect to property taxation?

Risks / points requiring care:

- Does this concern all religions?

- Does this concern all places of worship?

- What are the equivalents for non-confessional communities?

General survey

In most Council of Europe countries, property taxes are a source of revenue for local authorities and places open to public worship are usually exempt or receive preferential treatment. The reasons generally given are that places of worship belong to the authorities, public bodies or non-profit / religious organisations or are not regarded as generating rental income.

In some cases, taxation may come under another level of government, possibly being ceded back to or shared with the local authorities (e.g. the *précompte immobilier* [advance on income tax payable on immovable property] and *centimes additionnels* [local tax on property and businesses] in Belgium). In other cases, there is an autonomous local tax system, local authorities themselves setting the basis, rates and exemptions of the taxation concerned.

Whatever the level of the tax system, definitions need to be precise. Thus in Belgium, places of worship are exempt from the *précompte immobilier* (see previous paragraph); this also concerns:

- places of worship of non-recognised religions (on the basis of the fiscal argument mentioned above);

- buildings of various organisations providing non-confessional moral assistance;

- presbyteries, considered as places of worship because they are used as meeting places for local religious bodies as well as housing.

2g. Buildings – construction/funding/making available

Issues:

- to what extent should or can local authorities be involved in the construction of places of worship?

- some religions have comparatively few resources, and freedom of worship is thus hampered; should local authorities restore "some balance"?

- is there a danger that the fact that some communities do not have enough places of worship will result in "overpopulation" of existing ones or in ones that are a security risk or inconvenience the neighbourhood?

Risks:

- ideally, objective criteria should be laid down in order to avoid favouring a particular community (number of believers? community's financial resources?).

- and what about non-confessional communities?

General survey

The issue of buildings varies a great deal from country to country. Issues of ownership and use are linked. For historical reasons, situations also differ greatly from one religion to another, between "historic" churches on one hand and "more recent" philosophical and religious movements on the other.

For example, in **Belgium,** the Catholic Church has (too?) many places of worship, where attendance is uneven and that are a substantial financial burden on local authorities. Over the years, the Protestant and Jewish religions have received some assistance (land or buildings temporarily made available), but have generally been self-financing[53]. The problem arises in acute form for the Moslem community. Local authorities have in some cases made premises available or have made over a building for the symbolic sum of one euro to a religious association (e.g. the mosque in Andenne). As a comparison, it will be recalled that the non-confessional philosophical community has received a great deal of assistance from municipalities and provinces through premises being made available, purchase and renovation of buildings, ownership or sole use of which has been accorded to them, etc.

---

53   In Belgium, local authorities have a statutory duty to maintain places of worship but not to build new ones.

In **France**, as a consequence of the position of various religions with respect to the 1905 Act, most of Catholic churches built before that date are the property of the municipalities, which therefore have to maintain them, unlike Protestant and Jewish places of worship which belong to the local religious communities and do not benefit from this type of involvement.

Despite the prohibition on funding religions, the report *Islam in the Republic*[54] indicated several avenues that could be followed perfectly legally (extract):

- **municipalities may grant a religious association a long lease that gives it long-term use of a municipal site on which a religious building can be constructed** (with the implicit understanding that the lease will be extended under identical conditions when it expires). However this practice, introduced by Léon Blum, President of the Council, and Cardinal Verdier, Archbishop of Paris, complies with the law only if the rent is set at the market rate, otherwise the lease has to be considered a disguised subsidy;

- **the local authority may also let a building to a religious association by agreement at the market rate in order to avoid any indirect subsidy**;

- **Section 11 of the Amending Finance Act of 29th of July 1961 enables public authorities to guarantee loans** contracted by religious associations and other groupings for the construction of religious buildings;

- **while the authorities may not fund either religious associations governed by the 1905 Act or associations with combined (cultural and religious) purposes, they may subsidise associations with purely cultural purposes:** cultural centres, libraries, meeting rooms, etc. This possibility has been used during the construction of several religious buildings, such as the Mosque and Cathedral in Evry, when two associations with distinct purposes were established. However, this implies watertight financial and operational separation between religious and cultural activities;

- local authorities may **subsidise the upkeep of buildings used for public worship that are managed by an association covered by the 1905 Act** (Section 19 of the 1905 Act).

The flexibility of the law, which does not avoid the development of illegal practices, does not, as we have seen, provide a really satisfactory response to the situation created by the 1905 Act, characterised by the freezing of public religious property as it existed at the beginning of the 20th century and the impossibility of public funding to compensate Moslems for

---

54   High Council for Integration (2000), p. 38

the inequality in terms of buildings thus created.

A number of comments need to be made about this extract:

- first, several voices have been raised in favour of enabling the authorities to fund places of worship;

- in the meantime, the Minister for the Interior has suggested "developing use of the long-term lease" so that the authorities can make sites available to religious associations[55];

- the use of the "socio-cultural" argument by some municipalities has sometimes clashed with administrative court decisions:

27th September 2006 – Administrative Court of Montpellier overturns decision to fund mosque

A decision by the Administrative Court of Montpelier, handed down on 30th of June and transmitted to the Prefecture on 15th of September, has overturned a decision by Montpellier City Council dated 28th of January 2002 to finance the construction of a mosque. The controlling group, then led by Georges Frêche (Socialist Party), had submitted a plan to build a "multi-purpose community meeting hall", whose purpose was in fact Moslem worship.

"It is clear from the documents of the case, and in particular from the newspaper articles that quote the Mayor of Montpelier who was in favour of construction of a mosque and the discussions during the meeting at which the said decision was taken, as well as from the terms of use of this building which was allocated to the exclusive use of the Franco-Moroccan Association…, that the purpose of this facility is to serve as a mosque." Invoking Section 2 of the 1905 Act ("The Republic shall not recognise, fund or subsidise any religion"), the Court reaffirmed that "public authorities may not legally intervene in the religious field and in particular may not undertake the construction of a public place of worship".

It is precisely this aspect of the Act that the report of the Machelon Committee (see our issue of 25th of September 2006), set up by the Interior Minister, proposed to change to the point of allowing municipalities to fund the construction of places of worship.

"This judgment is a clear demonstration that the construction of places of worship cannot be funded without amending the existing legal framework," commented Didier Leschi, head of the Religions Office at the Ministry of the Interior. (*Le Monde*, 27th September 2006).

---

55   Maire-Info, 27th of October 2004, http://www.maire-info.com/article.asp?param=4912&PARAM2=PLUS

(Source: http://www.maire-info.com/article.asp?param=7417&PARAM2=PLUS)

Unlike in other countries, mosque-building has not been controversial in **Great Britain**. On the contrary, the construction of a mosque is sometimes a matter of pride for a city, which sees it as evidence of the successful integration of the Moslem community in the wider community. In Birmingham, the mosque appears in the city's publicity material, for example. The only discussions raised by building a mosque often concern only its integration in the local architectural landscape[56]. Building permission is granted by the local council.

The situation varies widely in **Germany**, where local authorities also have the main jurisdiction. One of the most successful buildings with respect to its management is the Yavuz Sultan Selim Mosque in Mannheim. The building of a mosque in a neighbourhood dominated by Turkish immigrants aroused concern among inhabitants, who feared that it would attract further Moslem immigrants. In order to alleviate this concern, Moslem leaders allied themselves with the municipal authorities and the local Catholic and Evangelical churches, particularly with the priest of the Catholic Church opposite the site where the mosque was to be built. Since its inauguration the mosque has been an example of Islam's successful integration in local life[57].

2h. Buildings – town planning/safety

Issues:

- places of worship receive large numbers of people; safety considerations cannot be ignored;

- because of their size and the numbers of people they receive, places of worship must be integrated in their urban environment and not disturb public order (e.g. traffic);

- good relations between communities.

Risks / points requiring care:

- risk of safety criteria being used to prevent a place of worship operating.

Town planning issues (car parking, minarets, etc.), even issues with neighbours (the call to prayer), arise quite frequently, as does the question

---

56   S. McLOUGHLIN, Muslims and public space in Bradford: Conflict, cooperation and Islam as a resource for integration, in *Islam in European cities*, research sponsored by the Town Planning, Construction and Architecture Plan, Ministry of Infrastructure, Paris, France - December 2001.

57   J.S. FETZER et J. C. SOPER, *Muslims and the State in Britain, France, and Germany*, Cambridge University Press, Cambridge, United Kingdom, 2005, p.118.

of fire hazards in places of worship. Permission to open to the public or build a place of worship is often refused on the grounds of non-compliance with safety or town-planning regulations.

When the place of worship is in a neighbourhood that includes other communities, the issue of compliance with such provisions is particularly sensitive.

Illustrations (France):

a. Car parking, town planning, public order and neighbourliness

Extract from the report *Islam in the Republic*[58]:

From the public order point of view, places of worship that are not purpose-built may give rise to significant problems. **Such places do not always meet the safety criteria for buildings open to the public laid down in legislation**. Access to them is not always such as to enable the faithful to drive to them and park and this may create critical situations during religious festivals. The comments made by Mr. Gérard Hamon, a Rennes town councillor, about the Islamic cultural centre in Rennes show how sensitive such situations are: "The council received letters about the haphazard parking during midday prayers on Fridays and the major feasts (Eid Al-Kabir and Eid Al-Fitr). The people in charge of the centre have always informed the police of these events and have constantly asked that "bad citizens" should be fined, since parking questions are not a Moslem issue but a question of individual public-spiritedness. The prevarication of the municipal officials responsible for parking has shown me how much work is still needed before Moslems are perceived as citizens like any others. A great deal of insistence was required over a long period before they decided to take action (and overcome) the fear of very negative reactions or accusations of racism".

b. Use of regulations in force

23rd of February 2005 – Interior Minister recalls that mayors may only oppose the construction of religious buildings on the grounds of the regulations in force

In a recent circular, the Minister of the Interior stated that Prefects should remind mayors and representatives of religious observance associations of the principles governing the construction or conversion of buildings as places of worship.

This reminder should avoid the proliferation of legal disputes.

58　High Council for Integration (2000), p. 37

The Minister recalled that "the principle of the separation of Church and State, laid down by the Act of 9th of December 1905, and the fundamental principle of secularism contained in the Constitution make neutrality the cornerstone of relations between the authorities and religious bodies".

He went on saying that "neutrality does not, however, mean indifference to the fact of religion, since, under the very provisions of the 1905 Act, the Republic guarantees freedom of religion, subject only to the restrictions contained in law in the interests of public order (Section 1)".

The Interior Minister, who is responsible for matters relating to religions, considered that, "the construction of a place of worship may only be prevented on the grounds of application of the regulations in force, in particular regulations on town planning and the construction of buildings open to the public".

He referred to three such principles, which should be complied with referring to case-law.:

- Town planning law should not be deflected from its purpose in order to prevent the construction of a place of worship. The courts may declare "illegal a municipal authority's inappropriate use of its right of compulsory purchase to prevent the construction of a place of worship".

- A land-use plan may reserve a site for the construction of a place of worship "because a place of worship may, in the light of the characteristics of the projected town-planning operation, be of general interest". (Conseil d'Etat)

- the Minister recalled, however, that any building project must obviously be the subject of an application for planning permission in accordance with national and local town-planning regulations or be legitimately refused.

But "conversely, where the regulations are respected, refusal to grant planning permission will be overturned".

(Source: http://www.maire-info.com/article.asp?param=5367&PARAM2=PLUS)

2i. Ritual slaughter

Issues:
- Respect for traditions

Risks / points requiring care:
- Public health, hygiene, animal welfare, environment, public cleanliness

General survey

From the authorities' point of view, whichever authority has jurisdiction, ritual slaughter raises many issues: public health and hygiene, animal welfare and sometimes public order and environmental protection. While the legal framework is often national, local authorities are in the front line as regards implementation[59].

Such issues are particularly significant during certain religious feasts, such as the Eid Al-Kabir, when the problem of illegal slaughter arises throughout Europe. While no single solution is adequate, it should be remembered that there has been a great deal of discussion between religious communities and local authorities in an effort to find appropriate solutions[60].

In many cases, ritual slaughter has to be performed by an authorised person (during the Eid, slaughtermen recognised by the religious authorities), as is required in France and Belgium. Some authorities have with varying degrees of success provided mobile abattoirs (see below) and opened up public slaughterhouses; they have distributed leaflets outlining legislation on slaughter and the facilities provided for performing the sacrifice in compliance with them[61]. The collection of waste and examination of the carcases by veterinary staff have also been organised on occasion.

The ritual slaughter issue arose as early as the 1960s in the Netherlands and no longer seems to give rise to debate since the Dutch authorities introduced a number of exceptions to the relevant legislation. Exceptions had already been made for the Jewish community in the 1920s and this facilitated the introduction of further exceptions for the benefit of the Moslem community. The position now is that slaughter has to take place in abattoirs designated by the authorities (115 abattoirs in 1999). The authorities distribute explanatory documents in Dutch, Arabic and Turkish for the annual Feast of Sacrifice and require all Moslems wishing to sacrifice a sheep to register at one of the official abattoirs a few days in advance (for organisational reasons). The slaughter itself is carried out by two qualified Moslem slaughtermen under the supervision of a veterinary surgeon, while the butchering is done by professional butchers. Only one person per family may attend the slaughter (for hygiene reasons). Despite all this, there are cases of unauthorised slaughter every year[62].

---

59 Animal welfare will not be discussed (e.g. the Swedish legislation requires animals to be anaesthetised, which is a problem for the Jewish community and part of the Moslem community) as it falls outside the framework of local authorities.

60 Report of the High Council for Integration, *Islam in the Republic*, November 2000 pp. 45ff.

61 "Over 1,200 register for Feast of Sacrifice"' *Le Soir*, 29th December 2005; C. BODART, "A Feast of Sacrifice within the regulations", *Le Soir*, 15th December 2006 ; Ma. C. "Containers or no containers", *La dernière heure*, 15th December 2006.

62 The exact date of the Sacrifice is based on the lunar calendar but not infrequently falls on different days in different Moslem communities, which means that agreement is needed not only between the authorities and the community of believers but also between Moslem communities, N. LANDMAN, *Dutch responses to Muslim religious practices*, Presentation for the Fachtagung der Katholische Akademie / Friedrich-Ebert-Stiftung, Muslime in Europa — ein Ländervergleich 9–10 februari 2001, http://www.euro-islam.info/pages/landmandutch.html

Illustration

a. Official regulation – Prefecture of Police, Paris (France)

19th of January 2005 – Conditions for observing the Eid Al-Kabir

On the occasion of the Moslem feast of the Eid Al-Kabir (which will take place on or around the 21st of January next), the Paris Prefecture of Police recalls that under the regulations in force the following are prohibited at any time of year:

- ritual slaughter, in particular of sheep, other than in a working abattoir, in application of Article R 214-73 of the Rural Code;

- to unload and sell live animals for slaughter in Paris (Prefectural Decree no. 94-10527 of 29th April 1994);

- to keep or hold, even briefly, within dwelling places, their outhouses, entrances or common parts animals of any species whose number, behaviour or state of health may threaten the safety, health or tranquillity of the neighbourhood, in application of Article 26 of the *departement* health regulations;

- to possess, allow to circulate, display, dispose of, sell or offer for sale unidentified sheep, in accordance with the provisions of Decree no. 2002-1544 of 20th December 2002;

- to sell and/or make available for consumption carcasses of sheep more than six months old without removing the central nervous system (brain, spinal cord, eyes), in accordance with the Interministerial Order dated 24th December 2003;

- to hand over to final consumers, as they are or after transformation, carcasses of animals of sheep or goat species or butchered parts of such species taken from the muscles attached to the spinal column, excluding the caudal vertebrae, from which the bones have not been removed without first removing the spinal cord, in accordance with the provisions of the Ministerial Decrees of 24th December 2002 and 7th January 2005.

There are establishments in the *departments* neighbouring Paris in which slaughter may take place according to Moslem rites.

(Source: http://www.maire-info.com/article.asp?param=5224&PARAM2=PLUS)

b. Organisation in a *département* with no abattoir

Extract from the report *Islam in the Republic*[63] describing the situation in Hauts-de-Seine, "an urban department with a high concentration of Moslems and no abattoir [that] has managed to find balanced solutions whose success

---

63   High Council for Integration (2000), p. 65

is largely due to preliminary consultation with religious organisations":

"Organisation of the Eid Al-Kabir in Hauts de Seine

Since 1995, the services of the Prefect's office have written to representatives of the Moslem community informing them of the measures taken to ensure that the Eid Al-Kabir runs smoothly. Sites where live animals may be displayed are made available to qualified people who have a contract with an abattoir situated in another department. People can choose a live sheep, which is then transported for slaughter in an abattoir and the carcass brought back in a refrigerated lorry.

Two or three sales sites are authorised each year. The departmental veterinary service, the police, the departmental amenities directorate and the animal protection society are represented. The veterinary services supervise, in particular, the return of carcasses from both abattoirs (Forge-les-Eaux and L'isle Jourdain) in the late morning so that the animals can be distributed to families in the afternoon.

In 2000, two periods in which families could reserve animals were arranged at each of the two authorised places of sale, Nanterre and Gennevilliers, during the two weeks preceding the feast on 16th March. A total of 632 sheep were sold.

Despite the pressure this system puts on government services, it enables the Moslem community's needs to be reconciled with hygiene, consumer, animal and environmental protection regulations, as well as public order, and complies with national and Community regulations."

c. Mobile abattoirs

In **France**, the AMGVF (Association of Mayors of French Cities) conducted a survey of cities on the renting of mobile abattoirs during the Eid Al-Kabir. This brief report followed an enquiry by the City of Angers as to the appropriateness of renting a mobile abattoir. Twelve cities replied to AMGVF's questions, but none had used such a system. The replies bring out the practical difficulties encountered and the practicalities of organising the feast[64].

Conversely, in **Belgium** the City of Namur considered using a mobile abattoir to be an advantage.

Newspaper article:

Le Soir – 10th December 2004

---

64   Association des Maires des Grandes Villes de France - Etude n° 217 – Online on 31th October 2006, http://www.grandesvilles.org/spip.php?article738

Namur – An abattoir for the sacrifice

A first for the City of Namur. The "compact", a specially fitted-out container, reconciles Islamic rites and hygiene standards.

In Islamic tradition, the Eid Al-Kabir commemorates the sacrifice God asked of Abraham (or Ibrahim) to test his faith. Hence the name "Feast of Sacrifice". For Moslems it is, along with Ramadan, one of the most important times of year. The social aspect of the Feast of Sacrifice is as important as its religious dimension. A sheep killed according to an established ritual is shared among the guests.

For the last three years, the City of Namur has made a number of arrangements to gather sheep carcasses. For January 2005, it has taken a further step in collaboration with Moslem communities.

Before 2002, nothing in particular was organised for the Feast of Sacrifice, recalled the deputy mayor responsible for the environment, Alain Detry. *Then for two years we have collected the animal waste resulting from ritual slaughter on the site of the parks department in Vedrin, the expense being covered by the Walloon Region. We collected 185 skins in 2002 and 290 in 2003*.

In 2004, the City made special arrangements with the Ciney abattoir. The very limited enthusiasm for this experiment, that can in part be explained by the difficulty of transporting animals to Ciney, led the Namur authorities to try something else. It should be remembered that it is illegal to slaughter animals at home. Anyone caught doing so would be fined €500 and the animal would be confiscated.

So a way of slaughtering in Namur that complied with both rite and legislation had to be found. The deputy mayor responsible for the environment found it: the "compact". From the outside it looks like a large container, the type that is seen on building sites. Inside, it is divided into two compartments. The first contains a cage that prevents the sheep from moving. With its head turned towards Mecca, the animal is electrically stunned and its throat cut.

There is a set of mechanisms to pump the blood away before it coagulates and to facilitate butchering. The butchered animal is passed through to the second compartment where it is examined by a vet. Forty animals an hour can be slaughtered.

The City of Namur hopes many Moslems will use the mobile abattoir. It has rented one this year but, if the threshold of 200 animals is reached, it may buy one next year. The cost of purchasing the container would be redeemed in ten years on the basis of a €40 fee per animal.

Luc Scharès

PRATICALITIES

Open day. The City invites people to visit the temporary abattoir on 12th December between 9.30 am and 1 pm at the Porcelaine, 57 chaussée de Liège, Jambes.

Forms. Application forms for slaughter can be obtained from City Hall and Moslem organisations from Sunday. Deadline for applications: Monday, 17th January.

Slaughter. The sheep will be brought to the site on 19th January. The slaughter will take place the next day and possibly the day after that.

2j. Swimming pools and sports facilities

Issues:

- enabling Moslem women to swim without men being present.

Risks:

- limiting periods when pools are open to everyone;

- risk of a proliferation of requests by particular groups (e.g. nudists).

Examples

Several municipalities have introduced women-only sessions in order to enable Moslem women to go swimming. Examples are Lille, Schaerbeek and Exeter.

1st of July 2003 – Martine Aubry justifies the introduction of a weekly one-hour session for Moslem women only at the Lille-Sud swimming-pool

During a municipal council meeting on Monday, the Mayor of Lille, Martine Aubry, justified the introduction of a weekly one-hour session for Moslem women only at the Lille-Sud swimming-pool as "an opportunity for some of them to emancipate themselves".

Ms. Aubry was replying to a question put to her by the head of the municipal opposition, Bertrand Decocq (UMP) who challenged "the exception to the republican practices of equality and mixing of the sexes", the session represented.

There is a large Moslem community in the Lille-Sud district. For Mr. Decocq, "demanding special conditions for using a municipal swimming-pool" was "a form of withdrawal and communalism."

"Let's diverge slightly [from our republican principles] so that these women can gain and achieve their emancipation," said Ms. Aubry, recalling that on their side they had "consistently requested a place where they could be together and talk".

According to the Mayor of Lille, the hour at the swimming-pool, set aside since 2000, was "for some of them the first opportunity to exist by themselves, to emancipate themselves".

(Source: http://www.maire-info.com/article.asp?param=3234&PARAM2=PLUS)

There are also women-only sessions at Schaerbeck swimming-pool (Brussels, Belgium) and in Exeter (Great Britain), where women-only swimming sessions seem to have been held since 2004. During the sessions, the lifeguard is female and children are also admitted (boys up to the age of 8)[65].

2k. Sects

Issues:
- avoiding contributing to the development of sectarian organisations

Risks:
- defining sectarian organisations (cf. "harmful sectarian organisations" = criminal organisations hiding behind a religious screen, to paraphrase the definitions given by several reports on the subject).

While several countries have produced reports – in particular, parliamentary reports – on the issue of sects, France stands out as having produced several reports dealing with the question in specific sectors. For example, in 2001 the Interministerial Mission Against Sects (MIVILUDES) published a 23-page guide for mayors called "Mayors and Sects", written by Alain Vivien, President of MIVILUDES, and Jean-Paul Delevoye, President of the French Mayors' Association[66]. The guide also covers issues such as premises, vaccination and education of children, allowing use of municipal halls, and so on.

Extract from the guide's editorial:

Sects are one of the dangers confronting our society. It is a particularly complex danger because our fundamental freedoms of thought, belief and association must be preserved at the same time as we take action against those who take advantage of human weakness by using spiritual and often

---

65   http://www.exeter.gov.uk/index.aspx?articleid=1725

66   Reaction to the report: http://www.sectes-infos.net/GuideMaires.htm

material alienation.

Because of the special role they have of listening attentively to the population and mediation, mayors, when they receive information, hear rumours or are questioned by zealous or fearful fellow citizens, very often wonder what their responsibilities are and what action they can take.

Another report entitled "Penser le risque sectaire - État de droit et acte éducatif" has been written and distributed on the initiative of the Ministry of Youth and Sport (n.d).

2l. Education

In most countries primary education is run by local authorities, although basic legislation is voted at a higher level.

In **Great Britain**, so long as a number of conditions are fulfilled, faith schools can receive state-funding of up to 85% of running costs[67]. State schools are run by local authorities which manage staff and the buildings they own. Conversely, and except for slight organisational variations, faith schools are managed by trusts, i.e. private bodies. At present, 4,646 Anglican schools, 2,041 Catholic schools, 37 Jewish schools, 2 Sikh schools, 9 Moslem schools and 1 Hindu school receive state funding. The partnership between faith schools and the British Government is particularly strong for financial as well as historical reasons because education in such schools is less expensive for the government. Evidence of this is the recent controversy over the imposition of a quota of 25% of pupils enrolled who are not of the school's religious faith. A voluntary agreement was reached with Catholic and Anglican state-funded schools to open their doors, making legislation unnecessary[68].

In Germany, with the agreement of the Land concerned, private schools, some of which are faith schools, can sometimes receive public funding. According to the information at our disposal, only two Moslem primary schools at present receive such funding. Access to public funding for faith schools seems not be a priority for the Moslem community in Germany.

The situation is similar in **Sweden** where the state funds 85% of public school expenditure. Such schools follow official curricula but may add their own curriculum to it. Access to such schools, about twenty in the territory, is free.

In the cases considered, the initiative for opening faith schools is always private, and such schools are expected to meet their needs unaided. Furthermore,

---

67 Recognised schools are part of the state network, as contrasted with education run independently of government, which has 2,500 schools and 620,000 pupils (http://www.isc.co.uk/).

68 D. CASCIANI, "Q&A: Faith schools and quotas", *BBC News*, 27th October 2006, http://www.bbcnews.co.uk

the demand for faith schools is negligible where the quality of public education provision is considered high (Germany) and more significant where private education is seen as performing better (United Kingdom, France).

2m. Police and public order

In most countries, local authorities have some responsibility for policing.

This question can therefore be examined from various angles, including:

- relations between local police and all sections of the local community;

- contacts with religious leaders to prevent tension;

- maintenance of order at large gatherings and special events[69];

- the question of sects (see above).

2n. Hospitals and healthcare

Many local authorities manage healthcare facilities as well as other services, such as retirement homes, family assistance, etc.

When people are hospitalised, they are unable to exercise freedom of worship in the same way as when they are fit and autonomous. Moral and religious assistance in hospitals therefore has a special dimension. There are additional considerations, such as the refusal of some Moslem women to be examined by a man, for example.

In most countries (including France) hospitals have chaplains and some have moral counsellors, but in widely varying forms[70].

Similar considerations apply in the case of people in retirement homes.

There are also other considerations regarding medical services.

In Sweden, for example, the number of local health authorities offering circumcision for religious reasons is falling. More stringent supervision since a new law entered into force five years ago has reduced the number of authorities performing such operations by half[71].

---

69 For example in July 2006 the Mayor of Lens regretted that the law did not allow him to oppose the annual meeting of the Jehovah's Witnesses (see http://www.maire-info.com/article.asp?param=7266&PARAM2=PLUS).

70 Vassart (2005)

71 http://www.thelocal.se/article.php?ID=5289&date=20061022. For a more detailed explanation, see: http://www.state.gov/g/drl/rls/irf/2005/51583.htm

Table 1. Statistical overview of the status of Islam by country

	Belgium	France	Netherlands
Muslims	400,000 (4%)	4,155,000 (8%)*	944,000 (5.8%)
Main countries of origin	Morocco, Turkey	North Africa, Turkey, Black Africa	Turkey, Morocco
Mosques	328	1,555 mosques, (2,147 places of prayer)***	453
Imams	Approx. 300	+/- 1,300	500
Other religious affiliations5	Catholic (4,800,000), Protestant (132,000), Orthodox (70,000), Jewish (50,000), Anglican (10,800), organised secularism (110,000)	Catholic (64.3% - 40,444,000), Protestant (4,900,000), Jewish (600,000), Jehovah's Witness (250,000), Orthodox (90,000)	Catholic (31%), Reformed (14%), Calvinist (6%), Hindu, Jewish and Buddhist (3%)

*   As in the Machelon report

**   Turkey and Bosnia and Herzegovina : recent immigration

*** Excerpt from *La Croix*, 24ᵗʰ October 2006: "*In 2001 the Ministry of the Interior counted 1,555 mosques and Muslim prayer rooms in France. Today, the latest directory of Muslim prayer rooms – the most comprehensive to date, available on the internet (http://annuclic. com) – contains 2,147 entries, including mosques, prayer rooms and cultural centres.*"

**** According to *La Croix*, 24ᵗʰ October 2006, there are 2,100 mosques in Germany.

Table 2. Overview of relations between Churches and the state (recognition)

	Belgium	France	Netherlands
Recognised religions	Recognised religions: Catholic, Protestant, Jewish, Anglican, Islamic, Orthodox. Recognition of non-faith-based philosophical communities (organised secularism).	Separation of Church and state. No recognised religion but some chaplains (Catholic, Prot., Jewish, Muslim) have their salaries paid by the state. Special status: Alsace-Moselle; some French overseas *départements* and territories. Islam recognised in Mayotte.	Separation from the Calvinist Church in 1983. Religions have private association status. Chaplains' salaries paid by the state.
Basis for recognition		Law of 9ᵗʰ December 1905 on the separation of Church and state; special arrangements for some French overseas territories and in Alsace-Moselle (e.g. Concordat of 1801)	Article 2, Book II of the Civil Code et seq., law of 1983 ending the financial relationship between Churches and the state
Official representative(s) of the Muslim community	Muslim Executive of Belgium (EMB), derived from the General Assembly of Muslims of Belgium (AGMB), elected by registered voters.	French Council of the Muslim Faith (CFCM)	- Contact-orgaan Moslims en Overheid (CMO) and - Contact group Islam (CGI)

United Kingdom	Germany	Sweden	Austria
1,600,000-1,800,000 (2.7%)	3,200,000 (3.7%)	350,000-400,000 (4.5%)	344,400 (4.2%)
Iran, Pakistan, Bangladesh, etc.	Turkey	Iran, Bosnia, Iraq, Turkey, etc.	Former Yugoslavia, Turkey, Bosnia and Herzegovina**, etc.
+/- 1,000	2,500 places of prayer****	112	
+/- 1,000			
Christian (72%, 42,000,000), Hindu (1%), Sikh (0.6%), Jewish (0.5%)	Catholic (26,200,000), Evangelical (25,800,000), Protestant (765,000-845,000), Orthodox (1,400,000), Buddhist (240,000), Jewish (189,000)	Church of Sweden (77%), Catholic (145,000), Orthodox (100,000), Protestant (Pentecostal and Missionary 400,000), Jewish (18,500-20,000)	Catholic (74%), Protestant (4.7%), Jewish (0.1%), Orthodox (2.2%), Christian (other 0.9%)

United Kingdom	Germany	Sweden	Austria
Church of England = the established Church; other religions (Catholic, Muslim, etc.) have chaplains. Chaplains' salaries paid by the state.	System of special agreements. "Recognised" religions can levy the "Church tax". Churches are bodies governed by public law. Islam is not recognised in this context. Chaplains' salaries paid by the state.	In 2000, the Church of Sweden (Lutheran) was separated from the state. Churches have religious federation status. (There are currently 19 religious federations, including the Church of Sweden and 2 co-ordinating bodies) Chaplains' salaries paid by the state.	There are 3 types of status for religions: 1. officially recognised religious society (public status), 2. faith-based community (private status), 3. association. Catholic and Protestant chaplains' salaries paid by the state.
Bill of Rights, customs, etc. "Established" Churches: Church of England (Anglican) in England since 1534, (Church of England Assembly Powers Act of 1919) and Church of Scotland (Presbyterian) in Scotland	Article 140 of the Basic Law, Articles 136 to 139 and 141 of the Weimar Constitution; Länder constitutions and agreements concluded between the Federation or the Länder and the religious communities	1999 law on religious communities and 1999 law on the Church of Sweden	1939 law on the financing of the Church (Catholic, Protestant and Old Catholic churches), 1874 law on the recognition of churches and 1998 law on faith-based communities
The most representative: Muslim Council of Britain (MCB)	NO Close contacts with the Directorate of Religious Affairs of Ankara (Diyanet) Several groups claim to represent Muslims in Germany: -Islamrat für die Bundes-republik -Zentralrat der Muslime im Deutschland	-Förenade Islamiska Församlingari Sverige (FIFS) -Sveriges Förenade Muslimska Församlingar (SMuF) -Islamiska Kulturcenterunionen (IKUS) -Sveriges Muslimska Råd (SMR)	Islamische Glaubensgemeinschaft in Österreich

Table 3. State funding of religions

	Belgium	France	Netherlands
Budgetary funding			
Salaries	Yes	No	No
Central body	Salaries: Yes Operating budget: Islam and organised secularism only	No	No
Places of worship	Yes	Yes (1908) Places of worship also receive state funding under the heading "heritage"	No
Chaplains	Yes	Yes (1905)	Yes
Tax benefits	Reduced gift/ succession duties.	Donations are tax-deductible.	Donations are tax-deductible.
Other main sources	Income from assets belonging to religious institutions (mainly in the case of the Catholic Church)	Donations	Funding for charity work

*   According to IRFR 2006, the number of members of the former state church, the Church of Sweden, and who pay tax to support it, is on the decline, mainly for economic reasons according to several surveys conducted by the church. The church tax is equal to 1.9% of the income of a religious community's members. The 8 officially recognised religions, moreover, receive state funding through the church tax or a direct grant, or through a combination of both.
IRFR 2006, v°Sweden

Table 4. Faith-based education (primary/secondary)

	Belgium	France	Netherlands
Faith-based education	Catholic, Protestant and Jewish education is recognised and grant-aided by the Communities. Also possible in the case of Islam.	State and private schools under contract are funded by the state (there is only one Muslim school)	Yes, with partial state funding. Islamic education classes, usually in Islamic schools.
Religious instruction in state schools	Yes, for all recognised religions + instruction in non-faith-based moral philosophy. Compulsory in the French Community. Possibility of exemption in Flanders.	No, except in special cases (e.g. Catholic, Protestant and Jewish religious instruction in Alsace-Moselle)	Yes, not compulsory. Including Islamic religious instruction.

*   As in the Machelon report

**   Turkey and Bosnia and Herzegovina : recent immigration

Sources: *Le Financement Des Communautés Religieuses* (2001) ; ANWAR, BLASCHKE, SANDER (2004).

United Kingdom	Germany	Sweden	Austria
			Funding for religious societies only
No	No	No	Yes
No	No	Denominations funded through a general grant (via the SST) which is redistributed to local communities	Religious societies receive an annual grant (for cultural purposes) (a fixed sum and a variable sum)
No except for tax benefits and funding received under the heading "heritage"	+/- *Länder* operations, tax treatment, heritage, substantial support for the Jewish community, repair and restoration of monasteries and churches expropriated in 1803, etc.	Yes (under the heading "protection of cultural heritage" in the case of the Church of Sweden and under specific arrangements in the case of the other officially recognised communities)	Yes
Yes	Yes	Yes	Yes (Catholic and Protestant)
Donations are tax-deductible.	Yes – Church tax paid by Church members; no additional tax for non-members.	Yes, in the case of certain recognised religions – "Church tax" paid by Church members – no additional tax for non-members*	Donations are partially tax-deductible and religious societies receive preferential treatment.
Income from movable and immovable assets belonging to the churches	Funding for charity work	Grants awarded to some officially recognised religions. Funding for charity work.	Funding for 5 theology faculties\n\nPreferential treatment for charities (including church-based)

United Kingdom	Germany	Sweden	Austria
Yes, with state funding for faith-based private schools (Anglican: 4,646, Cath.: 2,041, Muslim: 8, Sikh: 2, Jewish: 37)7.	Yes, with state funding.	Private education, granted-aided if under contract.	"Private" education provided by religious societies\n\n(there is only one Muslim school – the Islamic gymnasium)
Yes, possibility of exemption.	Yes, schools are required by law to provide religious instruction but attendance is not compulsory\n\nIncluding Islamic religious instruction in certain *Länder* only	Multi-faith religious instruction.	Yes, in the case of religious societies and religious communities and subject to certain conditions (minimum number of children: 3)8

Table 5. Examples of training relating to other religions

	Belgium	France	Netherlands
Institutions concerned	Seminaries and faculties of theology in Catholic universities. University Faculty of Protestant Theology (Brussels) Faculty of Evangelical Theology (Heverlee)	Faculties of Protestant and Catholic Theology of the University of Strasbourg which train Catholic and Protestant ministers.	The (state and other) universities train ministers of religion of various denominations. Universities which are affiliated to a religious or philosophical community are eligible for official recognition and grant aid.
Religions concerned	Catholic, Protestant	Catholic, Protestant	Catholic, Protestant (KPN and other denominations), Old Catholic, etc.
Situation with regard to Islam in particular	No training courses at present	*Grande mosquée de Paris* (which provides training for imams), Institut Européen des Sciences Humaines (IESH), Institut Français des sciences islamiques (IFESI)	Programme run by the VU
Faith communities	Spending on faith and secular communities +/- 1%	Local spending: p.m. (excluding Alsace-Moselle)	Optional direct shared competence
Ownership of places of worship	Made available for the community's use	Pre-1905 buildings: local authority Post-1905 buildings	Ownership transferred to the faith communities
Funding	Mandatory spending: upkeep of places of worship (reconstruction where appropriate) Optional spending: subsidies (for buying/ renting), donations, sale for token price of 1 euro, construction	Mandatory spending: upkeep and conservation of places of worship owned by local authorities (reconstruction where appropriate) Ban on direct funding (e.g. reduced rent, donations) for faith communities. Several possibilities for indirect funding, including special administrative long lease (99 years with token rent of 1 euro)	Temporary specific funding (construction of mosques, reconstruction of churches after flooding)
Safety			Mandatory shared competence
Heritage	Funding under protection of heritage	Funding under protection of heritage	Substantial funding under protection of heritage
Fire safety	Non-compliance with fire safety standards cited as a ground for refusing planning permission (mosques)	Non-compliance with fire safety standards cited as a ground for refusing planning permission (mosques)	Mandatory shared competence

* No record of any faculty of theology at the University of Münster, although it is mentioned in the FRB report.

United Kingdom	Germany	Sweden	Austria
The diplomas awarded by Protestant and Jewish training colleges and Catholic seminaries are recognised by the universities.	Training provided by churches, in association with universities and higher education institutions	Training provided by churches, in association with universities and higher education institutions	Minimum requirement for official recognition: certificate of secondary education Faculties of Catholic (4) and Protestant (1) Theology (funded by the state) The Islamisches Religionspädagogisches Institut (IPRI) trains Islamic education teachers for primary and secondary schools.
Catholic, Anglican, Baptist, Jewish	Catholic, Protestant, Jewish	Catholic, Protestant	All officially recognised religions
Muslim College, Islamic Foundation, Hawza Ilmiyya of London and Islamic College for Advanced Studies	DITIB, Johann Wolfgang von Goethe University*	No training courses at present	No training courses at present
	Local spending: p.m.	No (but the municipalities decide their cultural policy themselves)	Spending on faith communities: +/- 5%
	Owned by the faith communities	Owned by the faith communities	Municipality – local building police (competencies in town planning and spatial development)
General funding through the (federal) Church tax Upkeep and protection of places of worship by local authorities	Various funding options: protection of heritage, grant from the Faith Communities Capacity Building Fund (if the project is an intercultural one) Premises certified as a place of worship are exempt from council tax		Local inhabitants consulted about municipal authority construction projects
Direct mandatory shared competence (federal government and Länder Optional exclusive competence concerning abattoirs	Compliance with town planning and safety standards is policed by the local authorities. Appeal before the government.		Municipality – local security police and the local police in charge of public assemblies. Municipality – local police responsible for health and safety
Direct mandatory exclusive competence for town planning (spatial development: federal government)	Funding under protection of historic heritage (churches account for 45% of this heritage)		
			The municipalities have direct mandatory competence for fire safety

Chapter 3

Strategies for strengthening interfaith dialogue

Philippe Gaudin[*]

*   Head of training and research at the European Institute of Religious Sciences, Paris

Introduction

I am pleased to be able to contribute to the discussions organised by the Congress of Local and Regional Authorities of the Council of Europe, which I do on a personal basis but also on behalf of my Institute. The official objective of the European Institute of Religious Sciences, which forms part of the *Ecole Pratique des Hautes Etudes*, is to study the impact, at regional, national and European levels, of religious phenomena on contemporary society. We are therefore a sort of clearing house for university research, but are also active in the training and advisory fields.

I wish to speak about what secularism means in its French context and to cast some light on the current debates and challenges to which it gives rise, to improve our understanding of the place and role of religions in French society. I will also talk about the place of religious knowledge in state schools, and while this may seem a little remote from the theme of our meeting, I will nevertheless try to demonstrate its relevance.

I should also add that the very term "interfaith dialogue" means that this is a field in which our state, and therefore secular, university institute does not automatically have a place. I will therefore start by trying to explain why it is necessary for us to "side-step" this terrain, while at the same time, we hope, offering a valuable, enlightening and constructive contribution to the debate.

1. What interfaith dialogue? Three useful distinctions

We believe that many of the misunderstandings that arise, derive from failure to agree in the first place on the meaning of the terms being used. This applies particularly to "interfaith dialogue".

1a. Interfaith dialogue

This means that religions cease to be enclosed systems of beliefs and practices and that contact, interaction and perhaps even cross-fertilisation are possible. The history of this religious rapprochement dates back more than a hundred years ago and can be traced at least to the 1893 Chicago Congress of Religions. Nevertheless, considerable ambiguity remains. Should this dialogue be mainly conducted by religious authorities or reach out to all the faithful? Do the meetings, discussions and colloquies themselves have something of a religious element? Do they involve praying or worshiping together, or the joint study of sacred texts? It might be better to speak of intra-faith dialogue. From our standpoint, this is strictly a matter for the various confessions and their active members, not for government and the authorities.

1b. Citizen dialogue between persons of different faiths

We believe that this is what one normally has in mind when speaking of interfaith dialogue. Whatever our metaphysical and religious convictions, we all live in the same society and are subject to the same law. The very essence of secularism is to guarantee freedom of conscience and religion and not to impose either. How does the notion of humanity relate to that of citizenship? Humanity is more universal than citizenship since we are all citizens of the world and not of a single society. But it is also more specific, since human beings are concrete phenomena whereas citizenship is more abstract. Religious confessions are based on close relationships and the notion of community whereas citizenship is concerned with individuals and the public. It is not so much the confessions themselves that should be entering into dialogue – is that what they are really there for? – but this dual dimension within each individual that feels concerned by this type of dialogue. Faith instils knowledge in its own particular way, inspires and rouses to action, but it cannot ignore rationality with regard to knowledge or what is reasonable with regard to action. Individuals are not forced into a form of particularism, but have to look within themselves for shareable truths, based on the exercise of rationality. This is the role of the public domain, in the intellectual and political sense of the term. So what are the ingredients of this type of citizen dialogue? Firstly, a political approach that we characterise as republican and democratic, which means unity of the public domain coupled with diversity of points of view. Secondly, an intellectual approach that we deem to be based on reason. Finally, an approach, probably spiritual, based on mutual sympathy and interaction that requires a good general culture concerning the faiths of all those concerned and whose aim is to dispel mutual ignorance and prejudices. There is nothing to prevent local and regional authorities from promoting this form of dialogue.

1c. Religious knowledge

This is the third element of our initial distinction, namely establishing knowledge of religious phenomena, which is one of the duties of state schools. As Régis Debray has noted, it is not necessary to kneel to understand the notion of prayer, so why knowledge of religions should be seen as a religious act[72]? The type of activity which we referred to earlier concerns, or

---

72   *Aveuglantes lumières*, p. 126 Gallimard, 2006

should concern, everyone, with or without religious affiliation. It encompasses what we have called citizen dialogue and even specifically interfaith dialogue, however unclear that notion might be. There is thus no cause for concern that this form of knowledge might be detrimental to dialogue in any form, including that between faiths. What it can achieve is to show the adepts of interfaith dialogue how far religions entail a form of social conformism based on shared identity and that the formation of an "us" necessarily implies a "them". Such awareness is half the battle. Their new-found ability to distance themselves, however reluctantly, from an identity whose potential for conflict they now acknowledge will enable them to dialogue with themselves and make them more capable to deal with "others".

2. French secularism

This is the fundamental context in which we operate and whose developments need to be understood.

2a. Definition

Secularism is a great political idea according to which nothing should undermine the unity of the people, particularly any form of clericalism that would offer a small section of that people different rights and duties. More important, it is an ideal that must always be pursued since no people can become really worthy of the sovereignty it must exercise unless it forms an educated nation that is fully self-aware.

It is immediately apparent that the principle of secularism is in no way incompatible with a variety of faiths, but it is incompatible with a directly heteronomous organisation – for example, via a form of revelation and a clergy – of the social and political domains. Secularism will therefore constitute a legal framework that paradoxically offers a basis for religious freedom, with multiple beliefs and confessions, in a world where religion, if defined as a heteronomously structured society, has a diminishing or non-existent role.

In France, secularism was historically a complex process that took on the appearance of a war against religion, because of the attitudes of certain sections of society and resistance from the Catholic Church of that era. However, the so-called separation of Church and state law of 1905, with its subsequent amendments, eventually offered a liberal solution that made no claims to interfere with the right of confessions to run their own internal affairs. There is now general agreement with Jean Baubérot's description of secularism as a triangle, whose three points are religious freedom, equality of confessions and separation of the latter from the state. However, this freedom is regulated by law, equality is not complete for reasons of history and all sorts of arrangements mean that there is not a total separation.

This is the starting point for any consideration of the current debate on secularism throughout French society.

2b. Interpreting secularism – the two main trends...

The first is what we can call a strict republican secularism. Its main philosophical premise is that religion is a matter of personal opinion and only concerns individuals' private lives. Although religions are collective in nature, they should be denied all right of access to the public domain and thus any public funding. Those who hold this view criticise current secular practice - and even more any extensions of it - of giving wider role to religions in social and political life. Why does Alsace-Moselle retain a special governing relations between the state and four recognised confessions? Why do we grant tax advantages to cultural associations, and tax deductions to the taxpayers making donations to them? Why do we give massive subsidies to a quite distinct form of private education by paying the teachers of schools that have formal agreements with the state? Why are local religiously-based charities subsidised? Why do we meet the considerable cost of maintaining cultural monuments? Does this not simply open the door to the public funding of the places of worship of a religion deemed to be disadvantaged or even discriminated against by the burden of its historical heritage?

The other trend in secularism emphasises democratic and pluralist co-operation between the public sphere – central, regional and local government – and the different confessions, through the Churches and associations that represent them. Philosophically, this means that religions offer something other than simply individual metaphysical options that would put them on the same plane as atheism, agnosticism or any other personal belief. Religions are considered to be traditions rooted in the past and thus influencing all aspects of present social and cultural life. As such, they are major social factors, even in a secularised society, which makes them legitimate interlocutors and partners for government and the authorities. This means that secularism must be seen not as a new civil religion with its own intangible sacredness, but as an evolving framework for neutrality and equality between different faiths. Under these circumstances, there is no reason why the state should not become more actively involved in, for example, the organisation of the Muslim faith, as a newcomer to the republican table. It may then be quite acceptable to blur the distinction between the cultural and the religious in the use of donations and legacies. Why could we not establish a model of religious charity eligible for grant aid, so long as it is subject to supervision, the requirement not to discriminate in the services offered and so on? Why are religious authorities not considered as important instruments of social mediation that promote a sense of community?

Clearly, between the two extremes, there are an infinite number of nuances and intermediate positions.

3. Towards an intelligent secularism

Intelligent secularism contrasts with abstentionist secularism. In French, the notion of intelligence encompasses understanding not just of things but also of how they relate to people. An intelligent relationship between secularism and religion implies a better understanding of and ability to forge good relations with the confessions that are active in any particular society.

3a. Religious knowledge

The main question concerns the role fulfilled by this subject in the school curriculum. For an answer, it may be helpful to adopt a European perspective, drawing on the work of Jean-Paul Willaime[73]. In Europe, the relationship between state, religion and education reflects each particular country's religious history and legal system, but all face the same challenges.

These boil down to three main issues: lack of religious culture among young people, the presence of large Muslim minorities and confessional pluralism. Lack of religious culture among young people is a frequently noted phenomenon and is one aspect of a wider lack of culture that hinders our understanding of the past and the present. What is much more rarely commented on, however, is that it also contributes to social inequality since this lack of culture disproportionately affects more disadvantaged groups in society. The growing number of Muslims in Europe raises cultural and religious problems because it is such a new phenomenon. This is one of the most recent aspects of confessional plurality to which neither states nor education systems have properly adjusted. How does the French system respond to this problem? It is not confessionally based and does not seek to establish a separate subject within curricula. Instead, it tries to develop knowledge of religions as one factor to be taken into account within existing disciplines such as history, social sciences, languages, literature, art and philosophy. The aim is to benefit from "religious sciences" and to offer a context to the study of religions, particularly in documents and other written sources and in works of art. Even though there are wide variations in approach across Europe, there is

---

73 *Des maîtres et des dieux – écoles et religions en Europe*, edited by Jean-Paul Willaime and Séverine Mathieu, Belin 2005

still a general trend towards removing the confessional element from religious studies, which increasingly take on the features of "religious sciences".

Such teaching is now an integral aspect of the official objectives of French education. According to section 2 of the schools legislation of 23rd April 2005, these include the transmission of knowledge and the sharing of republican values. These values of liberty, equality, fraternity, secularism, anti-discrimination, social mixing and equality between women and men help to train citizens and create a common culture as a basis for co-existence. The common core of knowledge, as defined for pupils and teachers in, respectively, the official gazettes of 12th July 2006 and 28th December 2006, include knowledge of religions. The introduction of this ambitious programme is not on the agenda of interfaith dialogue but does help to establish a form of religious citizenship that is quite separate from any confessional allegiance or non-allegiance. There is nothing to prevent this process from taking place in a local government setting, for example through the organisation of lecture series, as happens in schools or in my own institute.

3b. Social action and culture

We have already seen that religions may have a valid role to play in contemporary secular societies. In the past, religions were more concerned with the invisible world and the hereafter, but nowadays they increasingly set out to help fellow citizens in this world. Whether through army, hospital or prison chaplains or in charities or other similar social organisations of religious origin but largely secularised and publicly funded, religions play an obvious and valuable part.

Naturally, from a cultural standpoint, anything that may encourage knowledge of religions, and of associated cultural artefacts and works, is to be welcomed. It is easy for schools and voluntary organisations and associations to organise visits to museums and exhibitions based on such an approach. Cultural centres such as the one in Fontevraud Abbey, funded by the Pays de la Loire regional council, organise conferences and lectures and other cultural and artistic events based on religious themes. At the local level, events such as meals, festivals, visits or excursions that encourage inhabitants from different backgrounds to come into contact are both feasible and desirable.

Conclusion

First, we have reservations about the title "strengthening interfaith dialogue", since from a secular standpoint, it only appears to concern individual confessions, and not the public sphere. While recognising the need for appropriate distinctions and clarifications, we have tried to show that French secularism is a reality and can offer the Europe of the twenty-first century a number of ways of or suggestions for achieving a more intelligent life style.

Part two

National situations
and local strategies

Introduction: Jacques Palard[74]

Given that each country has a different approach to organising the relationship between religion and politics, a comparative analysis is clearly of considerable interest and relevance. It is always instructive to identify the key points of differentiation, but this should not lead us to underestimate some degree of overall convergence. François Forêt quite rightly points out in this connection that "a certain vision of modernity, which finds its roots in religion itself in order to distance itself from it more effectively, is the *common heritage of Europeans* and is behind the clear trends towards deregulating faith and placing religion more in the context of society than of the state. To borrow the term used elsewhere, Europe today is "politically atheist" in the sense that political decisions are taken as though God did not exist, and yet the religious reference is still there but in another form. It is this "other form" that we have to understand"[75]. What is this "other form" exactly? It would appear in reality to be two complementary forms. First, religion is becoming a sub-culture, drawing its strength from the multiplication of social references and political preferences; it adopts the statute of a metalanguage demanding recognition; in this way, religion shapes perceptions of a political nature at a time when the strictly hierarchical mode of governance is giving way to new approaches, which function primarily by delegating the task of social regulation and by negotiating multiple and provisional compromises. In a manner of speaking, the process becomes more important than the result, or rather the process is an integral part of the anticipated results. Which is why national analyses are highly relevant, particularly as the growing number of religious identities cannot escape the various forms of power and domination built up over time nor the regional dimension of the type of action taken. From this point of view, religion is an appropriate vehicle for analysing politics, and this includes the new importance attached today to the decentralised regulation of social relationships. As Jean-Paul Willaime points out, "all political sovereignty says something about itself when it designates the status and position of religion in the society it administers"[76].

In the *United Kingdom* there is a historical agreement between the Anglican faith and the state, which are bound together by tacit relationships

---

74 Director of Research at CNRS, SPIRIT, Institute of Political Science, Bordeaux, France.

75 François Forêt, "Introduction", in François Forêt (dir.), *L'espace public européen à l'épreuve du religieux*, Bruxelles, Ed. de l'Université de Bruxelles, 2007, p. 19.

76 Jean-Paul Willaime, "Les reconfigurations ultramodernes du religieux en Europe", in François Forêt (dir.), *L'espace public européen à l'épreuve du religieux*, Bruxelles, Ed. de l'Université de Bruxelles, 2007, p. 31. The author adds that "it is because politics and religion, constantly regulating and adjusting their relationship (including in conflict), have a reciprocal impact on their respective spheres that the religious issue is a political issue and that an analysis of changes in the religious field may also contribute usefully to an analysis of the political field" (p. 32).

going far beyond the already formalised official and legal links. Anjum Anwar and Chris Chivers point out that "still, today, major doctrinal and liturgical changes have to be submitted for parliamentary approval, and the Church of England's General Synod has only, in this sense, been delegated powers by parliament and the crown. All of the measures that it passes have to be scrutinised by parliament and receive royal assent". This has prompted the other religious denominations to assert their identity more forcefully and to play the "difference" card. But this also impacts on the forms of inter-faith exchanges since the Anglican Church is an integral part of the structure of the state. In these circumstances, what for example does it mean for the Muslim community, to enter into dialogue with the secular authorities which are partly shaped by the Church?

It is now three decades since the end of the Franco regime in *Spain*, during which time there has been a fundamental reshaping of the links between religion and politics: Flora Burchianti and Xabier Itçaina start off by pointing out that "the formation of a new pluralist religious structure was one of the most significant issues in the political transition", bringing with it the end of state denominationalism. When the Socialists came to power in 1982, the loss of influence of the Catholic Church became even more acute, particularly in the fields of education and family legislation (decriminalisation of abortion, etc). Since then, the issues to be addressed, although of a different nature, have been just as crucial: the reversal of migration flows – Spain which for a long time had been a country of emigration has become a country of immigration – has given rise to a strong Islamic element in the religious landscape. Accordingly, the new conditions of the "religious market" have required a reformulation of relations between the various faiths and the state, in which so called "minority" religions need to be taken into account: in 1992, the Spanish government concluded co-operation agreements with Jewish, Protestant and Muslim federations. In the case of the latter two, the orders from on high to federate and become institutionalised were acted upon with clear but mixed results, affecting both representation and credibility. For example, the Islamic Commission comprises not only immigrants from the Middle East, but also Spaniards who have converted to Islam. The 11th March attacks marked the beginning of a completely new phase, which according to F. Burchianti and X. Itçaina is characterised by the involvement of new players: in April 2004, the association of Moroccan workers ATIME put forward a proposal to the Spanish government calling for the setting up of a Muslim Council in Spain, "whose functions, *inter alia*, would be to regulate Muslim religious practices and rituals, combat anti-Muslim prejudices and facilitate interreligious dialogue".

In *France*, the 1905 Act separating Church and State stipulates that "The

Republic shall not recognise, fund or subsidise any religion". Under the terms of the 1958 Constitution, France is "an indivisible, secular, democratic and social republic". The French republican model does in fact allow for links and forms of functional collaboration, particularly in two key areas: first of all in respect of chaplaincies – set up in the name of freedom of religion, which was also guaranteed under the 1905 Act – in hospitals, prisons and the armed forces, and second, recognition and funding of private schools (predominantly Catholic). Today, this model has to take into account a new situation to which it finds some difficulty in adapting. The sociologist Michel Wievorka, a disciple of Alain Touraine, holds that "the current burgeoning of identities is vigorous, and it is no longer possible to respond to it by republicanist retraction, this perversion of the republican ideal which requires the victims of exclusion to integrate without giving them the necessary wherewithal and which unreservedly rejects demands for cultural recognition as if they came from the worst form of communitarianism"[77]. In order to reconcile universal values and individual identities, the author puts forward the concept of "Neorepublicanism". Others, like Philippe Gaudin, have referred, with a similar aim in mind, to a "secularism of recognition".

In *Germany*, Protestantism and Catholicism have a special status, bearing the hallmark of the Reformation and the authority granted to them in the aftermath of the Second World War, insofar as they were the only institutions to survive the collapse of the 3rd Reich. The contemporary period of this bi-denominational country has been described as one of a "problematic separation of Church and State in a secularised society"[78]. Because, with the help of the State, Churches are able to levy taxes, and because of their status as public law corporations, they carry out acknowledged public service and socially beneficial tasks. The way in which the population has developed in cultural and religious terms and the reunification of 1991 have had a greater impact on the influence of these religious denominations than have any political arrangements, which as regards Church-State relations have remained fundamentally the same. N. Tietze quotes from a 2004 speech by Johannes Rau, former president of the Federal Republic of Germany: "The ideologically neutral state needs the convictions held in different, distinct communities, which have their own values and want to provide guidance. *These communities include the Churches and religious communities, which introduce their ideas into society*". In this connection, it is perfectly legitimate to speak of the religious regulation of politics insofar as the organisation of powers is the result of an undeniable cultural logic in which spiritual or

---

77   Michel Wievorka, "Le modèle néorépublicain", *Libération*, 13th November 2006, p. 31.
78   Jean-Marie Ouédraogo, "Églises et État en Allemagne: la difficile laïcisation d'une société sécularisée", in Jean Baubérot, *Religions et laïcité dans l'Europe des Douze*, Paris, Syros, 1994, pp. 15-27.

religious values, if not a religious paradigm strictly speaking, cannot be totally absent. This configuration, a result of both theoretical separation and close practical co-operation cannot but have a formative effect on relations with minority faiths, starting with Islam.

Like other predominantly Orthodox countries, the situation in *Russia* is very different. Agnieshka Moniak-Azzopardi notes that "as a result of their historical, traditional and religious Orthodox inheritance, citizens have an uncritical, affective sense of belonging, and transform this into an omnipresent religious ideology. This process embraces the entire sphere of politics in predominantly Orthodox countries, and even leads to a clear identification with the state and the nation, whose sources of Orthodox faith – the concept of the individual, the concept of God and the concept of power, to mention the three most important – combine to form a common base". Around 80% of the Russian population are Orthodox, of which probably only 5% are practising, and 10-15% are Muslim, the majority of whom are Sunni. The other religions are very much in the minority: apart from the Orthodox Church, other Christian denominations account for less than 2%. Of the 89 constituent entities of the Russian Federation (21 republics and 50 regions), 46 are predominantly Orthodox; in the others, the Muslim communities are in the majority. The fall of Communism in theory, meant that religious faiths, now legal, could develop but in practice this development, particularly as far as the Catholics are concerned, is largely shaped by the relations between politics at national and local level and the Orthodox hierarchy, which is in a situation of economic dependence. A. Moniak-Azzopardi comments that the most recent major crisis between the Russian Orthodox Church and the Catholic Church erupted in February 2002 following the creation of dioceses on Russian territory by Pope John Paul II. She also notes considerable hostility towards Evangelical Churches, new religious movements and the Jews. In contrast, the Orthodox and Muslim faiths generally come to an agreement over the sharing of areas of influence.

This overview helps clarify in a more informed way the underlying question at the heart of this initiative by the Congress of Local and Regional Authorities: *Why focus particular attention on the local dimension of inter-faith and intercultural dialogue?*

In her study on Germany, N. Tietze commented that "at the local and infra-political level, the regulation and diversification of the religious referents of users of public institutions can rely on pragmatic negotiations – *despite* the identity polarisation at the level of national and Länder politics"[79]. The concept of "governance" can legitimately be applied to this process, insofar as the organisational arrangements put in place require a relative non-hierarchical approach to the roles and establishment of networks founded not merely on the absence of suspicion, but also on trust and what the Canadian philosopher Charles Taylor terms the politics of recognition. The examples given by N. Tietze are particularly telling:

- the president of the Hamburg University Islamic Community, a member of the Schura (a federation bringing together some forty Islamic associations in Hamburg), joined forces with officials of the Jewish community to negotiate improvements in the practice of the Muslim faith with the university's vice-chancellor. This led to the provision of rooms at the university refectory to the traditional breaking of the fast during Ramadan, and the greater availability of vegetarian meals;

- in the Land of Hamburg, denominational teaching, entitled "Religious instruction for all" been provided for some thirty years in close co-operation between the recognised religious communities and the Ministry of Education. This instruction is "transdenominational" in nature and led, in 1995, to the establishment of the Inter-faith Religious Instruction Group, through which non-Christian communities were able to participate in drawing up the syllabuses. This initiative is typical of the Hamburg approach, the success of which is due not only to the personal commitment of the key players but also to the high-quality and strong relations that for a long time have existed between the political authorities and the North Elbe Lutheran Church and Protestant circles. This long process has brought about an ability to view all religions as a means of developing and implementing public action closely related to the expectations and values of the various population groups.

The relevance of the local dimension of inter-faith dialogue clearly depends on the political, institutional and ideological context. The personal experience of the two authors of the study on the United Kingdom is most informative: Anjum Anwar, a British Muslim of Indian and Pakistani origin, is Education Officer of the Lancashire Council of Mosques, and Chair of the Lancashire Forum of Faiths; Chris Chivers, a British Anglican, is Canon Chancellor of Blackburn Cathedral, where he is responsible for inter-faith

---

79   N. Tietze cites the case of a Berlin Islamic federation which in the year 2000, after a 20-year dispute with the Land education authorities, obtained the status of religious community within the meaning of the Berlin Education Act, enabling it to teach Islam at a publicly run school. She points out that the Berlin authorities attempted to circumvent such "breaches" and prevent further examples by enacting in March 2006 a law making ethical education compulsory, which has restricted the impact of optional denominational teaching and the diversification of normative references, by exercising control over the establishment of standards and values.

relations as director of the Cathedral's community cohesion, education, outreach, and development agency. They both take part in public dialogues in this Anglican Cathedral: the population of the municipality, comprising the industrial towns of Blackburn and Darwen, is two-thirds Christian and one-fifth Muslim. They attribute the problems encountered not to difficulties about faith but to the faith-secularist divide and the marginalisation of faith in public discourse, for which they consider the local authorities to be partly responsible: local authorities are obliged to take account of racial, ethnic and gender differentiation in terms of equal opportunities legislation, but they do not, in a statutory sense, have to take account of the faith paradigm. The authors note the absence of relations, other than purely ceremonial, between the Blackburn Interfaith Council and the Borough. More important, on the 229 initiatives in Lancashire using Neighbourhood Renewal Funding, only one was faith-based and two were multi-faith based. Drawing on the work funded by the Faith Capacity Building Fund, A. Anwar and C. Chivers believe that faith communities are a primary means of promoting community cohesion and that the faith and voluntary community sector is the best placed to enhance common values.

Judging by the studies on Germany and the United Kingdom, the situations there seem to be very different. In the United Kingdom, local government would appear to be ignoring central government recommendations issued by the Home Office (cf. for example *Working Together: Co-operation between Government and Faith Communities* of February 2004), which encourage the faith community involvement in decision-making at all levels of government. These communities play roles that are essential to economic and social development: emergence of a social capital founded on the voluntary sector and trust, contribution to the functioning of social support services, etc. While a recently published government report *Strong and prosperous communities: The Local Government White Paper* (October 2006) advocates a strong decentralising thrust, the study by A. Anwar and C. Chivers, which has a very meaningful subtitle – *A missed opportunity* – makes a very clear case, but without any excessive optimism, for local authorities to rethink their relations with faith communities so as to involve them more fully. It is with this in mind, that they make their own recommendations:

- initiating dialogue between local or regional authorities and faith communities;

- setting up a Royal Commission to look at the relationship between Church and State and of all faith communities to local, regional and national government;

- appointing a "faith tsar", a sort of ombudsman, tasked with finding the ways and means for exchanges and consultation/dialogue between partners.

However, in relation to the United Kingdom, Brian Pearce in this volume, sheds a somewhat different light and develops another approach, perhaps because of his position as Director of the Interfaith Network for the UK, set up in 1987 which has acquired experience in a different context, at supra-local level. He notes that "both central and local government have been making important contributions in recent years to the development of inter-faith activity in the UK". He believes that local authorities have been increasing significantly their engagement with faith communities in their areas, in some cases providing support for local interfaith structures.

With regard to Spain, F. Burchianti and X. Itçaina note a specific form of division of labour in the political regulation of religion: the national authorities have responsibility for official negotiations and the local authorities take care of practical arrangements, the symbolic value and social salience of which are considerable. The interest shown by local government varies according to the situation and context; it is much more structured in the urban metropolises, as they are home to many more different denominations. At sub-state level, the Spanish autonomous communities enjoy a high level of political autonomy and special relations with the municipal level. Many of the main players are to be found in Catalonia because of its leading role in promoting and giving structure to interfaith dialogue. For example, Barcelona is the headquarters of a UNESCO Forum for Interreligious Dialogue, a founder member of the United Religions Initiative, an international non-governmental organisation set up in 2000 to promote collaboration among faiths. There are also interfaith dialogue entities that have been set up, and a forum bringing together the main religions. The Catalan groups have joined forces in the *Xarxa Catalana d'Entitats de Diàleg Interreligiós* (Catalan network of inter-faith dialogue entities) which plays a major role in organising events to promote inter-faith dialogue and in establishing links with the authorities; in 2006 it organised for the second time the *Parlament Català de les Religions*. Such developments are all the more important since they are taking place in tandem with a process of institutionalisation of what is becoming a genuine "religious policy". For example, the new statute of Catalonia, approved by referendum in June 2006, provides that the Generalitat has "exclusive power over religious entities that carry out their activities in Catalonia", in the "regulation and establishment of collaboration and co-operation mechanisms for the carrying out of their activities within the jurisdiction of the Generalitat". The latter has a Directorate General for Religious Affairs, directly attached to the Presidential Department, which has played a mediation role in the controversy surrounding the building of a mosque in the town of Premià de Mar in the Barcelona region. Since the late 1990s close contacts have been established and agreements signed with representatives of minority religions. The initiatives include the training of imams in the Catalan language, allowing religions to enter hospitals and prisons, grants for denominational or non-religious activities, etc. Barcelona itself has made a commitment to inter-faith dialogue by setting up the *Centre Interreligiòs*, coming under the *Regidoria de Dona i Drets civils* (Department of Women's and Civil Rights). This department's role is to prevent and defuse conflicts that may arise between the various religions. It offers opportunities for minority religions who see it as a forum for expressing their views and providing support for interfaith activities.

Flora Burchianti and Xabier Itçaina note that there has been a change of scale in the political regulation of religion in Spain: on emerging from the Franco regime, the climate of institutional reform prompted a rethinking of the place of religion – at the time, the Catholic Church – in a centralised and vertical approach; today, local debates and controversies are calling this institutional order into question, mixing the international and local dimensions of the issues. From their observation of disputes that arrive in the public arena over plans to build mosques, they consider that local actors are unprepared for such problems and are slow to tackle them. But they also note that co-ordinated action between local, autonomous community and central government is becoming more frequent.

There continue to be strong contradictions in the Russian situation. Public statements in support of religious pluralism are undermined by numerous local conflicts: A. Moniak-Azzopardi notes the opposition encountered by minority religious groups: dissolution of the Salvation Army in Novgorod and Moscow; refusal to register the Greek Catholic communities in the okrug of Khanty-Mansiysk, etc. "Registration problems are the visible tip of the difficulties faced by local authorities in managing the different religious communities. Frequently, since 2004-2005, we have witnessed deliberate attacks on religious leaders and communities seen as a nuisance. […] The struggle against "sects" very often unites the authorities and the Orthodox hierarchy." In contrast, the Orthodox Church seems to benefit from the support of local authorities to carry out its church rebuilding plans, and, consequently, to assert its presence in public life.

These analyses confirm the validity of Louis Rousseau's comments drawn from his observation of changes in the religious landscape of Montreal: "In the growing confusion of differences which northern societies have to manage, the new increase in the number of religions prompts and doubtless speeds up a process of re-formulating identity which needs to be analysed. *Research on this issue should ideally be done at grass-roots level, in the very place where social interaction, marked by particular socio-historic decisions, occurs*"[80].

---

80   Louis Rousseau, "Recomposition identitaire et globalisation. Le travail de la référence religieuse dans la région montréalaise", in Michel Gardaz, Martin Geoffroy, Jean-Guy Vaillancourt (dir.), *La mondialisation du phénomène religieux*, Montreal, Mediaspaul, 2007, p. 69.

Chapter 4

Local authorities
and inter-faith dialogue in Spain

Flora Burchianti[*] and Xabier Itçaina[**]

[*]   Flora Burchianti has a Ph.D. in Political Sciences and ATER, at Sciences Po Bordeaux.

[**] Xabier Itçaina is in charge of research at CNRS, researcher at SPIRIT - Political Science, International Relations,
      Territory, at Sciences Po Bordeaux.

Relations between religion and politics in Spain have long been dominated by the recurring issue of relations between the Catholic Church, society and the State. We know how the formation of a new pluralist religious structure was one of the most significant issues in the political transition after the Franco regime in 1975. Similarly there has been ample coverage of the fact that winning over the Catholic Church and its most influential leaders contributed to acceptance of the new democratic regime by sectors of society that were still resisting (Brassloff, 2003; Pérez-Diaz, 1993; Anderson, 2003; Diaz Salazar, 2006, pp. 194-195). The reforming of the links between Catholic Church and State did not mean the end of politicisation of religion: far from it. Thirty years later Spain's final alignment with the other major European democracies can even be seen in fresh interweaving between politics and religion. Far from dilution into a kind of inevitable privatisation, religion is taking centre stage again in Spanish politics, and in a way very different from what happened during the transition, on one hand because the religious landscape itself has changed (the steady decline in the Catholic Church's grip on society has been accompanied by the claims of new religions and in particular by a Spanish Islam linked to the reversal of currents of migration) and on the other, because relations between religion, State and more broadly public authorities have had to adjust to new conditions in the religious market by revising the institutional organisation of the "coexistence" (*convivencia*) established on a quasi-consensual basis on emerging from the dictatorship.

This reforming of the links between religion and politics has had a dual aspect, one unobtrusive, the re-ordering of methods for political regulation of religion, the other, more visible, controversies thrusting religion into the centre of public debate. Undoubtedly, therefore, the crucial importance of the international context in national and local *perceptions* of religion should be underlined. Spain is no exception to the rule: doubtless the Madrid bombings on 11th March 2004 are a watershed in making a fully political issue out of inter-religious relations. Religious organisations have responded in various ways to this context of high politicisation, knowing how to alternate strategies of concealment and visibility in the triple relationship of withdrawal, affirmation and challenge that they maintain publicly as circumstances change (Bréchon, 2000). Perhaps we are seeing a change of scale in the political regulation of religion. On emerging from the Franco regime, the climate of radical institutional and political reform encouraged the parties to reconsider the new place of religion – at the time basically the "Catholic question" – in a centralised and relatively vertical fashion. Thirty years later it is local debates and controversies that are calling this institutional order into question, mixing internationalisation and localisation of the issues. Shifts in the levels of politicisation affect the political regulation of religion. Even if "religious affairs" are still within the jurisdiction of the State, the proliferation of initiatives coming from Autonomous Communities or local authorities tend to blur the boundary of the prerogatives[81], taking advantage *inter alia* of the ambiguous distinction between interreligious and intercultural. Thus the extent of autonomous communities' jurisdiction in education and cultural policy has helped to make the regional level an important player in the settlement, even indirectly, of religious questions, in particular in schools[82]. At this point, we shall bear in mind the hypothesis of a shift in the places where religion is politicised (from the national to the local/global level), trying to observe its effects on various scales. For the sake of clarity the account will follow the recommendations of the general outline document. We will begin by trying to show the reconfiguration of the religious market and of the political treatment of religion in Spain as a whole. Putting the issue into context in this way seems to us to be an essential prerequisite for a section more specifically devoted to local expressions of these religious and political rearrangements, seen here in the autonomous community of Catalonia.

1. National expressions: changes in the religious market and the institutional order

1a. New conditions in the religious market

Most observers of the Spanish religious landscape are in agreement on the progressive secularisation of society, at least from the viewpoint of the traditional indicators of religious observance (Requena, 2005). However, Catholic domination in the declaration of religious affiliation is still a reality, measured by a recent survey by the *Centro de Investigaciones Sociológicas* (CIS):

---

81 Jordi Moreras (Moreras, 2005) stresses, for example, that the Generalitat, the Catalan regional government, was the first autonomous community to set up a Religious Affairs Secretariat, in June 2000, although religious issues are not within its jurisdiction (cf. our second part).

82 In a European comparative study of the wearing of the headscarf in schools, the French Senate's Legal Studies Department noted the low level of politicisation of this topic in Spain compared with the situation elsewhere in Europe. The report states that "in the absence of specific rules, and having regard to the competence of autonomous communities in the matter of education and the relative independence of educational establishments, conflicts are settled locally, giving priority to the schooling of the children" (Legal Studies Department, *The wearing of the Islamic headscarf at school*, Paris, Senate, Senate working papers, Comparative Law Series No. LC 128, November 2003, p. 15, report available on http://www.senat.fr).

Table 1: Declaration of religious affiliation in Spain, January 2006[83]

Q: how do you define yourself in religious terms: Catholic, practitioner of another religion, non-believer or other?

	%	(N)
Catholic	77.3	(1919)
Practising another religion	1.7	(41)
Non-believer	13.0	(324)
Atheist	6.4	(160)
Unclassified	1.6	(40)
Total	100.0	(2484)

The number of those practising a religion other than Catholicism (1.7%)[84] is still very small in relation to non-believers and atheists. These findings should be moderated immediately in the light of the rate of practice: the same survey states that almost half (46.6%) of believers (Catholics and other religions) "never or hardly ever" practise their religion.

Table 2: religious practice in Spain (January 2006)[85]

Q: How often do you attend mass or other religious services, with the exception of social ceremonies (for example, weddings, communions or funerals)?

	%	(N)
Hardly ever	46.6	(913)
Several times a year	17.9	(351)
A few times a month	13.9	(273)
Almost every Sunday and feast day	17.9	(350)
Several times a week	2.4	(47)
Unclassified	1.3	(26)
TOTAL	100.0	(1960)

Although it is difficult to obtain reliable estimates regarding denominations other than Catholicism, various sources, particularly those supplied by the major denominational federations, make it possible to arrive at an order of magnitude. The Federation of Evangelical Religious Entities estimates the number of Protestants in Spain in 2006 to be about 1,200,000[86]. Of these 400,000 are faithful followers, the great majority of them Spanish, who meet

---

83　Source: Centro de Investigaciones Sociológicas, *Barómetro Enero 2006*, No. 2633, Madrid, CIS, January 2006 (http://www.cis.es) . The survey relates to Spaniards aged over eighteen.

84　According to other sources, in 1999 non-Catholic religions represented only between 1 and 1.5% of the population (A. Gómez Movellán, *La iglesia católica y las otras religiones en la España de hoy*, Madrid, Vosa, 1999).

85　Questionnaire confined to Catholics and those practising another religion (Source: Centro de Investigaciones Sociológicas, *Barómetro Enero 2006*, No. 2633, Madrid, CIS, January 2006 (http://www.cis.es) .

86　Source: Federación de Entidades Religiosas Evangélicas de España (http://www.federe.org/general. php?pag=estad), consulted on 19th October 2006.

regularly in Evangelical churches (about half of them are regular churchgoers, the other half being in the Protestant "area of influence"). Immigrants from the EU (particularly from Germany) and from non-EU countries (Latin American in particular) account for 800,000 of the total number of Protestants. The Federation of Jewish Communities in Spain estimates that the Jewish population of Spain is somewhere between 40,000 and 48,000[87]. Orthodox Christians come above all from Central and East European countries (Romania, Bulgaria, and Ukraine) and are concentrated particularly in Aragon and Valencia. The lack of comprehensive information is even more obvious with regard to Islam. Estimates of the number of Muslims fluctuate between 500,000 and a million, i.e. a variation of as much as 100%[88]. Most of the Muslims are Moroccan immigrants, but there are also Algerians, Pakistanis, converts and individuals from other Muslim countries. The two largest cities in the country, Madrid and Barcelona, also have the greatest number of religious denominations. The largest communities of immigrants from Muslim countries are in the autonomous communities of Catalonia, Andalusia, Madrid, Valencia and Murcia and in the enclaves of Ceuta and Melilla. Lastly the 9,000 practising Buddhists should be mentioned, for the sake of completeness.

In such a context, trying to make an overall assessment of the broad structure of the present-day "religious market" – the economic metaphor itself should be treated with care – is tricky. Putting too much stress on the recent increase in the number of Muslims is likely to minimise the importance of Catholicism. By sticking to individual declarations of religious adherence, we doom ourselves to overestimating the religious affiliation that this implies, and in particular the relationship to the institutions that are its legitimate mouthpieces. The same is true for the assessment of inter-religious relations: how can we see the true dimensions of a series of initiatives to promote inter-religious rapprochement (like the inter-religious dialogue cell set up by the Spanish Episcopal Conference) when we compare them with the local or national controversies that beset the representatives of religious organisations? This is a complex question, especially when religion cuts across

---

87 http://www.fcje.org, consulted on 16th October 2006. In 2000 Danielle Rozenberg estimated that there were about 15,000 Jews in thirteen communities in the territory. She stresses that the Jews of Spain "took a long time contemplating settling in the Peninsula (according to a report by the World Jewish Congress, in 1974 only 40% had Spanish nationality). At present the vast majority are Spanish –including second and third generations" (Rozenberg, 2000, p. 45).

88 Taking statistics from the Ministry of Labour and Social Affairs as a basis, Joan Lacomba arrives at a total of 512,706 persons from predominantly Muslim countries. Adding (legal) immigrants from countries in which Islam is not predominant, Muslim immigrants who have acquired Spanish nationality, Spanish Muslims from Ceuta and Melilla and Spanish converts brings the total estimate close to 700,000 (Lacomba, 2005, p. 49). Caritas (Italy), a Catholic organisation, estimated the Muslim presence in 2000 at 544,000 in Italy and 250,000 in Spain, figures to be compared with the figure of 2,700,000 Muslims in France or the 3 million in Germany (Caritas and Migrantes, 2002, p. 226).

but does not merge with other issues. The question of migration, for example, is kept separate from the religious issue by Catholic organisations (such as Caritas or Migrantes), which base their work on a principle of egalitarian and universalistic treatment for all migrants (Itçaina, 2006). However, when the issue shifts towards inter-religious relations the components of Catholicism no longer necessarily speak with one voice. When in February 2001, Cardinal Carles, the Archbishop of Barcelona, accepted the principle of opening mosques, he did so while asking for "fair reciprocal treatment in countries in which Islam is the majority religion"[89]. Similarly in February 2006, the Islamic Junta asked the Spanish and Turkish heads of government for a space for Islamic prayer in the Cathedral-*mezquita* in Cordoba and for ecumenical use of the Saint Sophia Basilica in Istanbul. Here historical memory is exploited by both sides in the light of contemporary religious requirements.

However, the politicisation of religion is not systematic. For example in 2002, during the controversy surrounding the building of a mosque in Premià del Mar (Catalonia), Mgr Carles refused to regard a "neighbourhood dispute" as religious in nature and reaffirmed that the Church did not oppose the building of mosques. In Spain as in Italy, Catholicism finds itself between the universalistic view of tolerance and the particularistic position of a party in contention on the religious market (Itçaina, Dorangricchia, 2005, p. 219). Open-mindedness does not amount to relativism[90], and the range of inter-religious relations varies according to the types of "systems of truth" (Lagroye, 2006) that are mobilised by religious forces. Here we find again the tension, analysed in France by Claire de Galembert, in the attitude of the Catholic Church between "compassion for the excluded" and anxiety when faced with "the emergence of a rival" (De Galembert, 1994). The temporalities are separate: though historically they follow each other in France (the 1970s for the charitable dimension, the 1980s for the emergence of the religious question), in Spain today the two phases seem to be chronologically closer together, even merged, and still more so in Italy.

1b. The two stages in political control of religion

The institutional order born of the transition

The source of the present-day organisation of the Spanish State's relations with religions is first and foremost the 1978 Constitution. Article

---

89 *La Vanguardia*, 17th March 2001.

90 Thus in the Catholic world the Vatican declaration *Dominus Iesus* in August 2000 responded to a concern for reaffirmation of the Christian identity by reasserting a distinction between theological faith, which is the only revealed truth, embodied in Catholic dogma, and belief in other religions, which is simply to a search for truth (Congregation for the Doctrine of the Faith, 2000).

16 proclaims the neutrality of the State and freedom of religion with no limitation other than the protection of law and order, while referring specifically to the Catholic Church[91]. Here we may share the interpretation of Claude Proetschel (Proetschel, 2003), for whom this reference to the Catholic Church (supported by the Communist Party), far from amounting to disguised denominationalism, is on the contrary a search for compromise characteristic of the transition. Juan Linz recalls attempts to "depoliticise the Church" in the transition from Francoism, to avoid having a fixation about the splits of the past (Linz, 1993). The system established at that time, while making a fundamental break with State denominationalism, is not the same as French-style secularism. Danielle Rozenberg refers to "secularism under construction" in Spain: some aspects of the separation between Church and State bring Spain closer to France, but the fact that this separation goes hand in hand with a recognition of religion – in the Constitution itself – is instead redolent of Swiss or German secularism (Rozenberg, 1996).

The 1980 Organic Law of Religious Freedom develops Article 16 of the Constitution by providing that Churches, Denominations and Religious Communities may acquire legal personality subject to registration with the Register of Religious Entities (RRE) (Mantecón, 2003). The law provides that the State shall enter into cooperation agreements and conventions with Churches, denominations and religious communities which, being entered on the RRE, are recognised as having significant roots in Spain by virtue of their size and number of believers. The same Law of 1980 provides for the creation of a general directorate for religious affairs within the Ministry of Justice. This department is responsible for managing the Register of Religious Entities, for maintaining normal relations with the religious entities, for drafting proposals or laws regarding cooperation agreements between State, Churches, denominations and communities, and for relations with international organisations dealing with religious freedom.

Two major challenges have faced the architects of this radical institutional reform of religion. The first was the renegotiation of the institutional effects of the end of the denominational system with the Catholic Church: a series of agreements between the Spanish State and the Holy See between 1976 and 1979 established the new framework for these relations. Apart from ending the denominational nature of the State and State control over the appointment of bishops, the agreements set up an endowment for the Church by the Spanish State and a system of subsidies for Catholic schools (Rozenberg, 2000, p. 41). This consensual climate, characteristic of the

---

91   "No religion shall have a state character. The public authorities shall take into account the religious beliefs of Spanish society and shall consequently maintain appropriate cooperation relations with the Catholic Church and other confessions" (Spanish Constitution, Article 16, 3).

transition period did not last long: the accession of the socialists (Partido Socialista Obrero Espanol - PSOE) to power in 1982 started with reforms conflicting the interests and causes defended by the Catholic Church, such as the law on the organisation of education passed on 15th March 1984, the decriminalisation of abortion (various legislative stages between 1983 and 1985), conflicts on the financing of the Church and of the Catholic NGO Caritas, etc. (Rozenberg, 2000, p. 42). All this raised the "Catholic question" anew in a Spain still affected by the memory of the divisions of the 1936 civil war (Mujal-León E., 1982) (Diaz-Salazar, 2006). During the transition, the split between "the two Spains" was compounded by the territorial question, Basque and Catalan in particular, whose repercussions were felt in the very bosom of the Catholic organisations (Itçaina, Palard, 2007).

The second challenge for the religious policy of the Spanish State concerned the regulation of the so-called minority religions. In formal terms the three cooperation agreements by the Spanish State with Protestant, Muslim and Jewish federations in 1992[92] grant recognition of so-called minority religions in a manner quite unprecedented in Western Europe. The effect of the injunction to join together was above all to persuade religious organisations to federate so that they could speak with one voice in dealings with the State administration. Thus, the Evangelical Defence Commission (*Comisión de Defensa Evangélica*) founded in 1956 gave way in November 1986 to the Federation of Evangelical Religious Entities of Spain (*Federación de Entitades Religiosas Evangélicas de España,* FEREDE*)*, which has become the leading representative of Protestants. Muslims also had to unify their own representative organisations in 1989 in order to present the State with a single negotiator (Moreras, 1996). Thus the Islamic Commission arose from the merger of two quite distinct entities: the *Federación Española de Entitades Religiosas Islámicas* (FEERI) and the *Unión de Comunidades Islámicas de España* (UCIDE). The UCIDE had its origins in a group of immigrants from the Arab Near East (Syria, Palestine) who came to Spain from the 1970s onwards to study or to pursue their professions, while the FEERI was formed at the outset by Spanish Muslim converts (Ramirez, Mijares, 2005). For this reason, "disappointment with the institutionalisation of Islam in Europe spurred the development in Spain of a model based on "institutionalisation from above", but which can be defined as a 'balance' between the two main Islamic federations of Spain" (Moreras, 2005a, p. 2).

In an instructive comparison with France and the Netherlands, Á. Ramírez and L. Mijares state that Spain's distinctiveness comes from the fact that in

---

92 Cooperation agreements were made by the State with the Federation of Evangelical Religious Entities of Spain (Law 24/1992, 10th November); the Federation of Israelite Communities of Spain (Law 25/1992, 10th November) and the Islamic Commission of Spain (Law 26/1992, 10th November).

1992, questions linked to Islam had but little to do with immigration as such and with models of immigrant integration (Ramírez, Mijares, 2005, p. 93). Jordi Moreras (Moreras, 1999) stresses the fundamental difference, as regards claims relating to worship, between the goals of immigrants and those of the Islamic Commission. The fundamental requirement of immigrants is the meeting of basic religious needs by a State with respect to which they feel fundamentally foreign. For the Commission, on the contrary, the issue is to seek recognition of diversity by the State of which they are citizens, or even natives in some cases. According to J. Moreras, Muslim communities have been doubly excluded from the Agreement: "on one hand [Muslims] are not overwhelmingly represented in the two federations (their registration as religious associations linked to one federation or the other can be observed only from the second half of the 1990s); on the other the Agreement makes no reference to "foreign Muslims" or "Muslims of immigrant origin". It is aimed at "Spanish Muslims" and at Islam in Spain, which is – theoretically – a very interesting position by the State (…), but which expressly negates the communalist conditions, requests and principles of these groups of immigrant origin, which form the overwhelming majority of Muslim populations in Spain" (Moreras, 2005a, p. 4). Á. Ramírez and L. Mijares point out that the agreement was signed at a time when Moroccan immigration, which accounts for the majority of the Muslim population in Spain, was already substantial numerically, but had not reached half the figure that it would reach in 2005. In addition, immigrant representatives played no part in the making of the agreement, as they were not focussed on religious issues at the time (Ramírez, Mijares, 2005).

The 1992 agreements settled fundamental points in the national regulation of Islam, including the status of religious leaders, legal protection of mosques, making marriage solemnised according to Islamic ritual valid in civil law, religious assistance in public centres or establishments, Islamic religious education in centres of education, tax breaks applicable to the property and activities of federations forming the Islamic Commission of Spain, recognition of food taboos in publicly run schools, etc. These provisions were supplemented by a 1996 agreement whereby the State undertook to respond to requests regarding education from Protestant, Jewish and Muslim denominations. Teachers, who, in the case of Muslims, would be chosen in agreement with the Islamic Commission, would be paid by the State. However, the strong disagreement between the two entities that signed the Cooperation Agreement with the State in 1992 is often given by the authorities as an explanation of the very low rate of application of the main provisions of that agreement[93]. For example, the 1996 provisions on education should have taken effect from the 1998 financial year; in practice they have remained a dead letter until 2005, when certain schools in the autonomous communities of Aragon, the Basque Country, Andalusia and the Canaries (in Ceuta and Melilla also) established optional courses in Islamic religion[94]. Among other problems, the two federations have experienced many difficulties in devising a joint proposal for the statutes of the Islamic Commission of Spain, one of the conditions required by the State for putting the provisions of the agreement into operation (Lacomba, 2005, p. 58).

In addition to the divisions within the Muslim community, Joan Lacomba (Lacomba, 2005, p. 59) states that these institutional negotiations should be put back into a more general context of cultural structuring of immigrants and their religion in the imagination of the receiving society. In this sense, Spanish history keeps alive a collective memory of distrust of the Moor, in spite of recent efforts to promote a positive memory of medieval inter-religious coexistence[95]. The explosions of violence in the Can Anglada quarter in the Catalan town of Terrassa in July 2001, and above all in El Ejido (Almeria province) in February 2000, illustrate this latent tension, as does the controversy surrounding the building of a mosque in Premià de Mar (Catalonia).

The complexity of political regulation also stems from the very nature of the religions concerned, which do not necessarily lead to a link to politics. In this connection Danielle Rozenberg stresses the difficulties of a strictly religious definition of Judaism and Islam: "These religions do not make the same separation between sacred and secular as Christianity does: they are a moral code, a culture, a way of life and a history, all at the same time... (Schnapper, 1991). Already the presence in Spain of a percentage of "secular" Jews (mainly of South American origin) intentionally putting themselves on the fringes of official Israelite communities, and at the same time the presence of Muslim or Jewish groups for whom expressing membership of a community goes some way beyond the strict limits of religious observance, lead to the assumption that other forms of affirmation of identity and probably

---

93 This lack of unity is reflected in the composition of the governing bodies of the Islamic Commission, whose general secretariat in particular is split between representatives of each of the two Federations (Mantecón, 2003). For a systematic account of the disparities between the 1992 principles and their application see (Moreras, 2005).

94 "Las clases de Islam en las escuelas públicas de varias Comunidades Autónomas comenzarán este mes", *Aula Intercultural*, 11th September 2005, Rosa Serrano "Los colegos de Aragón, Canarias y Andalucia serán los primeros en impartir clases de religión islámica", *La Razón*, 4th February 2005.

95 On the multiplicity of portrayals of the Moor, see (Pérès, 1999, p. 13). Since the controversy about the publication of caricatures of the prophet Mohammed in a Danish newspaper, some Valencian towns have decided to tone down their representations of Mohammed during traditional fiestas representing conflicts *entre Moros y Cristianos* (Lucia Galdea, "Pueblos valencianos suprimen de las fiestas actos ofensivos a Mahoma. Varias localidades suavizan la presentación de la efigie del profeta", *El País*, 2nd October 2006).

of institutional recognition (e.g. cultural or communalist) will make their appearance in the future, as is happening in the United States and in other European countries." (Rozenberg, 2000, p. 45). This analysis is confirmed in our own fields of interest focusing particularly on social mobilisation related to immigration: religious membership is only one of the multiple identities, individual and collective, on which claims for recognition are focused.

Present-day reconstructions

Though relatively stable within an institutional framework that is quite widely shared, the general pattern of relations between religions and the State in Spain has seen distinct phases of politicisation. The period beginning on 13th March 2004 with the accession to power of the Spanish Socialist Workers' Party after two Popular Party governments (1996-2004) seems to mark start of a new phase. Debates on the place of religions in the public space inevitably involve in return a discussion about institutional regulation of religion. Of course the tragic context of the changeover of power in the wake of the Madrid bombings of 11th March 2004 would tend to shift attention towards the organised forms of the Muslim religion. There is undoubtedly a pre- and post-11th March in the public management of Islam in Spain, at least in terms of work on perceptions: we will return to this. However (and the fact is given less media coverage), the return of a left-wing majority also meant an increase in tensions between the State and the Catholic Church. These tensions focus on two sets of issues. The first relates directly to the sectional interests of the Catholic Church, namely the reform of religious education in public schools and the debate about the method of financing the Church, while the second relates to new social policies, with certain symbolic measures rousing Catholic circles to anger: the easing of legislation on divorce in June 2005 and the Decree of the Council of Ministers of 29th October 2004 authorising research on embryo stem cells. But it was above all the Law of 29th June 2005 on the marriage of persons of the same sex that mobilised Catholics, the Spanish Church going so far as to ask Catholic mayors not to celebrate homosexual marriages and to invoke the conscience clause against the legal constraint[96].

This will to reform is intended to adapt the institutional edifice that emerged from the transition to the new political, social and religious conditions. The debate about the financing of the Catholic Church speaks volumes in this respect. In theory, the present system is based on the 1979 agreements between the Spanish State and the Holy See reforming the Concordat of

---

96 *La Croix*, 11-12th June 2005. This call was reiterated by the Prefect of the Congregation for the Doctrine of the Faith on the occasion of Benedict XVI's visit to the World Meeting of Families in Valencia in July 2006 (H.T., "Un appel à la désobéissance civile contre des lois jugées immorales par l'Église", *Le Monde*, 11th July 2006.

1953 and providing that the State should make an annual appropriation to the Catholic Church, updated in line with the consumer price index. In this connection Felipe Gonzales' socialist government made a transitional provision in 1988 allocating to the Church the 0.52% of personal income tax that taxpayers had chosen to allocate to the Catholic Church. In theory, the State's contribution was to be added to this 0.52% for a transitional period of three years. The system actually only began to function in 1988, and therefore the State's contribution to the Church has always been higher than what was actually collected from taxpayers. The number of taxpayers ticking the "Church" box on their tax returns has stabilised at around 33%. Apart from this "ordinary" financing, the Catholic Church is also entitled to tax exemptions[97] which other religions do not enjoy. Under the Aznar government, the bishops had asked for an increase in the rate of income tax allocated to the Church. The change to a socialist government reinforced this request: Lluis Martinez Sistach, the Archbishop of Barcelona, referred to the Italian example to justify increasing this appropriation from 0.5 to 0.8%. Since it came to power the Zapatero government has wavered between an *a minima* position that the government would go no further in financing the Church and a willingness to reform the system, announced in late 2004. The issue also affects the political balances within a left-wing coalition majority: for the PSOE it is about not letting itself be outflanked on its left by its two other parliamentary supporters (Izquierda Unida and the Catalan republicans of the Esquerra Republicana Catalana) while staying on course for the declared reforms. The rejection by 307 votes (Popular Party and almost all the socialist deputies) of the amendment tabled by Izquierda Unida in November 2005 to revise Church funding downwards is clear evidence of the fragility of political balances. However, the agreement reached in September 2006 between the Bishops' Conference and the government aims to put an end to this uncertainty by a compromise solution. The appropriation from income tax to the Catholic Church goes from 0.52% to 0.7%, but the annual budgetary supplement will no longer be paid by the State, and the Bishops' Conference will have to account every year for the use to which the appropriation is put. Lastly, the agreement puts an end to the VAT exemption, thus meeting the European requirement. The agreement, seen as "moderately satisfactory" by the Catholic Church[98], is viewed with mixed feelings by the so-called minority religions. According to the FEREDE, the main Protestant federation, and the Islamic Commission, the new system admittedly brings more clarity by putting

---

97   Prior to the agreement of 22nd September 2006 the Church hierarchy was not required to pay VAT or inheritance tax when the property or rights acquired were intended for worship, the maintenance of the clergy, the ministry and the exercise of charity. The European authorities have asked for explanations on this exemption from VAT on several occasions.

98   Agencias, "El Gobernio anuncia un acuerdo con la Iglesia que eleva al 0.7% la aportación voluntaria del IRPF", *El Pais*, 22nd September 2006.

an end to the supplementary contributions by the State but preserves a considerable advantage for the Catholic Church thanks to funding by tax[99].

Negotiating a redefinition of the institutional positions of a centralised and hierarchical religion that is both traditional and shrinking is one thing. Outlining a new pattern of State regulation for a religion lacking unified representation, deeply split by internationalised networks and under heavy fire from the media, is another. Present-day State relations with Islam bear the traces of this uncertainty. How can public officials manage the contradiction between promoting a stronger message on tolerance and the benevolent neutrality of the State towards the liberal and democratic components of Islam and keeping a closer watch on potential centres of Islamic radicalism? At the same time, a few token gestures assume great significance and reveal as much the unity as the fragmentation of the Muslim community. Unity prevails when extremism is rejected. On the State's part, there was the establishment in October 2004 of the Pluralism and Co-existence Foundation (*Pluralismo y convivencia*) chaired by the Minister of Justice and aimed at promoting inter-religious dialogue that seeks to restore the balance. The aim of this foundation is to help in implementing cultural, educational and social integration programmes for minority religious denominations that have entered into cooperation agreements with the State or demonstrably have significant roots in Spain, and to develop the full exercise of religious freedom. This refocusing on "socio-cultural" activities excludes support for any activity linked to actual worship.[100] Some have seen in this the germ of a funding system for minority religions, aiming at making up for the Catholic Church's built-in advantage. The *fatwa* declared by the Islamic Commission of Spain against Al Qaida on the occasion of the first anniversary of the Madrid bombings was also a strong signal from the Muslim partners of the State[101].

The outward show of unity cannot conceal the many forms of mobilisation. We readily agree with Á. Ramirez and L. Mijares (2005), who see the bombings on 11th March as opening a new phase characterised in particular by the mobilisation of new players on the question of regulation of religions. The new dramatisation of Islam and its representativeness is generating initiatives from players *a priori* remote from the religious issue, but who have gained greatly in legitimacy through their work with migrants: as a result,

---

99   While refusing to ask for public support for religious activities, pursuant to the principle of separation, the leader of the FEREDE Protestant federation has asked the government to offer them the same opportunities as the Catholic Church, reserving the right to accept or refuse this offer (Alfonso Mateos, "El resto de las confesiones quiere las mismas oportunidades", *El Mundo*, 23rd September 2006).

100   http://www.pluralismoyconvivencia.org. Consulted on 16th October 2006.

101   Comisión Islámica de España, "Comisión Islámica de España emite una fatua condenando el terrorismo y el grupo Al Qaida", 10th March 2005, http://webislam.com/?idu=399.

the opposition between religious and pro-migrant mobilisation valid in 1992 is tending to give way to new and competing views on the management of Islam. In April 2004, ATIME, the association of Moroccan workers, proposed to the government the creation of a Council of Muslims in Spain (*Consejo de Musulmanes en España*) whose functions, *inter alia*, would be to regulate Muslim religious practices and rituals in close collaboration with the Ministry of Justice and to channel and co-ordinate the official recognition of Islamic associations and mosques, accredit imams put forward by the communities of the faithful, organise teaching on Islam, combat anti-Muslim prejudices and facilitate inter-religious dialogue[102]. This proposal stemmed in particular from the recognition that the existing representative organisations were poorly integrated (Aierbe, 2004). Doubtless the substantial increase in workers of Moroccan origin together with and on top of the new situation generated by 11th March is encouraging the association to intervene in an area that is new to it. This positioning by an immigrants' association is unprecedented and paradoxical in that it asks for more State intervention in the control of religious activities, and it is out of step with an Islamic Commission that considers itself to be the sole legitimate body (Ramirez, Mijares, 2005, p. 95). The ATIME proposal also stresses that the Commission is not fully representative among the Muslim community itself. Mohamed Chaib, a Catalan Socialist Party member of the Catalan parliament and as such the first Muslim elected to the parliament of an autonomous community, is saying more or less the same thing when he proposes that the leaders of the Islamic Council should be elected, not appointed by the government[103]. All of these analyses demonstrate that Spanish Islam in 2005 is not the same as in 1992. So the picture of Spanish Islam that is emerging is that of an incomplete, composite and fragmented body that does not facilitate the task of a State administration in search of a partner. Increasing internal splits in the Islamic Commission[104], new religious interventionism by migrants' associations and international politicisation, the blurring or confusion of aims and issues is doubtless the new hallmark of present-day politicisation of this aspect of religion in Spain.

Two points can be made following this rapid review of the two great phases in the political regulation of religion. The first relates to uncertainty about the Spanish model of relations between the State and religions, as remote

---

102   Fdo. Mustapha el M'rabet, "Propuesta de ATIME para la creación de un Consejo de Musulmanes en España", http://www.atime.es/actualidad8.html, April 2004.

103   "Un diputado musulmán del PSC pide que las urnas, no el Gobierno, elijan el Consejo Islámico", *Webislam*, 26th September 2005 (http://www.webislam.com).

104   The shifts in the balance at the very heart of the two major federations making up the Islamic Commission testify to this instability. In January 2006, for example, a "heterogeneous alliance of Spanish converts, pro-Moroccan leaders and representatives of Saudi influence in Spain" became the majority in the governing bodies of the FEERI, isolating historic leaders such as Mansur Escudero (Luis Gómez, "Crece el poder de los líderes prosaoudíez y promarroquíes en la comunidad islámica", *El Pais*, 5th February 2006).

from the former denominational model as from French-style secularism. The second is that of constant interactions between local, regional and national levels in the management of religions, because local controversies, as the first stage in politicisation, compel a rethink of the extent of public authority action in the matter of religion. These controversies, given much media coverage, concern Islam in particular: we will observe their effects in one of the autonomous communities most exposed to this growing politicisation of religious issues: Catalonia.

2. Local authorities faced with the new religious issue

As we have said, local authorities are increasingly drawn into participating implicitly or explicitly in the regulation of religion. J. Garreta Bochaca puts it well: "national bodies negotiate the official position of Islam, while local bodies deal independently with problems that are more humdrum, though of highly symbolic value to the community" (Garreta Bochaca: 2000), and what is true in the case of Islam holds good for all minority denominations.

Although Spain took the minority religions in its territory into account quite early in a form of contract-based link that was to be a model for other European countries (particularly for Italy in its relations with Islam), the entry of minority denominations into the local public space is still a highly politicised issue. Thus anticipation at the national level has had but few knock-on effects at the local level, through lack of efficient transmission machinery. Political institutions' interest in inter-religious dialogue varies widely from locality to locality; it is much more structured in heavily built-up areas, especially as they are home to many more denominations than rural areas. Local issues are politicised in two opposite directions: they are integrated into the inter-religious dialogue as a constituent of "coexistence" policies in the town, while, at the same time, residents sometimes see demands by minority denominations as threats to peaceful coexistence. Very often these problems are tied up with the problems of inclusion policies for foreigners recently arrived in the town.

In the case study we are now going to develop, we have decided to pay particular attention to relations between local authorities and Islam, as Islam is the religion that has become most publicly visible in recent years. This development is associated with the increasing flows of migrants from countries in which Islam is the majority religion and Islam's political willingness to go into the public space as it gains certain stability. However, as Jordi Moreras says, "the visibility of Islam in Spain (…) is more the result of growing interest than of the resolute willingness of Muslim groups to make themselves visible socially" (Moreras, 2005a, p. 13). The fact remains that this visibility, whether acquired deliberately or reluctantly, means that for local authorities, Islam is increasingly an issue in political regulation "from the bottom"[105].

We will also focus more closely on case studies from Catalonia, not only because of its leading position in the promotion of inter-religious dialogue, but also because it is an area that has experienced the problems we have just described, particularly conflicts stemming from the increased visibility of emerging religions, principally Islam. We will have to address both the local (municipality) and regional (Spanish Autonomous Community) levels, because of the importance of the region in Spain as an area enjoying full political autonomy in most fields and because of the region's special relations with the municipal level. The cases described in detail here do not claim to give an exhaustive picture of the question in Spain generally; rather the aim is to present exemplars of the practices, tensions and politicisation that crystallise around the religious issue at the local level.

2a. Structuring of the inter-religious dialogue in Catalonia

It is in Catalonia that inter-religious dialogue is most highly structured through the existence of a multiplicity of platforms for dialogue and the vitality of the groupings and associations concerned. Dialogue is organised via interconnected platforms that pursue different aims. In the first place, Barcelona is the headquarters of a UNESCO forum for inter-religious dialogue (*Associació UNESCO per al Diàleg Interreligiós*) which has sought to federate initiatives in this area. This association is linked to many regional and international networks, which give it considerable weight in inter-religious dialogue: it is a founder member of the *United Religions Initiative* (URI), an international NGO set up in 2000 to promote collaboration among religions. At its initiative the *Parliament of the World's Religions* was held in Barcelona in July 2004 as part of the Universal Forum of Cultures.

In addition, there are inter-religious dialogue entities and a meeting platform for the principal religions. The platform – *Grup de Treball Estable de Religions* (Standing Working Group on Religions) – provides a collaborative working area, but above all an area of common visibility for the various religious entities[106]. The goal of the inter-religious dialogue organisations is different; it is to organise dialogue at the grass roots, among believers, and promote public initiatives in support of dialogue. The Catalan groups are

---

105 It is also Islam which is the subject of most scientific publications on this topic, thus testifying to its growing importance and to the interest taken in it by public decision-makers, who very often sponsor studies.

106 It includes the archbishop of Barcelona, the Orthodox Church, the Evangelical Council of Catalonia, the Islamic and Cultural Council of Catalonia, and the Israelite Community of Barcelona.

federated within the *Xarxa Catalana d'Entitats de Diàleg Interreligiós* (Catalan Network of Entities for Inter-religious Dialogue), which brings together sixteen groups based throughout Catalonia, understood in a broad sense to include Valencia, Alicante and Perpignan, on a geographical and a sector basis (cf. the CREA at the Autonomous University of Barcelona). This network plays a very important part in organising events to promote inter-religious dialogue and in hosting international events, as well as in establishing a link with the authorities, although this role devolves increasingly upon the hierarchy of each religion within the *Grup de Treball*. The *Xarxa Catalana d'Entitats de Diàleg Interreligiós* is also heavily involved in the organisation of the annual *Parlament Català de les Religions*, which sees itself as an important occasion for the various denominations to meet, as well as a manifesto for inter-religious dialogue; 2006 is the second year in which it has been organised.

Although dialogue is highly institutionalised in Catalonia, other Spanish cities host such platforms, as well as groupings and international events in support of inter-religious dialogue. A network modelled on the Xarxa d'Entitats exists in Madrid and in other major Spanish cities. Moreover, in December 2005 Bilbao hosted the *Congreso Internacional sobre el Diálogo Intercultural e Interreligioso*. Similarly, the *Pluralismo y Convivencia* Foundation, which is answerable to the Justice Ministry Secretariat for Religious Affairs and whose purpose is to assist minority denominations and encourage inter-religious dialogue, organised major conferences in 2005 in Santander, Madrid and Cordoba.

2b. Progressive institutionalisation of relations between local authorities and religions

To a large extent, the institutionalisation of religious practice in the local sphere through the creation of denominational associations and cultural groups and by the process of recognition of non-Catholic religions by the Spanish State since 1992, has put dialogue with religions onto the local political agenda.

The involvement of institutions in religious affairs varies widely from an Autonomous Community to another one and from municipality to municipality. In fact, it is dependent on several factors, first among which is the presence in their territory of substantial communities practising a non-Catholic religion. We must remember that Muslims are present mainly in Catalonia, Andalusia, Madrid, Valencia and Murcia and in Ceuta and Melilla. In addition, there is a substantial Orthodox community in Aragon and Valencia, and Evangelical communities linked to Latin American immigration are represented, *inter alia*, in the Community of Madrid and in Valencia. Secondly, institutional activism depends upon the proactivity of the authorities, either in the context of integration policies or as a distinct policy aim. Lastly, religion's powerful historical influence in Spain, and in particular the historical links that exist between local governments and Catholic bodies, must also be taken into account.

It is relatively difficult at this stage to decide whether local authorities feel compelled to take up these issues because of the demands placed on them by the vitality of the religious communities and of the dialogue between them, or whether they have sought to develop policies and partnerships in order to integrate recently arrived inhabitants through political regulation of new denominations. The fact remains that although the links between the Catholic Church and political institutions have always been very strong, the gradual "deprivatisation" of religion[107] should raise questions for us.

The religious policy of the Autonomous Community

We will take the Generalitat de Catalunya as an example in order to study the links that may be formed between political institutions and religions, in this case at the regional level. Although it is the most complete example as far as these questions are concerned, it nevertheless remains quite exceptional. In religious matters the powers of the Generalitat are particularly extensive. Thus Article 161 of the new Statute of Catalonia provides that the Generalitat has "exclusive power over religious entities that carry out their activities in Catalonia", i.e. "regulation and establishment of collaboration and co-operation mechanisms for the carrying out of their activities within the jurisdiction of the Generalitat". The Generalitat also has executive authority over religious freedom, which includes participation in the "management of the State Registry of [Catalan] Religious Entities", the "establishment of agreements and cooperation conventions with the Churches, confessions and religious communities registered in the State Registry" and the promotion, development and execution of these agreements[108].

To this end the *Generalitat de Catalunya* has instituted a whole series of actions intended to the various religions and a number of associated collaborative programmes, through its Directorate General for Religious Affairs answerable to the Presidential Department. This Directorate is responsible for:

«1 - Assisting the various religious entities established in Catalonia.

---

107 This analysis of a *deprivatisation* of religion or of a *counter-secularisation* of certain religious spaces is now normal in religious sociology. For an analysis of the emergence of Islam onto the political stage after the September 11th bombings, a parallel can usefully be drawn with Spain post 11th March (Zeghal, 2005).

108 Translations based on the Statute of Catalonia adopted in June 2006 in the Catalan Parliament.

2 - Application of Government agreements with bodies representing the various religious denominations in Catalonia and ensuring that they are complied with.

3 - Normal representation of the Generalitat before religious entities.

4 - Preparation of studies of and reports on religious affairs.

5 - Establishing and maintaining relations with officials of institutions for themes in the field of religion.

6 - The exercise of any other function in this area that may be entrusted to it by the incumbent or the general secretary of the Presidential Department[109].

This Directorate is attached directly to the Presidential Department, which enables it to act in collaboration with all other departments dealing with social, educational or cultural matters.

The *Generalitat* has entered into several agreements with representatives of Catalan religious denominations. In the mid-1980s, it signed conventions allowing Catholic clergy to enter and hold services in hospitals (1986) and prisons (1987). But it is since the very end of the 1990s, and at a much greater pace over the past two years, that minority religions in Catalonia have begun to make contact with the *Generalitat* and to sign new conventions with it. The Evangelical Council of Catalonia was the first to sign an agreement (1998), followed by the Islamic and Cultural Council of Catalonia in 2002, the Baha'i community in 2004, and the Agapé (Evangelical Church of Philadelphia) Christian Cultural Association of Catalonia and Jewish communities in 2005. The *Generalitat* also signed an agreement with the Secular League in 2004. These agreements are all based on the same principles (recognition of the various denominations by the authorities, recognition of religious freedom, and recognition of the secular nature of Catalonia) and are all intended to foster institutional dialogue. The conventions may also contain agreements regarding the training of imams (in the case of Islam) and support for learning and using of Catalan language (Islam and Agapé - Evangelical Church of Philadelphia).

On the basis of these agreements, the *Generalitat* is developing many programmes aimed at facilitating knowledge of a religion in society, giving it a recognised place, or encouraging dialogue among religions. In this context, it has instituted a programme for religions to be represented in all their diversity in hospitals, as well as a programme to encourage religious care for Muslim prisoners. Islam is still the religion on which public attention most

---

109 http://www.gencat.cat

focuses, in particular through programmes for training of imams conducted *in the Catalan language*. These programmes not only reflect a political will to supervise the practice of Islam, in return for its public recognition but are also an opportunity to encourage new arrivals to learn the Catalan language, which is a mainstay of Catalan immigration and integration policy.

Lastly, the *Generalitat* has a fundamental role as a provider of funds for religious entities, in particular the minority religions which do not have the resources that the Catholic Church enjoys nationally. In 2005, grants totalling €600,000 were made to various religions, either directly or through their associations, for specifically religious programmes. To these might be added the grants obtained by denominational associations for non-religious programmes (social assistance, immigration, education, culture, etc.). The *Generalitat* is thus the main provider of funds for the interreligious dialogue platforms referred to earlier, as indeed it is for the *Grup de Treball Estable* (Standing Working Group on Religions).

Institutionalisation and proactive policies are particularly strong in Catalonia, partly because of the presence of a great variety of religious communities with relatively large memberships and partly because of Catalonia's constant wish to be a leader in civil liberties and multicultural integration. But Catalonia is not an isolated case. Without describing them in detail here, we may mention the proactive policies of the Community of Madrid, which has *inter alia* introduced local regulations on the setting up of religious premises that are without parallel in Spain[110].

The "religious policies" of Catalan municipalities

The municipalities are also basic elements in encouraging inter-religious dialogue and in liaising with religions. Although most municipalities are faced with requests from emerging religious communities in Spain, few of them have really taken up these issues, either through their failure to anticipate these requests and relatively powerlessness to respond to them, or because there is no political will to take them up. And yet the requests to municipalities are often very practical and relate to everyday religious practice. J. Moreras has categorised them as follows in his study of the public regulation of Islam (Moreras: 2005a, pp. 7-8): request for premises, temporary use of public areas, assistance for mother-tongue and Islamic religion courses, occasional use of the municipal abattoir, requests relating to schools, reservation of a space in the municipal cemetery, licences and permits to open religious premises and

---

110 On the relationship between integration of migrants and religious provision, see the research in Madrid on 4 mosques, 28 Catholic institutions and 13 representing other Christian denominations (Aparicio, Tornos, Labrador, 1999).

exemption from municipal taxes thereon. In practice, there are fundamental differences in political investment between major cities, where there are large numbers of non-Catholic believers, and rural areas or smaller towns, which have neither a sizeable network of denominational associations nor a large number of believers to justify putting these requests on the agenda.

Larger towns and cities can respond to these requests but can also develop forward, proactive policies in this area. Here too we will pay particular attention to the example of Barcelona and the original experience of the Centro Interreligiòs de Barcelona. This Centre is a department of the municipality of Barcelona, but is run by UNESCO Centre for Catalonia and in particular by the Association for Inter-religious Dialogue that is answerable to it[111]. It comes more directly under the *Regidoria de Dona i Drets civils* (Department of Women's and Civil Rights). The City Council's intentions in setting up such a department are absolutely clear. Recognising the increasing diversity in religious beliefs in the city, the Regidoria reaffirms the necessity for dialogue and for mutual knowledge and understanding of religions. The role of the department is thus to contribute to defusing the conflicts that may exist among the various religions and their followers. For the city of Barcelona it is important to be in the forefront in questions of interreligious dialogue viewed as one aspect of a more global policy of minority integration and as going further than the mere promotion of "civic spirit" and "coexistence"[112]. This centre is above all a forum of opportunity for minority religions, which find in it a forum for expression but also a not inconsiderable source of help from the city council. It is a centre for encouraging initiatives, conferences and exhibitions and aid for the inter-religious activities previously mentioned.

Other cities in Spain claim to be in the forefront of interreligious dialogue. Thus the city of Saragossa's social affairs department recently organised seminars entitled "Diálogo interreligioso y convivencia para la Paz" (Interreligious dialogue and coexistence for peace) and claims to be politically proactive in this matter.

Logically, action by Spanish municipalities is proportional to the requirements, and above all to the size of the membership of the groups on the spot. Joan Lacomba shows that not all the requirements of communities, in this case Muslim communities, lead to requests to the local authorities

---

111 This delegation of municipal services management to specialist associations in the field is a method of organisation chosen by the municipality of Barcelona for emerging issues over which it has only partial jurisdiction (this is the case, for example, with its service to assist foreigners, the Servei d'Atenció a Immigrants Estrangers i Refugiats, SAIER).

112 The principles guiding the creation and operation of this centre can be found in the European Charter for the Safeguarding of Human Rights in the City (Saint Denis 2000), of which Barcelona is a signatory. Article 3 refers to religious freedom as a fundamental right. This charter also follows on from the "Barcelona Commitment" of 1998.

(Lacomba, 2005). Muslims are selective, resorting to the political authorities only if they cannot meet their requirements themselves or by recourse to the private sector. This is the case, for example, in Valencia, for the facilities necessary for festivals (Ramadan, Eid) or for Islamic ritual slaughter. On the other hand there is strong demand for the use of part of the local cemeteries, for the possibility for children to receive Islamic education in schools, and for social assistance, because the mosque and the various Muslim associations play a vital part in aiding members of the community in difficulty (non-compliance with legal requirements, accommodation problems, etc.). J. Lacomba shows that the responses given by local authorities in Valencia only partly meet Muslim expectations. Schools sometimes ignore requests for meals without pork in the canteens and do not have staff to teach Muslim religion, owing to a lack of appropriately trained teachers. However, since 2005 the first teachers of Muslim religion have been appointed in Spain, in schools in Andalusia, Aragon, the Basque country and the Spanish enclaves of Ceuta and Melilla, and in Barcelona and Madrid. However, although the Autonomous Communities were consulted, the decision came from the central Government, through the *Directora General de Asuntos Religiosos*, Mercedes Rico Godoy.

So relations between local political institutions and religions vary greatly from municipality to municipality or from an Autonomous Community to another one. Although some seek to be in the forefront on this issue, particularly since the bombings on 11th March 2004 and because of the presence in their territory of newcomers of various denominations, not all do so. There can be no public action if there are no structured communities and if there is no backup from denominational associations, which play an essential part in uniting the community of believers, especially in Islam. However, one of the reasons for the authorities' taking up these issues more and more is the conflicts that have arisen locally about public manifestations of new beliefs, in particular Islam.

2c. Political settlement of religious conflicts at local level: contrasted reality

As we have said, new denominations in Spain have been taken into account relatively recently. Islam is recognised by the Spanish State through the 1992 agreement, but it was only in the early 2000s that Muslims were effectively recognised at the local level. Muslim communities have been settled in Spain for much longer, mainly in the south, in Andalusia, but their vitality comes mainly through the involvement of Spanish converts. It was when immigration combined with the visibility of Islam on the public stage that major conflicts arose. We will see that it is difficult to give a univocal interpretation of this type of conflict: Islamophobia, xenophobia or simply a "neighbourhood dispute"?

Since the 2000s, the rejection of recently arrived immigrants and of Muslims has taken similar forms, bringing into play coalitions with a common cause involving the same parties, and the two views (rejection of Islam/ rejection of immigration) are frequently connected when conflicts arise. To date the most significant xenophobic conflict in Spain was the El Ejido riots in February 2000, rooted in the rejection of foreigners, mainly Moroccans, working in the region's agricultural economy. This region had seen a very substantial increase in the number of foreigners, needed as labour for intensive agriculture, and this went hand in hand with extremely poor living conditions for the immigrant body, the fact that most of the day labourers did not comply with legal requirements, and a very irregular pattern of days worked. Riots broke out after a woman was murdered by a mentally disturbed man of Moroccan origin, and any sign of an immigrant presence was attacked: makeshift dwellings, support associations and trade unions, bars, halal butchers' shops. The reason why we describe this event, in which Islam has so minor a place, is above all because it has left a negative historical mark in the Spanish consciousness and done much to bring the new reality of migration onto the political agenda, and because it foreshadows a whole series of after-shocks, albeit on a smaller scale and less widely reported. Yet Muslims were to play a more important part in these conflicts. The second significant event for Islamic institutions, as for the authorities, was the bombings on 11th March 2004, referred to above, which, like El Ejido, had a dual contradictory effect: criminalising Islam and immigration while bringing home to the authorities the need to promote dialogue and develop policies for stabilising both the Muslim religion and the immigrant groups.

The controversy surrounding the building of the mosque in Premià de Mar, a town with about 25,000-30,000 residents in the Barcelona region, is significant in this respect. The conflict broke out in 2001-2002, i.e. shortly after the El Ejido riots but before the 2004 bombings. To our knowledge this was the first major conflict to be brought into the public arena about the building of a mosque. It should also be pointed out that although the 1992 agreement provides for State and local authority assistance in the provision of places of worship for Islam, few mosques had been built in Spain at the time of the conflict: two mosques were in use in Madrid, one in Valencia, one in Cordoba, one in Marbella (Malaga Province) and a few in the enclaves of Ceuta and Melilla. On the other hand hundreds of prayer halls are in use, generally makeshift and in unattractive premises. J. Garreta listed 500 halls of that type in 2000 (Garreta, 2000), in which year Catalonia had over 100, but no mosque. This was the context in which the small Muslim community of

Premià de Mar, represented by the At-Tauba Islamic Association (AIAT), asked for a permit to build a mosque on a site that had belonged to it since 1997. It should be stressed that the 1992 agreements state that local authorities have a duty to grant land for the construction of places of worship. The conflict started in the late 1990s with the proliferation of neighbourhood complaints about the first Muslim prayer hall in Premià. When AIAT announced it wanted to build a mosque and give up the prayer hall, the neighbourhood dispute spread to the entire town, where an anti-mosque petition gained 5,000 signatures. The municipality, under pressure from residents, then proposed that the AIAT should build a mosque in the industrial zone, far from the town centre. Faced with the uncertain nature of this proposal, AIAT's new leaders, "young adults of Moroccan origin with a high level of culture and very well aware of their rights" (Gabinet d'Estudis Socials, 2002, p. 12), assisted by a lawyer, refused. The town council then broke off the negotiations and asked them to vacate the disused school that it had temporarily made available to them. The media began to report events. The AIAT, advised by its lawyers, handed back the keys of the school and used the site that it owned for prayer. The neighbourhood response was acrimonious: loud music, graffiti on walls, rubbish thrown onto the site, and the first demonstrations took place on Fridays as from the 19th April 2002. A turning point came on 26th April, when the municipal council voted in favour of granting the permit to build the mosque. The most hard-line residents then turned against the town council and a platform identified with the anti-immigration extreme right made its appearance, led by Josep Anglada, a resident of Vic. In response, the Coordinadora Premià per la Convivencia was formed in support of the Islamic and immigrant community. It called for a demonstration on 12th May which was attended by 1000 people. This platform brought together many associations, including IC-V, an ecological association that was part of the municipal majority. This brought out tensions within that majority, in which the PSC (Partido Socialiste de Cataluña) and the ERC (Esquerra Republicana de Catalunya – left-wing radical nationalists) refused to commit themselves. There were other demonstrations, giving rise to confrontation and to ever-increasing politicisation of the issues: Josep Anglada introduced his new party, the *Plataforma per Catalunya*[113], Jordi Pujol, the president of the Generalitat, published statements in the press stressing the duties of immigrants in Catalonia and the need to preserve the Catalan identity[114], while Pascual Maragall, a PSC candidate in the elections to the Autonomous

---

113 Xavier Casal argues in *El Pais* that this conflict allowed Anglada to benefit "freely from the political rostrum to defend his ideas and make known his organisation," at the time when his party did not have a political representation. Since then, still occupying a marginal place, PxC keeps developing and obtained as from 2003 posts of municipal councillors in Catalonia.

114 See the speech of Jordi Pujol in Madrid, 4 April 2000, published in the journal *La Factoria*, No 13, Oct.-Jan. 2001

Community, accused the right of playing on the immigration issued and supported the municipality.

At the local level, however, a meeting involving the municipal council, advisers from the Generalitat and the Muslim authorities reached a consensus: agreement by the Muslims to build the mosque in the industrial zone, in return for which they could continue to use the school that had been allotted to them. Although the PP criticised this agreement, it was finally put into effect, after much further prevarication, on 17th September. At the autonomous level, however, controversy swelled over the former imam of Premià, who refused to negotiate with a woman, in this case the mayoress. Heated exchanges on calls for the imam's expulsion then ensued between the ERC, the CiU (a centre-right separatist party, of wich Jordi Pujol was a member), the IC-V and SOS Racismo... although the imam had left Spain for the Netherlands nearly a year earlier. This conflict, coupled with an earlier and obviously xenophobic clash in the Can'Anglada quarter of the neighbouring town of Terrassa in 1999, led the Muslim authorities in Catalonia, though still criticised by some of the Muslim faithful, to organise more strongly and the authorities to recognise them in exchange for the training of imams to which we referred previously. The Generalitat's Director-General for Religious Affairs has acted as permanent mediator in the conflict since December 2000, at the request of the municipal council.

This long and complicated conflict is particularly instructive in that it combines all the problems and all the players involved in the establishment of Islam in Spain today. According to the various observers, religion is but one aspect of this conflict, the rejection of immigration in general, and of Moroccan residents in particular, being among the prime causes of tension (Gabinet d'estudis socials, 2002: 34). However, the controversy surrounding the imam of Premià and imams accused of advocating a strict form of Islam, running counter to the values of acceptance and coexistence, is significant and as revealing as the political outcome of these mobilisations (the Generalitat taking the training of imams in hand). Conflicts relating to religious affairs and migration carry the seeds of extensive politicisation of these issues, both by the social movements and causal coalitions involved and by politicians.

We must say, though without going into the details of other conflicts, that the same type of problem has arisen in several towns in relation to mosque building projects, inter alia in Lleida in 2003, in Reus (Catalonia) in 2004, in the Bermejales district of Seville in 2005-2006, not to mention Cornellà de Llobregat (Barcelona), El Ejido (Almeria) and Alicante (Valencia)[115]. So, this has in no sense been an isolated type of conflict since 2002. Most of the time, they arise in urban areas where there is already tension between native populations and those of foreign origin, even though the latter may be long-established[116]. This is particularly true for El Ejido, as already mentioned, but also for Reus, which has been the scene of attacks perpetrated against foreigners by neo-Nazi groups. The conflict over the Reus mosque also became more politicised because of its closeness to the March 2004 Madrid bombings.

Thus, it is conflict about the building of mosques that is most frequent in the local public arena, calling into question action by local authorities, in particular by municipalities. Analysis of all conflicts shows that local players are unprepared for this type of problem and are slow to tackle them. It also shows that the players cannot cope with the politicisation of these issues, while they are not even responsible for it, as was the case with El Ejido municipal council. Observation also reveals the frequency of coordinated intervention by the various levels of government (local, autonomous community and central) in settling conflicts, the higher levels acting as mediators in local conflicts, to which the municipal council is often a party. With the proliferation of these conflicts and under the impact of the Madrid bombings, local authorities are attempting to introduce preventive policies, combining interreligious and intercultural dialogue in order to defuse possible conflicts threatening the coexistence that is the political credo of municipalities with a substantial foreign presence.

In Spain the stabilisation of relations between religion and politics devised during the transition from the Franco dictatorship is being seriously challenged today. Changes in the local, national and international religious scene, shifting of political balances, and the interpenetration of levels of territorial jurisdiction in this matter are all joining together to reshape the politics of religion. The constantly interplaying manoeuvres of politicians and religious leaders can muddy the situation, with a sometimes imperceptible slide from the political regulation of religion to forms of religious regulation of politics which, though more fluid, are often less easily controlled by those involved.

---

115 Also in 2002, Alicante saw a series of attacks directed against Muslims, and a strong presence of groupings of extreme right. The City Hall closed down at the same time a certain number of businesses owned by Muslims who did not a valid authorisation, which they contest.

116 We have already seen that the arrival of Islam in the public arena, entailing in particular the building of places of worship, calls for an established network of associations and consequently a stable Muslim presence.

Bibliographical references

Aierbe P. M. (2004), « Entrevista con Mustapha El M'Rabet, presidente de ATIME (Asociación de Trabajadores e Inmigrantes Marroquíes en España) », *Mugak*, n°27, 1st April 2004.

Allievi S. (2005), «How the Immigrant has become Muslim. Public debates on Islam in Europe». *Revue Européenne des Migrations Internationales*, Volume 21, No. 2 , p. 135-163.

Anderson J. (2003), « Catholicism and democratic consolidation in Spain and Poland », *West European Politics*, 26 (1), 2003, p. 137-156.

Aparicio R., Tornos A., Labrador J. (1999), *Inmigrantes, integración, religiones*, Madrid, Universidad Pontificia Comillas.

Brassloff A. (reprinted 2003), *Religion and politics in Spain. The Spanish Church in transition, 1962-96*, Houndmills, Basingstoke, Hampshire : Palgrave, Macmillan New York : St. Martin's Press [1998].

Bréchon P. (2000), «Conclusion », in P. Bréchon, B. Duriez (dir.), *Religion et action dans l'espace public*, Paris, L'Harmattan, p. 287-301.

Caritas e Migrantes (2002), *Immigrazione, dossier statistico* 2002, Rome, Nuova Anterem.

Congrégation pour la doctrine de la foi (2000), *Déclaration Dominus Iesus sur l'unicité et l'universalité salvifique de Jésus-Christ et de l'Église*, Rome, 6 August.

De Galembert, C. (1994), « L'exclu et le rival. L'Église catholique et les musulmans en France », dans G. Kepel (dir.), *Exils et royaumes : les appartenances au monde arabo-musulman aujourd'hui*, Paris, Presses de la Fondation nationale des sciences politiques, 1994, p. 365-384.

Dietz G. (2004), «Mujeres musulmanas en Granada: discursos sobre comunidad, exclusion de género y discriminación etnorreligiosa». *Migraciones internacionales*, 6- Vol. 2 No. 3, 2004.

Estruch J., Gómez i Segalà J., Griera M. De M., Iglesias A. (2005), *Las otras religiones. Minorías religiosas en Cataluña*, Barcelona, Icaria.

Gabinet d'Estudis Socials (2002), *Estudio del conflicto de la Mezquita de Premià de Mar*, Barcelona, (in collaboration with MPDL and the Universidad pontifica Comillas de Madrid).

García Ruiz, M. (2006), Libertad religiosa en España. Un largo camino.

Garreta Bochaga J. (2000), *Els musulmans de Catalunya*. Ed. Lleida and Pagès.

Garreta Bochaga J. (2005), «Sécularisation et contre-sécularisation chez les immigrants musulmans en Espagne». *Revue Européenne des Migrations Internationales,* Volume 16, No. 3, p. 105-124.

Itçaina X. (2007), « Vers une nouvelle régulation religieuse du politique ? Catholicisme, espace public et démocratie en Espagne et en Italie », in François Foret (dir.), *L'espace public européen à l'épreuve du religieux*, Bruxelles, Editions de l'Université de Bruxelles, to be published.

Itçaina X. (2006), « The Roman Catholic Church and the Immigration Issue. The relative Secularization of Political Life in Spain », *American Behavioral Scientist Journal*, July 2006, vol. 49, n°11, p. 1471-1488 (special issue on Public religion and immigration across national contexts, dir. Cecilia Menjivar).

Itçaina X., Dorangricchia A. (2005), « Du répertoire de l'hospitalité : mobilisations catholiques et politisation de la question migratoire », dans E. Ritaine (dir.), *Politique de l'Étranger : l'Europe du Sud face à l'immigration*, Paris, PUF (coll. Sociologies d'aujourd'hui), p. 185-222.

Itçaina X. (2005), « La médiation vaine ? L'Église catholique et la question basque » dans J. Faget (dir.), *Médiation et action publique. La dynamique du fluide*, Bordeaux, Presses Universitaires de Bordeaux, p. 117-134.

Lacomba, J. (2005), "La inmigración musulmana en España. Inserción y dinámicas comunitarias en el espacio local", *Migraciones*, 18, December, p. 47-76.

Lacomba J. (2001), *El Islam inmigrado*, Madrid, Ministerio de educación.

Lagroye J. (2006), *La vérité dans l'Église catholique. Contestations et restauration d'un régime d'autorité*, Paris, Belin.

Linz J. (1993), « Religión y política en España », in Díaz-Salazar R., Giner S. (ed.), *Religión y sociedad en España*, Madrid, CIS, 1993.

Mantecón J. (2003), « L'Islam en Espagne », communication au colloque *The Legal Treatment of Islamic Minorities in Europe and in the United States*, Turin 19-21 June 2003, FIERI (Forum Internazionale ed Europeo di Richerche sull'Immigrazione).

Moreras J. (2005a), « Accords et désaccords. La régulation publique de l'islam en Espagne et en Catalogne dans sa dimension locale. », in Izquierdo Bricho F., Desrues T. (coord.), *Actas del Primer Congreso del Foro de Investigadores sobre el Mundo Árabe y Musulmán (Bellaterra- Barcelona, 17-19 de marzo de 2005)*, Barcelona, Fimam, 2005.

Moreras J. (2005b), « Sermons en la diaspora. La definició del perfil dels imams a Espanya i Catalunya » in J. Moreras, G. Aubarell (eds.), *Imams d'Europa : Les expressions de l'autoritat religiosa islàmica*, Bcn, IEMed, 2005.

Moreras J. (1999), *Musulmanes en Barcelona. Espacios y dinámicas comunitarias*, Barcelona, Ediciones del Cidob.

Moreras J. (1996). «Les Accords de coopération entre l'État espagnol et la Commission Islamique d'Espagne». *Revue Européenne des Migrations Internationales* , Volume 12 , No. 1 , p. 77-90.

Mujal-León E. (1982), « The left and the Catholic question in Spain », *West European Politics*, 5/2, pp. 32-54.

Pérès H. (1999), « L'Europe commence à Gibraltar : le dilemme espagnol face à la découverte de l'immigration », *Pôle Sud*, n°11, November, p. 8-23.

Pérez Díaz V. (1993), *The return of civil society : the emergence of democratic Spain*, Cambridge, MA : Harvard University Press.

Proetschel C. (2003), « Les relations Église-État dans la Constitution espagnole de 1978 », *Pôle Sud*, n°18, May, p. 135-149.

Ramírez Á., Mijares L. (2005), « Gestión del Islam y de la inmigración en Europa : tres estudios de caso », *Migraciones*, 18, 2005, p. 77-104.

Requena M. (2005), « The secularization of Spanish society: change in religious practice », *South European Society and Politics*, 10/3, November, pp. 369-390.

Ritaine E. (dir.) (2005), *Politique de l'Étranger : l'Europe du Sud face à l'immigration,* Paris, Presses Universitaires de France (coll. Sociologies d'aujourd'hui), p. 185-222.

Rozenberg D. (2000), « Espagne, l'invention de la laïcité », *Sociétés contemporaines*, n°37, April 2000, p. 35-51.

Rozenberg D. (1996), « Minorías religiosas y construcción democrática en España (Del monopolio de la Iglesia a la gestión del pluralismo) », *Revista Española de Investigaciones Sociológicas*, 74, April-June, p. 245-265.

Zeghal M. (2005), « L'islam aux États-Unis: une nouvelle religion publique ? », *Politique étrangère*, January-March, 1/2005, pp. 49-59

Chapitre 5

Local authorities
and inter-faith dialogue
in Germany

Nikola Tietze[*]

*   Nikola Tietze is a researcher at the Hamburg Institute of Social Studies.

The proliferation of religious referents and the diversification of the religious landscape that the German local authorities have to contend with, are mainly characterised by the establishment of Muslim communities and the erosion of majority religious identities, both Catholic and Protestant[117]. In the past 25 years, the public authorities have accordingly been confronted with a two-fold development: on one hand, new religious needs have appeared in the context of Islam that defy the existing regulation of relations between politics and religion; on the other hand, the structures and organisations of the Christian Churches have become weaker, leading to a change in the status of certain provisions of official religious policy (for example, denominational education at publicly run schools). The breakdown of stable memberships of the Catholic and Protestant faiths has at the same time led to an increase in the number of people with no religious affiliation, the proliferation of small religious groupings such as Buddhist groups or esoteric circles and, finally, the emergence of unstable religious identities, with people switching back and forth between different religious affiliations or constantly changing their religion according to their life situation and closeness to a particular religion. German unification in 1990 also resulted in a quantitative and qualitative increase in the number of individuals with no religious affiliation (often referred to in the public debate as the "third confession")[118].

This study of the situation in Germany focuses on the diversification of the religious landscape resulting from the establishment of Muslim communities in the large towns and cities following the immigration of foreign workers and their families in the 1970s. We shall initially sketch the history of the emergence of needs as far as Islam is concerned and outline how these needs have been managed by the public authorities over the years. Secondly, we shall set out the principles of the political regulation of religious matters in Germany and describe the current state of relations between politics and religion, paying particular attention to the relations between the public authorities and the Muslim communities. The third part will be devoted to the case of Hamburg and the relations between

---

117 In 2005, 31% of the population were members of one of the regional Lutheran churches (*Landeskirchen*), 32% were members of the Catholic Church and 0.1% belonged to the Jewish faith. The number of Muslims in Germany is estimated at 3.8% of the population.

118 It is estimated that 12% to 15% of the population of Western Germany and 65% to 75% in the east of the country do not belong to any faith. In the west, these people mainly live in the large cities, while in the east they are spread over a wider area and are to be found in villages and small, medium-sized and large towns. (cf. Groschopp (2003): Ostdeutscher Atheismus – die dritte Konfession? fowid. Textarchiv, TA 2003-1, p. 8. http://fowid.de/fileadmin/textarchiv/Atheismus_-_Dritte_Konfession__Horst_Groschopp___TA-2003-1. pdf#search=%22%22dritte%20Konfession%22%22)

the Muslim communities and the city authorities, in order to consider the practical aspects of these relations[119].

1. The history of the diversification of the religious landscape: the establishment of Muslim communities

1a. Phase one

Since the 1960s, German businesses have recruited workers in countries with Muslim populations, especially Turkey and, to a lesser extent, the former Yugoslavia and Morocco[120]. The large number of members of the Muslim faith present at that time in urban areas with industries in need of manpower did not, however, pose any political problems as far as religion is concerned. The workers and their families who followed them did, it is true, form a distinctive social group with specific problems but their identification with Islam raised no need for political regulation. On the contrary, the concessions that employers or administrative authorities granted the predominantly Turkish nationals with regard to the practice of their religion helped to guarantee social peace in the workers' households and at their workplaces. Considered as a temporary phenomenon that would theoretically disappear when the foreign workers went back to their countries of origin, Islam was in the eyes of the authorities and economic players an element of a culture alien to the Federal Republic – so alien in fact that it was considered negligible[121]. The co-operative attitude was at the same time a means of strengthening the foreign workers' links with their culture and of keeping the door open for them to return to their country of origin. The first phase of the history of the Muslim communities in Germany was characterised at the time by the lack of any public policy on Islam. The self-interested indifference towards Muslim practices was based on the conceptual exclusion of foreign workers from the nation-state and from social and political life in the towns and cities.

---

119 Hamburg is no doubt a special case as the city is not only a municipality but also has the status of a *Land*. Its religious policies thus combine the responsibilities of a municipality with those of a federal state, which is not the case in Munich, Frankfurt or Cologne, for example. Moreover, the example chosen limits the discussion to a city where the majority of the population is traditionally Protestant. This choice was necessary because our field research mainly focused on Hamburg. In our footnotes, we try to provide a number of comparisons with the situation in Berlin.

120 In 1970, 469,200 Turks were living in Germany, representing 15.8% of the foreigners in the Federal Republic. For 1998, the Centre for Studies on Turkey (*Zentrum für Türkeistudien*) counted 2,110,223 Turks in Germany, i.e. 28.8% of the foreign population (see http://www.zft-online.de/deutsch.php). In the same year, 190,119 persons from Bosnia and Herzegovina and 82,748 Moroccans were living in Germany, but it is important to note that the percentage of those who had come as foreign workers had declined by then. On the other hand, the number of foreigners living in Germany at that time had risen considerably. A study on the Land of North Rhine-Westphalia in 2004 revealed that only 13% of the Turks living in that region had arrived as foreign workers.

121 The German term *Gastarbeiter* (guest worker), which was used for foreign workers until the 1980s, is an indication of this conviction that they would return.

During this first phase, the Muslims themselves did not emphasise their religious identification in their relations with the representatives of the state. They organised themselves less in explicitly Islamic associations than in cultural associations based on references to regional and local issues or on political affiliations in Turkey[122]. In other words, the workers that German firms had invited to the country saw themselves as foreigners and practised their religion in the light of the issues they perceived in their relationship with their country of origin.

1b. Phase two

The phase of the authorities' self-interested indifference came to an end with the increase in family reunifications that followed the official halt to the policy of recruiting workers abroad. The resulting settlement of families who were Muslim both in terms of their culture and their faith towards the end of the 1970s and the beginning of the 1980s made Islam a visible phenomenon in the towns and cities[123]. New religious needs emerged for foreign workers (who had become immigrants) when they left their homes and settled with their families in districts with cheap rented housing (which, incidentally, was often poorly maintained and had been abandoned by upwardly mobile groups). It was necessary for them to find places to pray, celebrate religious festivals and teach Islam to their children brought from the country of origin or born in Germany. Muslim practice then changed its significance, losing so one of its external characteristics, which were based on a more rural conception of Islam, and (at least for a large number of immigrants) taking on the significance of a marker of cultural difference[124]. In other words, Islam constituted more a means for people to distinguish themselves from the groups with whom they were sharing the same urban living space. In this connection, neighbourhood disputes concerning the creation of Islamic spaces arose and issues relating to certain religious practices called for intervention by the public authorities (for example with regard to the consumption of halal meat or calling people to prayer through loudspeakers). The arrival of immigrants from an Islamic culture in the residential areas henceforth presented a new challenge to the German local authorities[125]. However, the latter began to identify the problems

---

122 For an analysis of the Muslims in this initial phase, see Werner Schiffauer, Religion und Identität. Eine Fallstudie zum Problem der Reislamisierung bei Arbeitsimmigranten (1984) in: *Schweizer Zeitschrift für Soziologie* 2, 485-516; Werner Schiffauer, *Die Migranten aus Subay, Türken in Deutschland: Eine Ethnographie* (1991), Stuttgart, Klett-Cotta; Hamit Bozarslan, Etat, Religion, Politique dans l'immigration (1992), in: *Peuples Méditerranéens* 60, 115-133.

123 See Aristide R. Zolberg/ Long Litt Woon, Why Islam Is Like Spanish: Cultural Incorporation in Europe and the United States (1999), in: *Politics & Society* 27/ 1, 5-38.

124 On the concept of "village Islam", see Werner Schiffauer, Religion und Identität (1984), op. cit.

125 See Claire de Galembert, La gestion publique de Islam en France et en Allemagne. Les modèles nationaux à l'épreuve (2005), in: Kastoryano Riva (ed.), Les codes de la différence. Race – Origine – Religion. France – Allemagne – Etats-Unis, Paris, Presses de Sciences, pp. 175-202.

associated with Islamic practices at a time when political Islam was beginning to shake international politics. "These developments transformed the image of Islam in the West from a passive to an aggressive civilization, while lending support to established Orientalist beliefs, especially the idea that Islam is inherently incompatible with liberal democracy and that individual Muslims function as docile instruments of ruthless secular leaders and equally ruthless ayatollahs[126]." The emergence of these negative portrayals of Islam following international events coupled with the visibility of Muslim populations, who are on the bottom of the social ladder, in German villages has had a lasting influence on the identification of Islam as an area of local politics.

The authorities responded to the challenges in the religious domain by introducing local solutions on a case-by-case basis and referring overall responsibility for the immigrants' religious needs to their countries of origin. For example, many *Länder* delegated the matter of the religious instruction of Muslims to the Turkish government, which included this subject in its courses on the Language and Culture of Origin (ELCO)[127]. The German authorities admittedly felt that they were responsible for social peace in the towns and cities but not for handling the general regulation of the place of Islam, which, in their view, constituted a cultural aspect of the foreigners living in their area. Moreover, since the Federal Republic pursued a policy during the 1980s of encouraging people to return, it did not see any need to intervene in the emerging field of Islam but saw it rather as a factor that would encourage people to go back to their countries of origin[128].

1c. Phase three

The third phase of the history of the establishment of Muslim communities, which began in the 1990s, no longer relates to the immigrants but to their children. It involves educational disputes (concerning, for example, the participation of Muslim girls in mixed physical education) and Muslims claiming their rights within the German legal and institutional system[129]. These Muslims, most of whom were socialised in Germany, began to become involved in community life by relying on Islamic organisations of Turkish origin

---

126 Aristide R. Zolberg/ Long Litt Woon (1999), p. 17.

127 In Germany, the teaching of religion is laid down in Article 7(3) of the Basic Law (the German constitution). It is carried out at publicly run schools in close co-operation with the confessional organisations recognised in the *Land* in question.

128 One of the consequences of this policy of encouraging people to return was a certain laissez-faire attitude with regard to Islam that some political organisations (on the fringe of the Turkish political landscape) were able to exploit (see Werner Schiffauer, *Die Gottesmänner. Türkische Islamisten in Deutschland* (2000), Frankfurt a. M., published by Suhrkamp.)

129 See, for example, the record drawn up by Thomas Lemmen of cases brought before the German courts: *Islamische Religionsausübung in Deutschland* (2001), in *Islamisches Alltagsleben in Deutschland*, Friedrich-Ebert-Stiftung, Bonn.

that had become firmly established in the districts with Turkish immigrant populations during the 1980s. They contributed not only to the reorientation of these Muslim associations towards the German public arena but were also able to exploit the rules of the German legal and political system, as evidenced by the many cases brought before the courts in the Federal Republic[130]. By claiming their individual rights, the Muslims have thus been able to take over a space for their religious practice that the public at large (preoccupied by the discussion on the Nationality Act and the reforms of the right to asylum) generally ignored during the 1990s. In spite of the authorities' policy of not recognising the immigration of Muslims into Germany, court decisions led to the inclusion of the Muslim communities in the institutional system that we see today: a fragmented and unstable inclusion considered unsatisfactory by the Muslims and the authorities. The latter were only made aware of this inclusion after the adoption of the new Nationality Act in 1999 (in force since 2000), which attaches more importance to *jus soli* to the detriment of the priority given in the old Act to *jus sanguinis*[131]. The Muslims in Germany – then seen as potential German citizens – from then on became a subject of domestic policy, their practices having ceased to be considered a cultural guarantee for the return of undesirable foreigners. This change in perception led at the same time to the heated public debates on Islam that have characterised the attempts to regulate and institutionalise Islam in Germany since the year 2000[132].

The division of the emergence of Muslim communities into three phases is based on a set of abstract criteria that merge in everyday politics or the everyday lives of Muslims, especially as certain factors are left out of account in our description, such as the role played by refugees in the situation of Islam in Germany (for example, Lebanese, Iranian or Afghan nationals). Both in the attitude of the political authorities and among the religious faithful, there are clearly some aspects that cut across the different periods, but the

---

130 The changing federal organisational landscape during the 1990s shows the beginning of this process of reorientation towards the German public sphere very well. The Central Council for Muslims in Germany (ZMD) was founded in 1994. It now comprises more converts than before, as indicated *inter alia* by the recent election of the convert Ayyub Axel Köhler as its president. The Islamic Council for the Federal Republic of Germany, which is characterised by its proximity to *Milli Görüş*, undertook a major reform of its structures in 1997, among other things in order to ensure greater autonomy vis-à-vis political developments in this Islamic organisation in Turkey.

131 The reform of the Nationality Act became possible after German unification in 1990 because ethnic criteria were no longer necessary to guarantee the national status of Germans living outside the Federal Republic.
In 1999, the CDU and CSU tried to occupy the position vacated by public policy on Islam by initiating a debate in the Bundestag. (cf. question for oral answer on Islam in Germany [*Große Anfrage. Islam in Deutschland*] asked by CDU/ CSU Group in the Bundestag (1999)). In response to the conservatives, the Social Democratic-Green Party coalition government, which had the new Nationality Act passed, declared Islam in Germany to be the core of a modern integration policy (Bundestag Doc. 14/ 4530).

132 The impassioned nature of these debates was clearly sustained by international events and developments, especially attacks by Islamic fundamentalists. However, failing to recognise the purely national aspects would mean not understanding the significance of these discussions.

characteristics of each phase make it possible to throw some light on the different trends that typify the policy on Islam and the different conceptions of Islam in the Muslim groups as well as their respective predominance in the course of history. The contradictions, ambivalences and changes in direction of public policy on Islam can be explained more in the historical development of social realities and political responses than in the ideological splits between the parties in power in the towns and villages, the *Länder* or the federal government. Among the 3 to 3.2 million people estimated to belong to the Islamic faith in Germany today, about a third conceive their Islamicness as religious in the strict sense and see their religious practice in relation to the German institutional system (characterising the third phase). Another third see their membership of the Islamic faith in cultural terms, either as a means to support and protect the differences between them and the dominant majority and their links to their country of origin (characterising the second phase) or as a vehicle for family memory. Finally, the remaining third move back and forth between the first two according to their personal situation[133].

2. The principles of regulating the separation of political from religious matters

The third phase of the emergence of the Muslim communities shows the important role of the courts in the diversification of the religious landscape in Germany. This process is bound up with two constitutional principles enshrined in Article 4 (1) and (2) of the Basic Law (the German constitution), which guarantees freedom of conscience and constitutes a basic right for anyone on German soil (i.e. irrespective of their nationality), and Article 140, which gives religious communities the right to set themselves up, under certain conditions, as "religious societies" and permits them to acquire the status of public-law corporations (*Körperschaften des öffentlichen Rechts*). German religious associations, which, under the law governing associations (*Vereinsrecht*), enjoy certain privileges compared with non-religious associations, can accordingly aspire to public-law status when they have demonstrated their respect for the constitution, proved they have existed for a certain period of

---

133 This quantification of different conceptions of membership of Islam is a rough summing up of a number of quantitative studies (see, for example, Katrin Brettfeld/ Peter Wetzels, Junge Muslime in Deutschland: Eine kriminologische Analyse zur Alltagsrelevanz von Religion und Zusammenhängen von individueller Religiosität mit Gewalterfahrungen, -einstellungen und –handeln (2003), in *Islamismus*, Bundesministerium des Innern, Berlin; Centre for Studies on Turkey, Euro-Islam. Eine Religion etabliert sich in Europa (undated), Zft-Aktuell Nr. 102, http://www.zft-online.de/deutsch.php [downloaded on 11th October 2006] (the survey on which this quantitative evaluation was based probably took place in 2003); Ludwig Ammann, 10th November 2005, Islam im Kreuzverhör: *Die Debatten in westlichen Zuwanderergesellschaften seit dem 11. September 2001*, unpublished lecture in the series "Muslim cultures and integration policy in the Federal Republic of Germany" at the Hamburg Institute for Social Research).

time and shown they have the ability to command a sufficient membership in the same *Land*. This public status, which dates back to the State control of the Protestant Church in Prussia (repealed in 1918), was initially designed for the Christian Churches and is still characterised by their specific features. As a result of their status as public corporations, the Churches possess internal autonomy, which is guaranteed by the State and allows them to make their own body of law in the form of their internal regulations. The State neither controls nor regulates the internal order of the churches, so that issues concerning the church but also relating to matters of public importance (such as religious instruction at publicly run schools, representation in audiovisual councils or the management of a hospital) are not regulated by the law but by "church contracts" (*Kirchenverträge*), which are contracts that the state has concluded with the public-law religious corporations. The regional Protestant Churches (*evangelische Landeskirchen*), the Catholic Church and the Central Council of Jews in Germany (*Zentralrat der Juden in Deutschland*) are thus considered as partners of the state authorities and not as bodies subordinate to them[134]. This way of regulating relationships originates from the notion of state neutrality, which, according to the German conception of law, results from the interaction involved in negotiations between the state and religious or ideological groups in society (traditionally between the state and the two Christian denominations represented by the regional Lutheran Churches and the Catholic Church). The German state is thus not considered the bringer or agent of a predefined neutrality imposed on the social players, its role being limited to supervising the rules established for the purpose of organising the relations between itself and the various religious and ideological groups. However, the linchpin of this system of regulation is the state's obligation to give equal treatment to all the secular or religious communities that have been identified as such. Constitutional law relating to religious matters does not grant any cultural privilege to the Christian Churches on the basis of their historical predominance in the German political arena[135].

During the 1990s, Article 4, paragraphs 1 and 2 of the German constitution, the guaranteeing of which is of paramount importance in the Federal Republic in view of the country's experience of National Socialism, enabled the Muslims to introduce their religious practice into institutional life

---

134 The regional Protestant churches (*evangelische Landeskirchen*), the Catholic Church and the Central Council of Jews in Germany are only the largest and most important public-law corporations at the federal level. Depending on the *Land*, there are other religious communities with this status, for example Baptist communities or the Jehovah's Witnesses. Communities of individuals who adhere to specific world views (*Weltanschauungsgemeinschaften*) can also be recognised as public-law corporations.

135 Hans Michael Heinig/Martin Morlok, Von Schafen und Kopftüchern. Das Grundrecht auf Religionsfreiheit in Deutschland vor den Herausforderungen religiöser Pluralisierung (2003), in *Juristenzeitung* 58/15-16, pp. 777-785.

(for example, at schools) and economic life (for example, at the workplace)[136]. Freedom of conscience and, in particular freedom of worship have indeed created and provided spaces for the observance of Islam in institutional and social bodies, even though these bodies are based on the idea of the cultural homogeneity of the body politic. The priority that the German courts attach to the individual's rights enshrined in Article 4 of the Basic Law has accordingly not only obliged the state and social organisations to demonstrate more neutrality but also forced them to recognise and respect the diversification of the religious referents in the population – and it is the Muslims who have brought this diversification into the social relations.

The incorporation of this diversification into the management of political affairs nevertheless reaches its limits when the diversification of the religious sphere has to be transposed to the regulation of relations between religious groups and the state. Court rulings in favour of individual freedom of religion that guarantee a framework in social life for the practice of Islam mainly concern the official handling of specific cases at the local level, such as the resolution of a conflict concerning a girl's participation in mixed physical education at a specific school, a specific company's organisation of working hours according to times for Muslim prayer, or the provision of halal food for an army conscript[137]. Even if these judgments provide the legal basis for solving similar problems elsewhere, they do not affect the institutions as such. On the other hand, the rights granted to recognised religious communities or the recognition of the latter as public-law corporations involve the very status of the national institutions. The legal and institutional concept of a

---

136 In 1985 an employment court in Düsseldorf forced an employer to reinstate a worker who had been dismissed for praying at his place of work, the judges deciding that the freedom of worship of the individual concerned took precedence over the employer's economic interests. They accordingly called for working time to be managed in such a way as to enable a Muslim working in the company to avoid a conflict of conscience. (Düsseldorf Regional Employment Court, ref. 4 Sa 654/85). At the beginning of the 1990s, several courts were confronted with complaints from Muslim girls or their parents requesting exemption from physical education lessons. The final court of appeal, the Federal Administrative Court, ruled in the complainants' favour (ref. BVerwG 6 C 30/92). In one of the decisions handed down in the girls' favour by the courts it was stated: "*The fundamental right to freedom of religion not only concerns the inward freedom to believe or not to believe but also the outward freedom to bear, manifest or spread one's belief in public. [...] On the basis of this finding, obligations relating to clothing are also protected by Article 4, paragraphs 1 and 2 of the Basic Law*" (ref. OVG 8 A 287/89). This "outward freedom" to manifest one's religious conviction in public through one's clothing was subsequently confirmed by a judgment in 2002 delivered by the Federal Employment Court, which ruled in favour of a saleswoman who had been dismissed by a large store for wearing a headscarf at her workplace. Before that court, she challenged her dismissal for wearing a headscarf at work and won her case against her employer. Although the judges recognised the employer's freedom to define the dress code for its employees according to its economic interests, they ruled that this freedom was limited in the light of the employee's freedom of religion (ref. BAG 2 AZR 472/01). However, the priority attached by the courts to the individual's free practice of their religion is not, as in the above case, always in line with the Muslim's personal wishes but may lead to an obligation for an institution to provide more space for individual Muslim worship. Accordingly, a complaint by a Muslim refusing to do military service owing to his membership of the Islamic faith was rejected by the Hamburg Administrative Court in 1994, but the judges called on the Army to create conditions for serving Muslim soldiers to practise their religion (ref. VG Hamburg 3 W 2411/93).

137 Cf. the litigation cited in the previous footnote.

religious community refers to the official role played by the recognised faiths in Germany, a role that leads to their participation in developing the common national good. This was stated in a speech on relations between the state and religion given by Johannes Rau, a former President of the Federal Republic of Germany, who went on to say: "The ideologically neutral state needs the convictions held in different, distinct communities, which have their own values and want to provide guidance. These communities include the churches and religious communities, which introduce their ideas into society[138]." The incorporation of religious diversification in the definition and portrayal of the common national good proves much more confrontational and painful than that at the level of individual, more or less local cases.

The way the nation is portrayed stems from Germany's federal structure, which undeniably has a confessional-cultural dimension. The way the German states were formed means that regional differences are largely the result of the states' historically-based confessional identities (Catholic or Protestant) at the time of the religious wars and as confirmed by the peace settlement. The way in which the *Länder* portray themselves and the perception of their distinctive characteristics within the country still include this confessional dimension today, even if the distribution of Catholics and Protestants has not followed the present *Land* boundaries for quite some time. It is thus not only the official status of the recognised religious communities but also the religious outlook that can be observed among those who intervene in support of regional interests that guarantee political recognition of the religious dimension and legitimise respect for the Catholic and Protestant confessional cultures. In this pattern of relations, non-Christian religions become "the Other" and are considered as minorities compared with the national culture, which is defined by reference to Christian and Western values. That is why the Jewish communities, although recognised as public-law corporations, are virtually only seen in public space through the memory of the Holocaust and why Muslims, despite the reform of the Nationality Act, are considered as Turkish *foreigners*. The conception of the state's neutrality as the resultant of the interaction of politics and religion is now shot through by the contradiction that emerges from the importance attached to the Christian Western culture.

In addition, the *Länder* are the most important political authorities regarding official policy on religion, especially Islam: they have the power to take decisions on the recognition of religious groups as public-law corporations; they negotiate contracts (*Staatskirchenverträge*) between the

---

138 Johannes Rau, 22nd January 2004: Religionsfreiheit heute – zum Verhältnis von Staat und Religion in Deutschland, speech at a ceremony marking the 275th birthday of Gotthold Ephraim Lessing. http://www. epd.de/dokumentation/print/dokumentation_index_19878.htm [downloaded 10th October 2006], p. 3.

state and the recognised religious community; their administrative authorities are responsible for determining the conditions for religious practice (for example, with regard to the question of Muslim plots in cemeteries, the slaughter of animals, or school education)[139]. The federal system accordingly leads to some variation in the situation from one *Land* to another – a variation based *inter alia* on the importance that the authorities attach to the majority confessional culture in defining the identity of the *Land* in question.

No Islamic organisation has yet been able to acquire the status of a public-law corporation, although the first attempts by some federations date from the end of the 1970s. The diversity characteristic of associations within the Muslim communities in the 1980s has always been an argument used by the authorities against recognition and makes it extremely difficult to identify an interlocutor, which the German system of regulating relations between the political and the religious sphere demands. During the 1990s, the Islamic organisations grouped themselves into federations, both at the federal level (the Central Council of Muslims in Germany (*Zentralrat der Muslime in Deutschland*) and the Islamic Council for the Federal Republic of Germany (*Islamrat für die Bundesrepublik Deutschland*) and the level of the *Länder*, which are trying to overcome the ideological and national splits within the Muslim communities. One such association at *Land* level is *Schura* (the Council of Islamic Communities in Hamburg), which unites some forty associations of many different persuasions and origins[140]. The aim of these groupings has mainly been to establish themselves as a single Islamic interlocutor for the state authorities.

Nevertheless, the Muslims have been able to obtain collective rights reserved for recognised religious and secular communities. A Federal Constitutional Court judgment delivered in January 2002 concerning the right to slaughter animals without stunning them (ref. 1 BvR 1783/99) relaxed the definition of the concept of community, ruling that anyone claiming an exception to an existing law in the name of their religious conviction (in that case, Islamic) had to belong to a group of persons linked together by a common belief. "In this context, it is accordingly also possible to consider as religious communities those Islamic groups whose views differ from other Islamic communities. This interpretation of a religious community complies with the Constitution and

---

139 The problem of the local authority financing of places of worship does not arise in Germany. Public-law corporations are privileged to receive a church tax collected by the *Land* government as a percentage of the taxes paid to the state (in addition to their income taxes) by citizens who are members of a religious community. State grants for various public services provided by public-law corporations (hospitals, nursery schools, retirement homes etc), are regulated in the contracts between the state and the recognised religious community. Lacking the necessary institutional recognition, Muslim communities have no access to the tax-collection system or to state grants for their social and educational activities (such as school support).

140 The Alawites do not, however, belong to Schura, although it does comprise Sunnis and Shiites.

takes particular account of Article 4 of the Basic Law[141]." From then on, the principle of heterogeneity recognised with regard to the religious community made it possible to avoid the difficulties encountered in defining and forming a united group of Muslims in Germany. The judgment paved the way for including Islam in the institutional system while changing, albeit incidentally, the very definition of the community. In addition, in the year 2000 and after a 20-year-old dispute with the school authorities of the *Land*, an Islamic federation in Berlin (*Islamische Föderation Berlin*, IFB) obtained the status of a religious community within the meaning of the Berlin Education Act. This enabled it to teach Islam at a publicly run school[142]. These two examples show that the diversification of the religious sphere is becoming subject to institutional regulation, although it is coming up against considerable political resistance. The authorities are therefore trying to circumvent the breaches that have been opened to diversification by enacting legislation. For example, the Berlin government passed a law in March 2006 making ethical education compulsory. This law does not abolish optional denominational education but it does restrict both its impact and its appeal for the pupils' parents[143]. The introduction of an ethics course developed and provided by the state shows the political determination in Berlin to exercise greater control over the normative socialisation of future citizens and to establish a core set of values that neutralise the diversification of standards in the school environment. It should be noted that the discussions on the law relating to the introduction of ethical education began after the Administrative Court's decision to grant the IFB the status of a religious community within the meaning of the Berlin Education Act. The amendments to their education laws that a number of *Länder* made following the Federal Constitutional Court's decision in 2003 on the wearing of the Islamic headscarf by women teachers is also evidence of the political authorities' determination to curb religious diversification in schools. Germany's highest court stated that the wearing of the Islamic headscarf by Muslim teachers fell under the protection of individual freedom of worship for as long as the legislature did not limit general religious expression at schools. This reason given for the judgment led virtually all the *Länder* to review their education acts in order to prevent women teachers who wear an Islamic headscarf from becoming civil servants. A judgment by

---

141 Bundesverfassungsgericht, Pressemitteilung 15.01.2002, *Schächterlaubnis für muslimischen Metzger* (1 BvR 1783/99).

142 Cf. *Deutsches Verwaltungsblatt*, 1st July 2000, pp. 1001-1006: (translation) "The so-called 'Bremen Clause' in Article 141 of the Basic Law applies to the whole of Berlin". It should be noted that denominational education is not compulsory in Berlin because Article 7 (3) of the Basic Law does not apply there. If pupils at the city's schools so wish, they may participate in such classes, which are held on an extracurricular basis under the sole responsibility of the religious communities but at publicly run schools.

143 See Rolf Schieder, Kontroversen um das religiöse Gedächtnis in der Schule – das Beispiel Berlin, unpublished lecture given at the conference *Öffentliche Religionskontroversen in Frankreich und Deutschland – auf dem Weg zu einem europäischen Modell* held at the University of Bamberg on 1st July 2005.

an administrative court in Baden-Württemberg in 2006 nevertheless leads one to doubt that the legislatures wishing to reaffirm the predominance of the Christian Western culture by amending the law will succeed: despite an amendment to the Education Act prohibiting teachers from wearing a headscarf, the court in that *Land* reinstated a teacher who did this, giving as its reason the equality of all religious communities. This equality, it said, meant that a Catholic nun wearing a religious habit could not give lessons at a school if a teacher in an Islamic headscarf was excluded from doing so[144].

A host of contradictions thus characterises the institutional and political regulation of religious diversification, which, as things stand at the moment, leads to a hardening of attitudes. For organised Muslims, all the issues associated with religious practice are becoming touchstones for the recognition and institutional inclusion of Islam in Germany, which is transforming each individual dispute into a symbol of comprehensive demands and fundamental principles[145]. The Muslims thus tend to stick stubbornly to their positions and refuse to enter into local negotiations aimed at solving a particular problem. The authorities, on the other hand, increasingly see the management of the Muslims' religious needs from the standpoint of integration in the nation rather than from that of the rule of law. This policy endorses the assimilation of religion to culture, which shifts the focus of any official policy on Islam to the question of identity. The search for solutions to the problems posed by the emergence of the Muslim communities then easily degenerates into heated discussions.

3. The interaction between the authorities and Muslim communities at the local level: the case of Hamburg

The Hamburg-based federation *Schura* (the Council of Islamic Communities in Hamburg), which was founded in 1999 and brings together some forty Islamic associations of many different national origins, theological persuasions and ideological dispositions, published a declaration in 2004 on "Muslims in a pluralistic society"[146]. The signatories to this declaration state: "The guarantee of human rights, democracy and the principles of the

---

144 See article "Streit über Kopftuchurteil" in the 12ᵗʰ July 2006 issue of *Süddeutsche Zeitung*.

145 By "organised Muslims", we mean believers who not only attend the meetings of an Islamic organisation but also become involved in its internal politics or its external representation. They are often operators who act collectively.

146 Schura – Rat der islamischen Gemeinschaften Hamburg e.V., Grundsatzpapier: Muslime in einer pluralistischen Gesellschaft, 18ᵗʰ April 2006, http://www.schura-hamburg.de/Downloads/Grundsatzpapier.pdf#search=%22%22Hamburg%22%22Muslime%22%22 [downloaded 12ᵗʰ October 2006]

rule of law is of existential importance for us. [...] It is for this very reason that Muslims are called upon to foster, develop and actively defend [true democracy]. [...] We want to play a full part in organising this society because we, as Muslims living here, consider ourselves part of it. Our commitment is for all the members of society and the community as a whole and is not based on a particularist policy in favour of Muslim interests[147]." The wording of this declaration reflects the conceptions of the social and political action of Muslims who have been socialised in Hamburg and are upwardly mobile after studying at university or completing vocational training[148]. These Muslims are actively seeking contacts with the authorities, are professionalising the public relations of Islamic associations and are closely examining the working methods of other socially committed groups[149].

The president of the Islamic University Community (*Islamische Hochschulgemeinde e.V.*), an association that was founded in 1999 and is a member of *Schura*, explained in an interview that he gave us in 2005 how he tried to negotiate improvements in the practice of the Muslim faith at the University of Hamburg with the university's Vice-Chancellor and the body responsible for its catering service and how he sought contacts with senior officials of the Jewish community, which had no specific facilities for its religious practice at the university either. His aim was to be able to link the demands of his association with those of the Jewish students. What he told us testifies to a determination to find pragmatic solutions to problems experienced by believers while at university and to avoid getting into identity politics. The young man felt he was being listened to and taken seriously by his interlocutors even though he was unable to ensure that all the Muslim students' needs were met. Under a more or less tacit agreement with the Vice-Chancellor, students would be permitted to use part of the basement for Friday prayers, but other concessions were currently not possible owing to a lack of space. The university would also officially place rooms at the Islamic association's disposal free of charge for its activities, such as seminars on theological subjects or public debates on current affairs. Discussions were,

---

147 *ibid.*

148 They represent the Muslims that characterise the third phase of the history of the Muslim communities in Germany outlined in Part I.

149 A study on the Muslim communities in Berlin reached findings comparable to what we were able to observe in Hamburg. The results, a summary of which has just been presented by the Berlin government's Integration Commissioner, highlight the intensification of the co-operation between the Islamic associations and the administrative authorities of the various city districts. (see press release of 26th September 2006: *Integrationsbeauftragter stellt erste Ergebnisse einer Studie über islamisches Gemeindeleben in Berlin vor*, http://www.berlin.de/lb/intmig/presse/archiv/20060926.1000.48048.html [downloaded 6th October 2006]). 80% of the 40 associations of places of worship surveyed said they had regular contacts with public bodies at the level of their district (schools, police stations and district mayors), while a 1998 study on the Muslim communities stressed their isolation and limited contacts with the local authorities (see Gerdien Jonker/ Andreas Kapphan, *Moscheen und islamisches Leben in Berlin* (1998), Ausländerbeauftragte des Senats Berlin).

we were told, under way with the body in charge of the catering service in order to improve and increase the number of vegetarian dishes, but it was impossible to offer halal food. Finally, our interviewee said he was proud of being able to rent the rooms of the university restaurant for breaking the fast during Ramadan, in which between 180 and 200 persons participated each year. This quite ordinary example, which involves everyday issues concerning the management of the Muslim aspect in the diversified religious landscape of university life, shows that, at the local and infra-political level, the regulation and diversification of the religious referents of users of public institutions can rely on pragmatic negotiations – despite the identity polarisation at the level of national and *Länder* politics. However, our interviewee's description of his negotiations with the university representatives also teaches us that there is a fundamental precondition for any pragmatic negotiations, namely the absence of suspicion. The Muslim militant does not feel identified by his interlocutors as a result of his membership of the *Milli Görüş* Islamic Community (IGMG), so this frees him from any obligation to put up an ideological defence[150]. The dialogue can then be limited to material and practical issues and does not have to include affirmations or justifications of the dialogue partners' ideologies. The negotiations described are guided by the rules and regulations and by material constraints at the university, not by either side's convictions[151].

Nonetheless, reducing the problems associated with Muslim practices to mundane matters like the allocation of rooms or the organisation of meals or

---

150 The IGMG (*Islamische Gemeinschaft Milli Görüş*), a transnational organisation of Turkish origin, is regularly mentioned by the German Office for the Protection of the Constitution (*Verfassungsschutz*) for its anti-Semitic publications and its Islamist ideology because the aim and purpose of its basic texts is the establishment of an Islamic state. It should, however, be noted that the *Milli Görüş* federation in the Netherlands is the preferred interlocutor of the Dutch state, which considers it pragmatic and a trustworthy partner (see Gerdien Jonker, Probleme der Kommunikation zwischen Muslimen und der Mehrheitsgesellschaft – Analyse und praktische Beispiel (2002), in: *Vom Dialog zur Kooperation. Die Integration von Muslimen in der Kommune. Dokumentation eines Fachgesprächs.* Nr. 12, Beauftragte der Bundesregierung für Ausländerfragen, 9-26, p. 13) According to our own research on Muslims in Hamburg, the associations affiliated to the IGMG gather together individuals and officials of associations with diverse political ideas and conceptions of Islam. The aforementioned declaration on Muslims in a pluralist society published by Schura, many members of which are associations affiliated with the IGMG, is evidence of this heterogeneity even within the German arm of *Milli Görüş*. To regard the signatures of these associations on the declaration as a means for people to conceal their true intentions of overturning the democratic and pluralist system rather than defending it would be to misjudge the intellectual dynamic and the change from one generation to another within this movement in Germany. The IGMG's German arm is a haven for people with Islamist and anti-Semitic views while at the same time offering scope for engaging in activities to Muslims who are sincere in defending the dovetailing of Islamicness with pluralist and democratic principles. In this, it testifies to the complex interlocking of continuities and discontinuities that characterise the field of Islam in general in Germany (see Werner Schiffauer, Die Islamische Gemeinschaft Milli Görüş - ein Lehrstück zum verwickelten Zusammenhang von Migration, Religion und sozialer Integration (2004), in: Klaus J. Bade, Michael Bommes & Rainer Münz (ed.). *Migrationsreport 2004. Fakten - Analysen – Perspektiven*, Frankfurt; New York: Campus Verlag, pp. 67-96.)

151 Gerdien Jonker (2002) provides the example of a dispute concerning the construction of a mosque in Berlin, where, *inter alia*, suspicions about the convictions of the parties to the dispute (the urban planning and construction authority and the Islamic organisation) led to an escalation of the confrontation to the detriment of pragmatic negotiations (see Gerdien Jonker, Probleme der Kommunikation zwischen Muslimen und der Mehrheitsgesellschaft (2002), op. cit.)

timetables is not always successful, as many other examples show us, especially with regard to the management of everyday life at Hamburg's schools. One school in the working-class Veddel district, situated south of the city centre, was the focus of media attention in 2005 owing to the difficulties that some Muslim pupils and parents were causing to the everyday running of the school (girls forbidden to go on class trips, refusal to participate in biology classes on sexuality, contempt for women teachers, etc). The Hamburg foundation *Körber-Stiftung*, in co-operation with the Conference of *Land* Ministers of Education and the Islam and Me (*Islam und ich*) project, developed by Sanem Kleff (a Berlin teacher and member of the GEW teaching union) and Eberhard Seidel (a journalist), subsequently organised a discussion between teachers, pupils and inhabitants of the district[152]. This discussion made it possible to revisit the media coverage and speak about the problems experienced by the various players in the district. Muslim practices were core issues in the debate, not at all in their theological dimension but insofar as they interlock with social issues: generational conflicts, difficult relations with the school authority, relations between men and women, competition between immigrants, etc. It was not possible to solve any of the problems that day, but the debate in this microcosm helped to give the participants confidence in the possibility of engaging in a social dialogue, which is a not insignificant outcome in view of the media reports on deadlocked cultural conflict situations. The local level, more than any political authority, can provide the freedom for people to speak together without being compelled to produce a result, so it gives them the opportunity to learn how to express and listen to the many different views in a pluralistic society.

A comparison of two initial examples of social dialogue provides information on the importance of distinguishing between the groups of individuals that local authorities have dealings with. The negotiations that the President of the Muslim students' association is trying to hold with the representatives of the university world can be conducted in the manner described because this Muslim has been well-educated in the German system (all the more so as he seems to have learned the institutional rules). He acts like a German from Hamburg while stressing his religious "otherness". In the case of the open discussion in the Veddel district, the majority of the authorities' interlocutors (in this case teachers) and of the civil society mediators (the Körber foundation and the project's designers) are Muslim immigrants and their children (more typical of the second phase of the history of the Muslim communities). Their views are necessarily based on different social experiences, concerns and conceptions of the public space from those of the representative of the Muslim students at the university. The two types of dialogue, both of which

---

152 See *Zwischen Moschee und Eiscafé*, Die Zeit, 17th March 2005.

focus on the subject of Islam, cannot necessarily be evaluated according to the same criteria and categories. A shortcoming of the political discourse and the public debate conducted through the media is precisely the fact that they often (intentionally) confuse statements by the two groups of Muslims and their ways of expressing their respective thoughts. In other words, people like the President of the Muslim student association are easily suspected of concealing their intentions and actually thinking like the immigrant parents of the children at the school in Veddel. The latter, on the other hand, are expected to think and behave like the Muslim student at the University of Hamburg.

The third example of social dialogue that we wish to mention concerns the organisation in the *Land* of Hamburg of denominational education, pursuant to Article 7, paragraph 3 of the Basic Law. This means this instruction is provided through close co-operation between the recognised religious communities and the Ministry of Education of the *Land*. The numerical domination of the Protestants in Hamburg has made this region's Protestant Church, the North Elbe Lutheran Church (*Nordelbische Evangelisch-Lutherische Landeskirche*) the state's only interlocutor on religious instruction[153]. Denominational education professionals have proclaimed the opening up of Protestant education at Hamburg's schools since the 1970s and developed a "transdenominational" curriculum in collaboration with the school authorities. This has been taught for about 30 years now under the title "religious instruction for all" (*Religionsunterricht für alle*)[154]. In 1995, the promoters of this model institutionalised the drawing up of the curricula and the development of "transdenominational" teaching methods by establishing the Inter-Faith Religious Instruction Group (*Gesprächskreis Interreligiöser Religionsunterricht,*) which made it possible to stabilise the involvement of the non-Christian communities in drawing up the syllabuses[155]. Today, members of *Schura* represent the Muslims on this body.

This structure of religious education in Hamburg, which is essentially based on the position of the Protestants and their place in politics in this *Land*, has not only calmed the debate on the teaching of Islam at publicly run schools

---

153 The Catholic Church has waived its right to determine Catholic education in the public sector since 1945, preferring to focus on setting up private schools. The Jewish community, on the other hand, offers (extracurricular) religious instruction to Hamburg pupils within the community itself. Participation in this Jewish education releases the pupil from the obligation to choose between ethical education and classes under Protestant control.

154 See Folkert Doedens, Dialogisch orientierter "Religionsunterricht für alle" in Hamburg (2002), in *Vom Dialog zur Kooperation. Die Integration von Muslimen in der Kommune*. Dokumentation eines Fachgesprächs. Nr. 12, Beauftragte der Bundesregierung für Ausländerfragen, pp. 39-52.

155 See Wolfram Weisse, Der Hamburger Weg – Dialogisch orientierter "Religionsunterricht für alle" (2000), in *Islamischer Religionsunterricht an staatlichen Schulen in Deutschland. Praxis – Konzepte – Perspektiven*. Dokumentation eines Fachgesprächs, Beauftragte der Bundesregierung für Ausländerfragen, pp. 25-48.

(which is causing the authorities in the other *Länder* some concern) but also facilitated, indeed legitimised, the dialogue with the Muslim communities in other fields: involving these communities in the resolution of neighbourhood disputes, inviting Muslims to work as trainers for the in-service training of Hamburg's teachers, and drawing up the plans for an interdisciplinary Centre for Dialogue between the World Religions (*interdisziplinäres Zentrum Weltreligion im Dialog*) at the University of Hamburg[156]. The success of the "Hamburg approach", as the promoters of "religious instruction for all" refer to it, is no doubt due to a particular group of individuals, such as the professor of education sciences Wolfram Weisse, who, *inter alia*, has had a university education in Protestant theology, and the director of the Islamic Scientific and Educational Institute (*Islamisches Wissenschafts- und Bildungsinstitut*), Ali-Özgür Özdil, who has a degree in Islamic studies, ethnology and religious studies from the University of Hamburg. However, it is also due to the efforts by the protagonists on both sides – the Muslims and the public and university authorities – to separate religious matters from their entrenchment in cultural, political and ideological issues. For this reason, those involved in the negotiations on the involvement of Muslims in the institutional system succeed in treating Islam as a system of belief and theology conceptually equal to that of Christianity. In other words, they try to leave identity politics out of account when they meet for their talks on Muslim participation in the established system.

The example of institutionalised co-operation with Muslims on preparing "religious instruction for all" is also evidence of the combination of two situations in Hamburg's religious scene: the strong emergence of Muslim communities and the collapse of Protestant identities in the city. In the 1950s, 90% of Hamburg's population were members of the region's Protestant Church (the North Elbe Lutheran Church) and about 5% were Catholics. At the beginning of the 21st century, less than 40% of the population are represented by the Protestant Church, while the proportion of Catholics has now reached 10%, due in part to the immigration of people from countries that traditionally have a Catholic majority, such as Spain, Portugal or Poland[157]. Statistics on the origin of foreigners and naturalised people living in Hamburg suggest that Muslims constituted about 10% of the population in 2000, while the statistical services only recorded 61,885 individuals claiming

---

156 See Thorsten Knauth/Wolfram Weisse, *Akademie der Weltreligionen. Konzeptionelle und praktische Ansätze* (2002), Dokumentation Erziehungswissenschaften, University of Hamburg; Ali-Özgür Özdil, Interreligiöse Integrationsprojekte in Hamburg (2002), in *Vom Dialog zur Kooperation. Die Integration von Muslimen in der Kommune. Dokumentation eines Fachgesprächs*. Nr. 12, Beauftragte der Bundesregierung für Ausländerfragen, pp. 53-60. The author of this article is the director of the Islamic Scientific and Educational Institute (*Islamisches Wissenschafts- und Bildungsinstitut*), which is the Muslim side's linchpin in the process of involving Muslims in Hamburg's institutional system. (cf. http://www.iwb-hamburg.de/index_html.htm)

157 Weisse, Wolfram, 2000, op. cit., p. 33.

to be Muslim (3.9%) in 1987. In less than 15 years, the Muslim population has thus more than doubled. In the light of these figures, the opening up of Protestant education and open-mindedness of the North Elbe Lutheran Church and representatives of the state authorities (which are to a greater or lesser extent products of this Protestant environment) are an intelligent way of protecting the power over the drawing up of religious policies.

The examples of social dialogue in Hamburg, all of which more or less recognise the diversification of the religious sphere in general and the place of the Muslims in particular, should, however, not mislead anyone as to the tensions between the communities and between the Muslim communities and the authorities. These tensions exist in the same way as they do in the other *Länder*. There is also a considerable mistrust of Muslims among Hamburg's population, which makes the city's inhabitants no different from the rest of the country[158]. Nonetheless, relations do exist between the Muslim communities and representatives of the local authorities and dignitaries of both the *Land* and the city of Hamburg. As Claire de Galembert described in her detailed report on the position of Muslims in public politics in Berlin and Hamburg, the Muslims have, in comparison with Berlin, been discovered somewhat belatedly as a political domain by the Hamburg government[159]. The first report commissioned by the *Land* of Hamburg on the city's mosques was published in 1990, whereas the Berlin Senate called for an inquiry into Islamic associations as early as 1980[160]. However, after identifying the Muslims as a subject of domestic policy beyond the management of immigrants of various national origins, the Hamburg authorities took account of the needs of the Muslims by according them a certain respect for their religious beliefs from the second half of the 1990s onwards. Most attention is paid to Islam in the field of education, where, incidentally, we see the majority of contacts between the authorities and Muslim organisations, especially through discussions on pedagogical matters. The *Land* authorities' excellent relations with the

---

158 A survey among the viewers of a debate televised by a Hamburg channel in 2004 established that 32.5% of them thought Muslims enriched life in the city, whereas 67.5% regarded them as a threat to the city. (Cf. GAL Bürgerschaftsfraktion, press release of 21st April 2004: Wir brauchen den interreligiösen Dialog (http://www.gal-fraktion.de/cms/default/dok/25/25157.wir_brauchen_den_interreligioesen_dialog.htm) [downloaded on 13rd October 2006]. A possible explanation for this high proportion of people who felt threatened is no doubt the fact that two of the 11th September terrorists studied in Hamburg for several years. However, there is no study that analyses the impact that Hamburg's role in the preparation of those attacks had on the opinions of the city's inhabitants and their image of Muslims. Incidentally, the weekly magazine *Stern* published the results of an opinion poll conducted in the whole of Germany on the image that people have of Muslims. It established that every third German was afraid of the Muslims living in the country. The figures provided by the Hamburg survey thus broadly reflect the state of opinion in the country as a whole.

159 See Claire de Galembert, *Musulmans à Mantes-la-Jolie, Berlin et Hambourg. Au seuil du droit de cité?* (2003), Plan Urbanisme Construction Architecture, Programme "villes et hospitalité".

160 See Ursula Mihçiyazgan, *Moscheen türkischer Muslime in Hamburg, Dokumentation zur Herausbildung religiöser Institutionen türkischer Migranten* (1990), Behörde für Arbeit, Gesundheit und Soziales; Christoph. Elsass, *Einflüsse der islamischen Religion auf die Integrationsfähigkeit der ausländischen Arbeitnehmer und ihrer Familienangehörigen* (1980, Senatskanzlei/Planungsstelle, Berlin).

North Elbe Lutheran Church and the Protestant community – relations that have been important for the history of Hamburg and still to some extent characterise the city's political life today – are no doubt crucial in this context. In Berlin, the government has responded to the political challenge posed by the needs of Muslims with much more scepticism towards religious matters in general, as evidenced by the dispute about lessons on Islam in the city's schools. The courts have had to adjudicate between the *Land* authorities and the Muslim organisation that was claiming the right to this instruction and which even (at the very beginning of the dispute) enjoyed a certain amount of implicit support from the Churches in Berlin.

The core area of relations between the local authorities and the Muslim communities seems to be the education of children, who are future German citizens. School is now not only the place where the diversification of the religious landscape is handled on a daily basis but is also, because of Germany's political structure, the foremost place where local and national issues interlock. It is within their walls that the nation's normative integration with the Muslims is negotiated – a process that, when all is said and done, is always based on the portrayal of the nation as a body politic with a Christian culture and that, despite the weakening of the traditional faith-based cultures, always refers to the predominant public roles of the Catholic and Protestant Churches. In this context, the mission of the local authorities is to confirm the diversification of religious referents in the German population, irrespective of the conflicts of ideas concerning the nation as a whole. Like it or not, they legitimise this diversification by a pragmatism in everyday matters that transcends court decisions which have long been forcing the political authorities of the *Länder* to accept greater pluralism.

Chapter 6

Local authorities and interreligious dialogue from a United Kingdom perspective - A missed opportunity

Anjum Anwar[*] and Chris Chivers[**]

[*]   Anjum Anwar MBE is Education Officer of the Lancashire Council of Mosques and Chair of the Lancashire Forum of Faiths. She broadcasts frequently on radio and television to advance her belief in the positive role that faith can play in the life of any society and her passion for education in all its forms. She was awarded the MBE for her work to promote community relations in Lancashire.

[**]   Canon Chris Chivers is Canon Chancellor of Blackburn Cathedral where he has responsibility for inter-faith relations as the Director of the cathedral's community cohesion agency, Exchange. He is the author of several books and writes for various publications including Church Times, The Tablet, The Witness and Cape Times. He is also a frequent broadcaster on BBC Radio 4 for whom he is a Daily Service presenter.

Introduction: the rhetoric of "clash" as "meta- or macro-narrative"

Since 9/11, if not before, the chief paradigm or prism through which "Western" nations have increasingly understood their identity and their place in a moral order or framework, has been that of the typology which Samuel P. Huntington advances in his book *The Clash of Civilisations and the Remaking of the World Order* (1996). Indeed, this typology has become a driving force behind social, educational and other policies across the "Western" world.

Within hours of the attacks on the World Trade Centre and the Pentagon, President George W Bush was analysing the events, and what he supposed would have to follow them in thoroughly apocalyptic terms. In so doing, he was playing into an epic narrative of cinema-screen proportions, a narrative which marshalled the forces of good in "Western" trenches to pit these against the forces of evil beyond. The specific "beyond" that he had in mind was later to be described by him – using an approach at once simplistic and neo-biblical ("either you are for us or against us") – as "an axis of evil".

One has only to mention the primary foreign-policy narratives of Afghanistan and Iraq, together with the lesser narratives of Iran and Syria, to name but two, to see the full extent in international terms of the way in which this particularly assertive, combative and conflictual mode of thinking has penetrated the whole western psyche via an overt American imperialism.

Like poodles to the slaughter – literally – the armed forces of the United Kingdom were marshalled to support this Huntingtonian view of the world from which, as we write in October 2006, they are now rapidly seeking to retreat. In what, briefly, does such a view of the world consist?

Samuel P. Huntington's theory is, in essence, very straight forward. Surveying the complexity of the relationships between people and nations, Huntington seeks to proceed by reducing each nation – or transnational grouping – to an essence. In essence, therefore, Western Civilisation (which would include most of Europe and North America) is Christian in its core values, aspirations and beliefs. By contrast, a grouping of various Middle Eastern countries would represent "Eastern" or Islamic civilisation. In such a typology, India would be a Hindu civilisation.

For Huntington, history and international relations are thus perceived to be articulated through a series of civilisational "clashes" with varying degrees of intensity. In the rhetorical world-view of President George W. Bush et al this means that we are at present caught up in a fundamental clash between Western Christian Civilisation and Eastern Islamic Civilisation (the upper versus lower case is intentional here). This is a clash of world-views stemming from what is perceived (wrongly) to be a fundamental clash of religious beliefs. It is a clash which, however, has become a self-fulfilling prophecy in the context of the intervention in Iraq, for instance.

This brief summary of course risks caricature. But there is almost always more than a half-truth in caricature. And the "more than half-truth" in this potential caricature of Huntington may, for our present purpose, briefly be sketched as follows.

Huntington's analysis puts great stress on single identity ways of looking at the world. Over-against Michel Foucault, for instance, who, in a very similar vein to the African philosophy of *ubuntu* (briefly summarised as "a person is a person on through their relationship to other persons") argues in *Discipline and Punish: The Birth of the Prison* (1975) that identity is not innate, it is always "something which results from interaction" with others, and which cannot therefore be stationary or categorised in a single-form way, since it is forever changing, Huntington advances a typology which suppresses a multi-layered reading of identity.

It is an approach which of course plays into an existing language of delineation: the way in which people are labelled as foreigners and immigrants, for instance. As with such linguistic labels, the Huntingtonian typology gives no account of the way in which interaction of civilisations and cultures is for Foucault a fundamental way in which identity is forged. Rather, it puts "immigrant" communities in an impossible position. It asks that they "be at home" within a given "civilisation" whilst in reality saying that they will "never be at home" because they do not, in essence, "belong". It is no surprise in this regard to see "immigrant" communities act-out the labels assigned to them. His critics, of whom the most searching so far has been this, as we shall see, as Huntington's most searching critic, Amartya Sen, argues in his book *Identity and Violence: the illusion of destiny* (2006) – has severe consequences for both the macro and micro levels. Furthermore, the particular single-identity characteristic upon which Huntington draws is the paradigm of faith. Why this single-identity characteristic and not any other?

Doubtless there are multiple not single category reasons for Huntington's apparent "projection" into and on to the realm of faith of difficulties which other realms (political and social among them) are struggling to deal with. But whatever the reasoning here, one sure consequence is the way in which Huntington takes communal-garden prejudice – a latent fear of the "other" which seems to bedevil all human systems, religious or otherwise – and writes this into a grand, over-arching theory.

We can see a significant and, of course, highly contentious instance of this consequence – of such prejudice writ large – in the present Pope's attitude to the accession of Turkey to the treaty of Rome. Taking a communal-garden, simple prejudice against the "other", in this case the Islamic other, Pope Benedict XVI has actually been pretty up-front about his reasons for opposing Turkish accession.

The language may be somewhat tortuously "cloaked" – as we shall see later that faith is so often cloaked by talk of "culture" – but the reality is simple: Turkey is not wanted in the European family because it is of another world view (one feels that the Pope stops short of seeing it as part of a civilisation). This world view would "pollute" (our interpretation of the Pope's attitude) what the Pope strongly views as "Christian Europe".

Now, there are certainly many critiques of such an approach which could be levelled within the context of this specific issue. The assumption, for instance, that Europe can be or has ever been able to be seen as monochrome "Christian" or even "Judaeo-Christian" civilisation, flies in the face of ethnic, or racial, or any accepted form of religious or faith-based statistics. Just as the designation of India as a Hindu civilisation sets its face against the 100 million Muslims in that great country, not to mention the fact that India was the birth-place of Buddhism. But one can of course navigate the world with greater ease if one deploys such reductionist tools.

The "clash of civilisations" approach thus appears to be a logical – even a rather ingenious – way of "reading reality". It also has the added credential of being the work of a distinguished academic. But whatever Samuel P. Huntington's credentials, the truth of the matter, as Amartya Sen has so coolly demonstrated, is that Huntington takes base prejudice and projects it into an over-arching theory which is at best an illusion and at worst produces the nightmare of an Iraq. It is, in the words of one trenchant critic, "spreading the most terrible cancer at grass-roots levels".

Its strong tendency to oversimplify is especially dangerous. As Christian and Muslim people, for instance, we reckon that we have all sorts of multiple layers of identity that both divide and unite us. We are British. But one of us has heritage with the complexity of both Indian and Pakistani roots. One of us is adopted and knows not the genetic heritage which is much clearer for the other. So one of us is inevitably, perhaps, more reliant on those aspects of identity that come through nurture than the other, who is more reliant on natural genetics. In addition, there is gender differentiation between us, though we share a common interest in certain issues, and even take a similar view on many of them. Yet there are obvious differences between us in terms of taste and hobbies and the multiple communities and identities into which these characteristics and interests link us.

One could elaborate further. But this is unnecessary since the point is obvious. Huntington is too un-nuanced to be useful in any meaningful sense even as the roughest guide-map to the world's political geography because human beings and human societies are simply too complex as the raw data from which to advance such a simplistic approach.

But the Huntingtonian paradigm is also dangerous in another profoundly arresting way which has a direct impact on the attitudes experienced by faith communities from many elected and appointed officials in local government. This is so since it projects onto religion – itself described by Huntington in a misleadingly monochrome way – the nuance of conflicts and divisions which, again, come from multiple identity sources. These sources may be difficult to define but this does not mean that they should be projected onto religion in an unsophisticated way which actually ends up making religion the problem.

Neither of us as members of faith communities would wish to shirk the blame or the responsibility which our several traditions would need to shoulder and share for the part that they have played in fuelling many of the world's problem issues, both in an historical and a contemporary sense. But the transference of them onto the generic label "religion" transforms them into a caricature, cartoon or comic-picture-book version of transnational relations.

It also fuels a perception – common, in our experience, among so many in local government – that religion is part of the problem not the solution. By projecting the problems onto religion, it encourages others to do so. A case in point at local level would be the issue of faith schools towards which many local politicians have consistently shown much opposition. Such politicians argue that these schools deepen segregation. Statistically, several important studies have shown that they actually serve to break it down because of the core values that they encourage and inculcate. But the charge in a very Huntingtonian sense remains that they are the problem, the source of conflict.

It may well be that many of the world's elected leaders feel unable to do anything other than to place the problems that beset nations and transnational units into a drawer marked "too difficult". Subconsciously, and very understandably, this reaction to the complexity of reality causes them to project the difficulties into the religious sphere. As understandable as the bafflement is in this regard, it nonetheless has dangerous and unhelpful consequences at international, national, regional and local levels.

Inevitably, we are painting with broad brush-strokes in order to show the dynamic which we would contend pertains between the macro and the micro levels, the latter of course being our primary focus. Before we move on to discuss this micro level, in equally broad and general terms, we would wish to add one observation.

The clash of civilisations rhetoric – which we do not feel able to ennoble by describing it as a world view (so slip-shod is its thinking) – whilst seemingly all-prevalent is actually completely inaccessible to people. It is deceptively simple – and simplistic – but it is out of reach in the sense that a science-fiction film is out of reach. Its scale and scope is such that it can only mean something to people when it is reduced to the micro level. Here it is at its most dangerous, as we've tried to illustrate, because it operates as a validating mechanism for communal-garden human prejudice. Indeed, we would contend that it encourages a deepening of prejudice to the point where this spills over into outright conflict.

1. At a micro or local authority level: the absence of religion

If life at the macro and meta-narrative level is problematic, discourse at the micro level is equally fraught.

As well as seeing the tragic events of 9/11, 2001 was also the year which saw civil unrest in the UK cities or towns of Bradford, Burnley and Oldham. Following this unrest, which was felt to have arisen as a result of interracial conflict exacerbated by the low wage economies and deprived circumstances of these communities, a UK Government task force, chaired by Professor Ted Cantle, produced a report analysing the causes of the disturbances which advanced a new responsive language and rhetoric of "community cohesion". This was swiftly adopted as a national policy, a policy very much directed at the micro level.

In the five years since the initial Cantle Report (and another three years later), the language of community cohesion has become all-pervasive in civil society. It has led to considerable restructuring in terms of central government, in that part of what was once the Home Office has now been separately structured as the Department for Communities and Local Government, headed by a minister of cabinet rank. One of its chief objectives is, of course, the promotion of community cohesion.

Paradoxically, as Samuel P. Huntington was advancing the meta-narrative of a world-wide clash of faiths – a narrative which was attracting the attention of the British Government in foreign policy terms; indeed, a narrative from within which British foreign policy was being framed – Ted Cantle was cautioning against what he saw both as the increasingly strident self-definition of citizens' identity along faith lines or the imposition upon citizens of a heavy-handed definition in terms of the faith paradigm.

In this sense, though Cantle's approach may have the disadvantage of paying too little attention to the importance of faith in terms of identity – a feature of his approach that we shall see in relation to the way local authorities have responded to the policy – his is nonetheless an approach with the advantage that it throws the focus away from single-identity categories towards an umbrella concept of citizenship.

For this is the concept which Cantle's typology would suggest UK society needs most pressingly to explore, enhance and strengthen, in order to unite diverse people across national, regional and local contexts. Hence, for example, the development by the UK Government of a citizenship test for immigrants.

This test is, however, but one aspect of a root and branch examination of the way in which people of different communities relate to one another. Its existence and its nature nonetheless strongly suggests that a real problem with Cantle's focus on citizenship – and the way government has responded to it – is that it also begins to look at things in too narrowly, single-identity-category a way.

The UK is of course a member of the EU. Logically, then, its identity should be framed in a transnational way. Added to which, given the UK's former status as the seat of an empire, now transformed into its commitment to a world-wide Commonwealth, one might expect the definition of citizenship advanced to be somewhat less rigidly and narrowly nationalistic. But these European and Commonwealth dimensions seem largely to have slipped off the radar in terms of the concept of the common citizenship to which all are to aspire.

When it comes to the concept of community cohesion itself, the situation is similarly problematic. The term was defined by the UK Government[161] as follows:

A cohesive community is one where

- *there is a common vision and a sense of belonging for all communities;*

- *the diversity of people's different backgrounds and circumstances are appreciated and positively valued;*

---

161 See Local Government Association, Office of the Deputy Prime Minister, Home Office, Commission of Racial Equality, *Guidance on Community Cohesion*, 2002

- *those from different backgrounds have similar life opportunities;*

- *strong and positive relationships are being developed between people from different backgrounds in the workplace, in schools and within neighbourhoods*

Perhaps the most striking thing about this definition is that while in a Huntingtonian sense it sets out, at the macro level, to provide an over-arching narrative framework – one in which there is "a common vision" – the language of faith which is so all-pervasive for Huntington is totally absent here. For faith is subsumed – if it is in any way present – in an expression of "people's different backgrounds and circumstances" which are to be "appreciated and valued". The phrase "different backgrounds" is used no less than three times, which shifts the focus onto a (welcome) acknowledgement of difference to be both embraced and transcended (this is also of course welcome) by "common vision", "relationships" and "a sense of belonging". But not, it would seem, by faith.

It would be tedious to read too much into the minutiae of the language used, but the contours of difference between Huntington and Cantle are certainly instructive when it comes to examining the relationship between faith communities and local authorities.

Whereas Huntington deploys the language of "clash", Cantle shifts the language to one of "difference". And again, whereas Huntington uses the meta-narrative descriptions of "civilisations" at war with one another on the basis of "faith" or "religion", Cantle sees difference in terms of "background". This is certainly a much weaker English word and one which, in a very literal sense, sidelines all sorts of realities: religion, as we have already noted, among them. What stands in the foreground for Cantle is a sense of common "national" identity, won through citizenship.

Implicit in such an approach is the sense in which identity is largely non-negotiable and static. Indeed, over-against the likes of Foucault or Wittgenstein – who see identity emerging from context in a thoroughly permeable and re-negotiable way – Cantle's typology treats language in a way reminiscent of Augustine's view of language and identity, namely that it can be learnt in a "building block" fashion, where we all know or learn what each component means. The latter approach, of course, plays into the territorial, border-based delineations which have dominated the international scene at east since the eighteenth century. But the reality for so many people is that such fixed borders are not an important part of their identity – as, presumably, the pan-European ideal would acknowledge – since they carry their identity with them in the religious stories they share. Its portability – the profound sense, as George Steiner, for example, has argued in his collection of essays, *No passions spent* (1996) that the Jewish homeland is not a place but the text, and its interaction with context – suggests a multiple-identity approach which cannot be treated in a reductionist or minimalist way, since identity is diminished where plurality is diminished.

The return to an inward-looking nationalistic approach is, as we suggested above, perplexing to say the least because it so clearly comes at a time when right-wing nationalism has been causing such widespread consternation across the EU, and follows a decade marked by the severest and most overtly nationalistic of conflicts in and between nations of the former Soviet Union. Here is not the moment to rehearse a complex history of the UK's relationship with continental Europe and the European ideal, but it is certainly striking that the increasing ambivalence in the 1980s and 1990s to the foundations laid by the generation of Edward Heath and Roy Jenkins – a generation which had been determined to free not just Europe but the whole of the world from the very intra and inter-civilisational clashes which lay beneath the surface of the Second World War's presenting issues – has led so clearly to a seemingly introspective redefinition of "British-ness". The dominance here of "nation state" theory may be conducive to the control of citizens within carefully-delineated boundaries and borders, but it is not conducive to community cohesion.

It is a matter for speculation as to the cause and effect linkage between the thought world of a Huntington and that of a Cantle. But the reality at the micro level is that a definition designed to reflect the complexities of cohesive living is being predicated from a similarly single-category standpoint. Instead of faith, one has the single-category of citizenship which is itself defined in too narrow way, one which does not take enough account of the UK's current commitments and responsibilities in identity terms vis-à-vis the EU and the Commonwealth, let alone the complexity of its history as a product of wave upon wave of migration. This tendency to "exclude" – felt to be an especially pervasive feature of the UK national landscape by British citizens who belong to more recent immigrant communities – may not have been the intention of those who sought to see citizenship defined so carefully, David Blunkett when he was Home Secretary, among them. The popular perception, however – and the reality of the handbook published to prepare candidates for the citizenship test – is that citizenship is now being defined in a too narrow way. Added to which, this narrow definition is being fashioned by subsuming what is the all-pervasive category at the macro level – faith or religion – which at the micro level is consigned to the "background", or subsumed within it.

Perhaps one of the problems here is that the UK has, over the centuries, become used to faith being subsumed in this way amidst the national discourse, faith or religion in the form of an established Church?

2. Anglican assimilationism

The lack of a written constitution makes the UK's constitutional arrangements notoriously difficult to pin-point with exactitude. They are, for the most part, a matter of precedent, often stretching over a very considerable period of time, sometimes centuries. But unlike some of the UK's continental neighbours – Holland, Germany or Switzerland, for example – the historical settlement between religion and state has taken a very different course in the UK context.

Taking the UK as a whole, it can certainly be argued that it has never experienced in its national life a religious reformation of the sort that was experienced in northern continental Europe in the sixteenth century. That said, and in the spirit of our implicit plea for a multiple-identity approach in the discussion thus far, it is even difficult to speak about the UK itself in single-identity historical terms. Since, as recent parliamentary devolution in Scotland and Wales, or as the intermittent Northern Ireland Assembly have emphasised, the UK has very distinctive and constituent national identities, the roots of which stretch back hundreds of years. These are also, of course, thoroughly multi-layered.

To stay with the example of reformation history, there are certainly regional differences within the UK itself, the Scottish post-reformation arrangements, for instance, being more akin to those on mainland Europe. But in England, the reformation – which saw the Church of England "established by law" emerge from the vicissitudes of Henry VIII's marital difficulties – was almost entirely a political expedient rather than a religious necessity. Monasteries were of course dissolved in great number, suggesting a reaction to those features of religious life which in continental Europe were seen by the reformers to represent the excesses of late medievalism. But in the English context, a programme of dissolution was enacted as much to satisfy the crown's need for greater revenue as for anything else. Many of the monasteries, after all, weren't abolished or destroyed but were in fact re-founded with stream-lined communities whose worship showed much more continuity than discontinuity with the pre-reformation Church when compared with the situation pertaining to pretty-much any other "reformed" Church in Europe.

Ultimate authority changed of course Henry VIII vested what had previously been papal authority in himself. And the authority of the crown – and therefore of parliament – in matters of the Church of England extends of course to our own age. Still, today, major doctrinal and liturgical changes have to be submitted for parliamentary approval, and the Church of England's General Synod has only, in this sense, been delegated powers by parliament and the crown. All of the measures that it passes have to be scrutinised by parliament and receive royal assent.

The consequence of all this is hard to quantify. But it does seem fair to observe that prior to the *Catholic Emancipation Act* early in the nineteenth century – an act which provided equality for the sovereign's Roman Catholic subjects – being an Anglican and being a citizen were effectively one and the same thing.

Whilst such a view of citizenship in no way pertains in contemporary Britain, there is a lingering sense nonetheless in which Church and State are inter-linked in all sorts of unspoken ways beyond their clear linkage by law. When, for instance, the Church of England in the 1980s effectively performed the function of an opposition party to Margaret Thatcher's administration – critiquing many of its policies' negative social impact on the UK's poorest citizens – this was felt by some to be wholly appropriate, given the Church's role in the nation's constitutional affairs – the seats in the upper chamber of the UK parliament reserved, for instance, for a number of diocesan bishops. Others, of course, saw things differently and perceived such a stance on the part of the Church to be a rejection of what they saw as the Church's "neutrality" as an established Church.

Whatever view was taken, the pivotal and privileged access that the Church had to the machinery of government even as critic was undeniable. It had perhaps been assumed for too long that the Church of England was simply an assimilated part of the establishment, or the "background", and that it functioned rather like a maiden aunt, always there to pour the tea but largely silent when it comes to conversation. Suddenly the aunt woke up to scold some of the guests at the tea party and to initiate some of the liveliest, most radical of conversations! The seemingly assimilated aunt reasserted an aspect of identity that had perhaps long been forgotten, as much by her as by her fellow tea-drinkers.

The questions raised by this episode clustered around what it meant to have unelected (appointed) representatives assimilated into the machinery of the state in a manner which, to an age of obsessive "accountability", seems to allow them to be largely unaccountable. Such questions persist today. Indeed, they feed directly into the way in which the Church of England relates to elected representatives and officers in national and local governmental contexts.

An assimilated religion at the heart of the state can, for instance, mean that elected representatives and officers do not feel the need to bring religion to the table because they believe that it is already there. The fact that the Secretary of State for Communities and Local Government recently felt it unnecessary to include Christian representation on an important commission on community cohesion, is entirely indicative of the problem here. Equally, and by contrast, elected politicians and officials may feel disinclined to deal with religion and its leaders because they resent their unelected and what is perceived to be "unaccountable" presence at the heart of the establishment.

These are just two of many possible reactions, of course, though they are two of the commonest in our experience; the reality and irony of which means that often Christianity – which is after all the majority religion by far in the UK – does not have any voice in the discussions of the local context. Minority "faiths" get a place at the table not by virtue of their faith but by virtue of their "race" or "ethnicity", an invitation which local government is bound to extend to them, by statute. But, there being no statutory obligation to recognise "faith" *per se*, the Christian voice is frequently marginalised in local discourse, whilst the minority faith communities can seem much more strident, though they invariably do not sit at the table in their faith so much as their race or ethnicity or culture capacity.

It has to be said here that Christians must shoulder some of the responsibility for their recent marginalisation. It may well be the case that this relates to the "assimilated" nature of a state Church since in the past Anglicans have so often acted as a "conduit" for the other faiths. To this day, they are often lauded as the "guarantor of our place at the table" by minority faith communities. This perception is inaccurate in statutory terms, of course, so far as the local context is concerned, since statute guarantees the minority voices a place in the discourse by virtue of ethnicity and race. It is, however, perhaps much truer in the national context.

Either way, the proprietorial nature of a state Church (a Church whose neo-colonial instincts have been slow to die) can set up an unhelpfully tiered layering of engagement – "your place at the table comes through my presence". No doubt this has created a degree of resentment too. Added to which, there is the problem of over-assimilation: the Anglicans have frankly, at times, been so indistinguishable from the machinery of the state – so "establishment" – that other faith communities, indeed other Christian denominations for that matter, have sought, more obviously to define a religious identity for themselves. They may not have done so in the absolute singular terms of Huntington – indeed, this is a logical impossibility – but they have often done so in a readily identifiable, indeed very distinctive way.

As Mohammad Siddique Seddon, Dilwar Hussain and Nadeem Malik make clear from the Muslim community perspective, in their recent paper, *British Muslims, between assimilation and segregation* (2004), if one relates the insights of Abraham H. Maslow's "hierarchy of needs" theory – as he annunciates this in *Motivation and Personality* (1954 revised 1970) – to the contemporary British Muslim community, their need for distinctiveness is all too apparent. As economic migrants in the early 1950s, their priority was to fulfil their "deficiency needs", in other words to focus not on integration with the wider community at a philosophical level, but on survival: housing, employment and education. Arguably, with these needs still not satisfied for so many British Muslims they are trapped in "infancy", unable to progress further up Maslow's hierarchy of needs towards "growth needs" where negotiated integration is much more possible.

But there are others reasons for this stridency, and for what many have identified as the reassertion of religious identity *per se*. Chief among them is the actual and underpinning clash of world views which pertains in the UK, as across continental Europe and elsewhere, namely, the clash between a world-view in which faith predominates and a secularist (rather than secular) world view in which faith has absolutely to be marginalised.

Undoubtedly, that such a clash emerges in the UK context is attributable to the Church-State fusion of the Anglican polity has historically seen a gradual coming-together of secular and religious values. To some, this is viewed as a watering-down or accommodating of Christianity to secularism. To others, it is seen as common sense, as indeed "the answer to modernism". But however it is seen, there is no doubting its impact on religious communities which a) lack the privileged position of being "established" and b) have no desire to accommodate themselves to what they perceive as the "mish-mash" of values at the heart of the Church-State polity.

3. The post-enlightenment paradigm

At the start of the twenty-first century, societies across Europe find themselves rehearsing arguments which have been thrashed out in public discourse since the age of scepticism or enlightenment in the eighteenth century. Then, the question for so many countries – France would be an excellent example – was how to move beyond what was perceived as a confusion of Church-State authority.

To put it simplistically, what was required was a replacement for the superstitious "hocus-pocus" of religion. Reason and rationality – and the liberal democracy that seemed to be their best products – were seen as the glittering alternatives. In such an intellectual cauldron, science was set against religion, reason against faith, the latter being firmly pushed to the margins as a purely private enterprise. It had no place on the public stage – since it couldn't earn one, being literally "irrational". The way to deal with it was to allow it as a private option, but thereby firmly to ensure that it was "managed" by being kept out of the public political domain.

The older alliance which had seen the private and public as intertwined, and viewed religion as St Anselm saw it – as faith in search of understanding (reason) – and which had thus kept the two as bedfellows, now sought to separate them. As a result, societies across the globe have, to varying degrees, been playing these post-enlightenment tunes, and their counter-melodies ever since.

To put this whole trajectory into a single image it is – as one recent writer, the theologian-bishop N. T. Wright, has characterised it – as if a beautiful garden was being turned into a patio, whilst all the roots of the best plants (the religions) nonetheless remained underground. The hope from the patio-constructors was doubtless that the roots would die, or at least be forced to grow in the opposite direction, and that what was once a flourishingly diverse garden above ground would become, if it must survive at all, an under-ground project. But religious roots are of course of amazing strength and vitality. Small wonder then, given the attempt to suppress or redirect them, that their inherent vibrancy should have led, in our own age, to their bursting back through the concrete, and doing so not always in the most helpful of ways.

Some of the shoots, some of the melodies, for the reasons hinted earlier, have recently re-emerged with considerable vehemence, provoking a variety of responses, at their most condemnatory from the secularists. But no less edgy, perhaps, are some of the liberals – who had hoped that their own straddling of the above and below-ground, secular-religious divide was an accepted way forward. The conservatives or the neo-cons, to use American terminology, are of course most often hysterical. Interestingly, the neo-cons[162] with their Moby Dick-like quest for a beast to slay – whether it is Osama Bin Laden or Al'Qaida, without, abortionists or stem-cell researchers, within – are, in temperament and philosophical standpoint much more "fundamentalist" than their perceived enemies. But such is the bad fruit that grows amidst the branches of Huntingtonian trees.

The labelling we use here is of course religious and political short-hand, and unsatisfactory as more than a lose guide to the terrain. But it goes some

---

162 As former US President Jimmy Carter has demonstrated in a bestselling rebuttal

way to explaining the universal complexity of the issues pertaining to the clash between faith and secularism right across Europe and beyond, as also to the distinctiveness of this clash in a country with an established faith community at its heart.

The current controversy around the issue of faith schools, many of which are within the maintained sector of education in the UK system – and thus in receipt of government funding whilst able to set their own criteria for entry – is but one of many flashpoints, in the relationship between faith communities and secular authorities, national and local. No doubt the vociferous opposition of the Roman Catholic and Jewish communities to the recent proposal that 25% of places in their schools be reserved for pupils not of their faith, indeed of no faith, relates to the insecurity faith communities feel about their voice in society, as the proposal itself comes from an insecurity about the place of faith in the national and local context.

4. Local government and faith communities in relationship

At this point, having explored some of the key issues which form the "undersong", to use the poet WB Yeats' evocative image, of the terrain in which relationships between faiths or religions and secular authority is set, we should like to draw out and to point up one aspect of the discussion thus far. This is that the framework for the writing of this paper is itself, we would contend, an illustration of a predominant tendency we discern amidst the contested terrain of the faith community to local authority relationship. Since, to be discussing local authorities in relation to the business of interreligious dialogue is already to have set up the dynamic in a very particular way.

One might caricature the approach as follows. Huntington's analysis of the world suggests that the problems, flash-points and actual conflicts are caused by religious systems rubbing each other up the wrong way. The answer to this is obvious: to get people to talk with one another, hence interreligious dialogue. How then can secular power, in the form of local authorities, promote such a dialogue? But to pose the question in such a way is of course to accept and to advance the Huntingtonian premise on which it is founded, which is content to project the issues into the religious realm, as if they somehow did not pertain or originate from public policy in both national and local arenas. Pose the question in such a way, and you accept a distancing between secular power in the form of local authorities – seen as more "neutral", when it certainly isn't so – and the faith communities, where the real problems are to be found. Pose the question this way and it becomes possible for the role of secular power to be seen as "managing", "facilitating" or "encouraging" a dialogue which is outside of itself, a dialogue which is the business of faith communities. But this is to accept a "virtual-reality" scenario which cannot be said to pertain, however nations seek to divide the secular and the sacred.

Our critique of this approach takes the form of a two-fold rebuttal. For one thing, in the UK context – for good or ill – the question cannot be posed in this form, as in historical terms, secular power is religiously influenced in a root and branch way by virtue of the presence of an established Church. Even if, indeed perhaps precisely because, this Church's assimilation within the structures of the state makes the presence of religion a less overt thing, its covert presence is undeniable and alters completely the dynamic of the way in which other faiths relate with one another and with secular authority. For another thing, we contend over-against Huntington and Cantle, that the issue at stake is not one of faiths in dialogue and how such a dialogue may be supported by local authorities. Rather, it is a question of how faith *per se* may be in dialogue with and influence secular power, and be accorded its proper place by local, regional or national political authorities.

That the fundamentalist extremism shared, for instance, by neo-cons and terrorists alike, is one which sets itself against what is perceived to be "secularist, capitalist Western degenerate living", surely indicates the need for a dialogue not between faiths, but across the actual divide in the global context which sees such extreme reactions against "secularism". In this sense, and to emphasise the point, we need more urgently to put together those who most need to be in conversation, which is those who clash over the absence or presence of faith on society's stage.

One underlying aspect of this twin contention – we point it up again from the analysis thus far since we are not of course suggesting that there isn't a need for interreligious dialogue – is the question as to what it may mean, for the Muslim community, for instance, to be in dialogue with the Anglican Church as part of the business of interreligious dialogue, when the Anglican Church is part and parcel of the state structure? As also, we would ask what it might mean for the Muslim community to be in dialogue with secular authorities inescapably shaped by the Church-State fusion?

Would, consequently, the UK context be helped by the disestablishment of the Church of England (the Church in Wales already having been disestablished)? Interestingly, there appears to be most resistance to such disestablishment not from within the Church of England but from within the leadership and membership of other faith communities. Perhaps, inevitably, given the overt "secularist" agenda experienced in the media and political arenas over the last twenty years, and our earlier observations in relation to Maslow's hierarchy, this is not surprising.

Other faith communities, as we have suggested, see the presence of the Church of England, as a guarantor of the place of faith at the table in any shape or form, partly because it has a head start on some of them – it is not dealing with Maslow's "deficiency needs" as they are. But, conversely, clinging to the thin end of the wedge argument – disestablish and we shall all lose our place at the table amidst the ravages of secularism – may be a circular argument. It may, of itself, be preventing the persistent deficiency needs from being recognised, as equally it may prevent the flourishing of a new relationship between faith and secular power.

We also recognise that part of the contemporary dynamic which sees Islam, for instance, adopting a much higher profile in terms of its public presence, sees the issues raised by Maslow combine themselves with the post-Enlightenment view of religion as a private enterprise, to doubly-strengthen the community's reaction to its context. For whilst Christianity – in its established form – could be perceived as having "bought into" or "sold out to" a privatised view through its assimilation with the structures of the state, this is in contrast to a religious community, like the Muslim one which has sought, over-against such a tendency, to maintain a strong, independent identity in faith terms, and not, thus, in any way to collude with the predominant secularist agenda of the political realm. These are certainly issues which we hope can inform a pan-European discussion.

5. Blackburn with Darwen: a thumb-nail sketch

We shift gear now and move towards the grounding of these more philosophical, sociological and speculative trajectories within one specific context, that of the Borough within which we both work and in which one of us resides: Blackburn with Darwen.

The Borough consists of the recent amalgamation into one unitary authority of two post-industrial former mill towns, Blackburn and Darwen, together with their (mainly) rural surrounding areas. The Borough is predominantly urban in context, with suburban and rural aspects. It has recently been the focus of a considerable amount of (physical) urban regeneration work for the excellence of which the Borough has justly won several awards.

From an analysis which the Borough has made available on its own website, using the statistics of the UK 2001 Census, one can summarise some of the Borough's key features as follows:

Ethnicity: 77.9% of the residents are white. 20.6% are Asian. Two of the Borough's twenty-three wards are 98% white, two others are 73% and 79% Asian, amongst the most densely populated Asian wards nationally (for the purpose of these statistics national means England and Wales; Scotland having published separate statistics), the split between Indian and Pakistani Asian heritage being roughly equal.

Religion: 63.3%, a majority of the borough's citizens are Christian. 19.4% are Muslim: the largest proportion in the North-West Region. As with ethnicity, the wards line up in a similar pattern with wards where three quarters or more of the population are Christian at one end of the spectrum, and wards where the same percentage are Muslim. One ward has 1.6% Hindu population, the largest in the Borough. An overwhelming 92% of the Borough in response to the question "What is your religion?" stated that they had one. Only 8% stated that they had no religion. For ease of reference, the detailed percentage figures may be tabulated as follows:

Religion	Blackburn with Darwen	North West	England & Wales
Christian	63.39	78.01	71.74
Buddhist	0.12	0.18	0.28
Hindu	0.31	0.4	1.11
Jewish	0.04	0.42	0.52
Muslim	19.4	3.04	3.1
Sikh	0.1	0.1	0.07
Other religions	0.14	0.16	0.29
No religion	7.99	10.48	14.49
Religion not stated	8.62	7.23	7.69

Health: 20.3% of the Borough's citizens reported a limiting long-term illness. This was a rise from 15.5% in the 1991 census, but a rise nonetheless in line with national trends. When questioned about their health generally, 11.1% reported that it was not good. Inevitably, the poorest wards accounted for this statistic.

Employment: 55.1% of the Borough's citizens of working age (16-74) are in employment. The proportion across wards varies considerably, from 76% at its highest to 36% at its lowest, in a ward with many indicators of poverty and deprivation. 4.1% of the Borough's citizens are unemployed.

Education: 37.2% of the Borough's citizens have no educational qualifications whatsoever, well above the national average which is 29.1%. In one of the poorest wards, 53.3% have no qualifications, whereas, unsurprisingly, in one of the wealthiest wards, only 17.2% of the population lacks qualifications. In one ward, 34.2% of the population is qualified to degree level or above, whereas at the other end of the spectrum one ward contains merely 7.3% educated to this level.

Wealth and deprivation: In the Borough as a whole, just over a third of the population (33.5%) does not own a car. This is above the national average (26.8%). In the poorest wards, over half the population does not own a car. 3.6% of the population owns three or more cars, compared to 5.9% nationally. The average household size in the Borough is 2.54 people. In one ward the average is 2.16, at the other end of the spectrum it is 3.75. Overall, 14.7% of the Borough's houses lack central heating. The national figure is 8.5%. The range in Blackburn with Darwen runs from 24.8% in one ward to 1.4% in another. Very few households have a shared bath/shower or toilet (0.4%). In one ward the figure is 1.2%.

Housing: The proportion of owner-occupied housing (70.5%) compares favourably with the national average (68.9%). The ward range is from 95.6% at one extreme to 46% at the other. In terms of terraced housing, the Borough has a much greater proportion (47.9%) of such housing (some of which is rental stock), when compared with the national average (26%). This housing is located in the urban town settings of Blackburn and Darwen themselves. It is perhaps one of the features which most encapsulate the identity of these towns to the casual observer. One ward contains 69.4% of such housing. The contrast between detached homes – one ward has 51.2% and another but 3.6% – is illustrative of the considerable economic divides across the Borough's wards.

Comment: From this statistical snapshot, it is clear that in terms of ethnicity, race, and religion the Borough is not so much multi-cultural as bi- or duo-cultural, with dominant White heritage-Asian heritage, Christian-Muslim populations. It is also clear that in terms of deprivation and poverty indicators, the Borough scores highly especially in terms of the number of citizens without educational qualifications, and the number living in terraced housing. It has a high concentration of urban priority areas. It has very little extreme wealth, but the contrasts between wealth and poverty are certainly as extreme as almost anywhere in the UK. Taken as a whole – and especially when analyzed at ward levels, where the disparities between the extremes are striking – the statistics suggest the strong possibility of "parallel communities" and "segregated living", or as some have come to term this 'self-segregation'. These are contested terms since, historically, the notion of "segregation" suggests a state-sanctioned system. This is of course not the case. But the degree to which the "parallel living" one can observe is a result of choice or circumstance is equally contested. What cannot be doubted, is the reality of separate living and schooling that pertains.

6. The marginalisation of faith in local authority thinking

Having painted this thumb-nail sketch of the Borough that we wish to use as a prism for our observations, and given the trajectory of our argument thus far, we find at this point that we are frankly struggling when it comes to giving examples of good practice in terms of the relationship between local authorities and the faith communities. The endemic problems we have outlined all pertain to this, as to other, particular contexts in the UK.

What we would wish to say in defence of the Borough here, is that the confusion over who gets to sit at the local authority's "discussion table" and on what grounds (Christianity being treated as a faith and being less present than minority faiths which are treated differently in terms of race and ethnicity) doubtless means that from the Borough's perspective they see themselves engaging with the minority racial or ethnic communities on cultural terms, as they are obliged to do by law. Hence, but incidentally, they also find themselves dealing with minority faith communities by virtue of the race or ethnicity agenda but not with the majority faith community to whom they owe no statutory obligation in respect of formal dialogue.

From correspondence with councillors and officers which is in the public domain, it would seem that the Borough very much regards the majority of Christians as "cultural" Christians (in other words, they move them out of the faith and into the culture "box"), further supporting our contention that they struggle to recognise the issue of faith *per se*, not least because they have no legal obligation to do so.

Even if we cannot therefore, in all honesty, see much to celebrate in the relationship between the Borough and the faith communities as faith communities, we would certainly wish to record some of the many positive ways in which faith communities themselves are relating one to another.

Focussing therefore on interreligious activity, we could instance – though the reader would have to seek independent and more objective verification of this – the work which we have sought to advance over the past year, especially since 7/7, within Blackburn with Darwen, and also the wider Lancashire (regional) context.

One key aspect of this has been the way in which the two of us have been regularly in public dialogue in Blackburn's Anglican Cathedral on Tuesday lunchtimes. Visibility has been especially valuable since 7/7, following which all sorts of unhelpful aspects of Huntingtonian analysis have played themselves out in community discourse at the grass roots, fostering considerable tension around the Asian, majority-Muslim community. So far, we have hosted two series of such dialogues. The first, under the title *Clash of civilisations or chance to co-operate,* and the second, with the title *Discovering how to be human* were opportunities to demonstrate that "clash of civilisations" thinking is both inaccurate and dangerous.

Differences were certainly very much in evidence – we did not in any way seek to disguise them – but in the forty minutes of questioning from the 150-200 people who attended most sessions (including large groups of young people in the 16-25 year old age range) which followed twenty minutes of introductory dialogue from the two of us, it was evident that many people realised that the problems were not about difficulties between faiths but, as our analysis has suggested, about the faith-secularist divide, and the marginalisation of faith in public discourse of which local authorities are one factor. It was perhaps significant in this regard, that despite repeated invitations only 4 local councillors and 2 officers of the Borough attended any of these dialogues.

In the UK context, as we have pointed out already, local authorities are obliged to take account of racial, ethnic and gender differentiation, and even to do so in relation to culture in terms of equal opportunities legislation – so that they can ensure equality in terms of public policy – but they do not have, in a statutory sense, to give an account, or to take account of the faith paradigm.

To point up the sense in which there is little or no inherent tension between the faith communities as faith communities, and to emphasise the way in which when tensions arise they do so not for religious but because economic and social reasons (the poverty of Asian heritage working class and White heritage communities is notable in the Borough) we might instance the fact that we also took the dialogue model to a mosque in Burnley. Indeed, several dialogues were hosted there. As with the cathedral dialogues, they engaged the two majority faith communities and all minority faiths, alongside those who claim no religious affiliation, in a mature and nuanced discussion. A further series begins in November 2006, specifically to engage with the Hindu, Sikh, Jewish and Buddhist communities.

Joint work in schools – which are deeply "segregated" in a place like Blackburn; and some of which are in the extraordinary position of being Church of England Voluntary Aided Primary Schools with almost wholly Asian (majority Muslim) intakes – has seen the two of us advance an 'exchanging communities' methodology. This has twinned schools across the divide so as to give pupils the chance to document (chiefly to photograph) their community as they see it (using the term of "home" as a way in), and to share perceptions once the resulting captioned photographs have been shared in facilitated workshops.

Much of this work has been funded nationally by the Faith Capacity Building Fund which was initially based at the Home Office, now at the Department for Communities and Local Government. From within the context of the national arena, this fund recognises what many local authorities at the grass roots seem to find difficult to acknowledge, which is that faith communities are a primary means of promoting community cohesion and therefore need to be funded to grow their considerable capacity to deliver cohesive communities. Enhancing the capacity to do so is quite simply in the fundamental interests of society. The availability of this funding also represents a recognition on the part of central government that increased decentralisation of power to local authorities has not produced the kind of relationship between these authorities and faith networks that is needed if cohesive communities are to become a reality.

In our own Blackburn with Darwen context it is, for instance, clear that "New Labour" in central government terms needs to make strategic interventions into what is very much an "old Labour" way of doing things, a way which tends to divide the community into its constituent racial and ethnic groups and to address them as separate entities. There is no doubt an element of short-term electoral gain to be had by doing so – because of the ethnically divided nature of the current ruling group – though this undoubtedly counters the long-term political objective which must be that one integrated community at ease with itself is the only way forward.

In this regard, one could explore, for instance, the way in which Blackburn with Darwen's flagship arts and cultural projects – spanning successive summer weekends each year when a large local park becomes the venue for an Asian Festival, the Mela, and an indigenous white festival, the Arts in the Park (including a last night of the proms with fireworks display) – are directly predicated on a recognition of parallel lives rather than one of unity in diversity.

Clearly, community "cohesion" in such an approach means dealing with communities "separately". It means an institutionalised "divide and rule" approach, which does not set out in any way to bring the community together as one. Rather it presupposes that there is no desire to be one but only to inhabit constituent communities. Much anecdotal evidence suggests that the public at large wishes to see the two cultures (in reality a plurality of cultures) united in one visible and tangible expression of the possibility for cohesive living. Quite simply, an arts and culture festival presents a golden opportunity to get to know people across the divide. In this sense, to segregate them merely perpetuates a community where ignorance at the most basic cultural levels breeds fear and reinforces communal-garden prejudice.

Set against this particular critique of the Borough's approach, however, we would both wish to applaud the work that Blackburn with Darwen has done in terms of their continued promotion of the racial and gender equality agenda which has been a feature of the UK landscape since the first Race Relations Act in the mid-1960s. An extension of this work, and perhaps one of its most successful initiatives in this regard, is the *Belonging to Blackburn with Darwen* campaign, which has sought to use representative members of the community in a highly visible poster campaign, so as to reflect the diversity of the Borough and project the sense in which it is a place or home for all. In visual terms alone, this has been an enormous success. And it has included some significant members of the faith communities. But, significantly, once again, they have not been recognised as people of faith so much as because they fit into other categories – as senior citizens, members of ethnic minorities, and so on. In a sense, it is all the more frustrating that such an imaginative tool should so glaringly omit the faith perspective, especially in terms of the Christian community (the Muslim, Sikh and Hindu communities being more obviously represented, by virtue of recognisably distinctive "cultural" dress).

If the relationship of local authorities has primarily been one with ethnic minorities, and cultural groupings, how has the faith paradigm, in fact, been drawn into this network of relationships or partnerships if at all?

Two common features in almost any local or regional authority structure are the presence of an Interfaith Council and of faith community representatives on Local Strategic Partnerships.

Both of the present writers are members of the Blackburn with Darwen Interfaith Council, whose recent history illustrates the positive relationships at a personal and institutional level between the faiths themselves (evinced elsewhere by an Anglican-Muslim forum, for instance, built upon a relationship between the Lancashire Council of Mosques and the Anglican Diocese of Blackburn) and the negative lack of any real engagement and relationship between this Interfaith body and the Borough.

Indeed, the Interfaith Council is a construct of the Borough, drawing together "the usual suspects", who play a ceremonial role on certain civic occasions – they are at their most visible at the Borough's Holocaust Memorial Day commemoration – but who receive no realistic funding from the Borough to enable their capacity to deliver interreligious dialogue to be extended, little in the way of administrative support, and no encouragement to feel that they have a role to play in dialogue with council leaders.

The fact that this is the case is emphasised further by the occasional meetings organised by the leader of the council not with the interfaith council as representative of faith "as a whole" across the Borough, but with a select group of Christian leaders, on one hand, and a similarly select group of Muslim leaders on the other. This would tend to the obvious conclusion that a policy of divide and rule – whether intentional or not – is nevertheless being practised. It is a policy which also excludes the Hindu, Buddhist, Sikh and Jewish faith communities from the discourse altogether, which is again damaging to community cohesion.

The reality for the Interfaith Council is that beyond a very few number of concrete projects[163] and the tireless work of several individuals either to represent the Council at events across the Borough, or to produce a much-needed directory of places of worship[164], there is no desire to see the Interfaith Council perform anything other than a ceremonial role. Its presence, in short, simply enables a box to be ticked. There is no funding or support being made available by the Borough to give the body real teeth and a role in public discourse, not least with the Borough itself. Anecdotal evidence suggests that this is a pattern replicated in many other local authorities in the UK, where the representatives of faith communities can all too often fail to notice that they are actually being seduced by chains of office, photo-opportunities and what we characterise as "cucumber sandwich and samoosa" interfaith (really intercultural) relations.

The lack of funding to support the visibility or status often accorded such bodies, and their real value as representative of a huge segment of the community, subtly undermines the public perception of such bodies. They are perceived as talking shops – which are as "unaccountable" as is the presence of a State Church – because this is all they are allowed to be. This underfunding and undermining is sadly replicated when it comes to the involvement of faith communities in Local Strategic Partnerships (LSP).

The Borough's own website defines the purpose of its LSP as follows:

The Local Strategic Partnership is the Borough's largest and most influential partnership body. It is an overarching body, made up of representatives from the public sector, local business and the faith, community and voluntary sector. The aim of the partnership is to create a vision for the Borough and set mechanisms to deliver on the vision which is known as the community plan. The partners works together to

---

163 An interfaith sculpture, for instance, about which a team from the nterfaith Council is currently in negotiation with the Borough's regeneration team

164 Which the Borough will not fund though in terms of access to community spaces alone, it would be in the interests of the wider community to do so

improve services to all the people of Blackburn with Darwen.

The Local Strategic Partnership is responsible for delivering the Community Plan. The priorities in the Community Plan were drawn up after widespread consultation with local people.

Each LSP appoints a variable number of faith representatives, on a varying denominational or multifaith basis. Given the overwhelming self-definition of the Borough's citizens, the Lancashire-wide and North West region's population in faith terms, one may question the low level of representation when compared with the number of councillors, for instance, represented: 9 councillors to 2 faith representatives on Blackburn with Darwen's LSP. Lancashire-wide, 44 councillors on 6 LSPs represent Lancashire County Council, a unitary authority or a District Council, when compared with but 9 faith representatives (only three of whom were clearly appointed on a multifaith basis). Leaving this aside, however, some statistical research carried out using the Freedom of Information Act, in relation to Neighbourhood Renewal Funding (NRF), a prime source of funding for the community cohesion work of LSPs[165], revealed the following alarming situation in relation to the financial year 2004-2005:

Of 229 pieces of work undertaken in Lancashire using NRF, with a total budget of £14.4m, only one piece of work was faith-based and two were multifaith based. This accounts for but 1.05% of the fund. In addition, one further project has an implication for the development of partnerships between faith communities and statutory bodies (local government, health, police, etc.). As the figures tabulated below reveal, most of the NRF was spent not by any of the voluntary or community sector members of the LSPs, or by other partnerships, or even by schools and colleges – where, arguably, much of the renewing work to break down "segregation" is needed – but by the local authorities themselves.

It is small wonder, in this sense, that many faith leaders have little confidence in the LSP process, given that this one potential chink of light in the statutory relationship between faith communities and local authorities has borne such meagre fruit. A perception is again being reinforced that boxes are being ticked through the presence of faith representatives, indeed of voluntary sector representatives' altogether, since their presence is not translated at the chalk face into funding. They are often merely there, in effect, to rubber-stamp the decisions of councillors. Yet, all the sociological evidence points consistently to the faith and voluntary community sector as that most likely to enhance common values, shared perceptions and cohesive living.

---

165 Research that was carried out by The Reverend Dale Barton, Interfaith development officer for Churches Together in Lancashire

Summary Table: Neighbourhood Renewal Funding in Lancashire 2004-2005

© Dale Barton 2006

LA	Blackburn with Darwen	Blackpool	Burnley	Hyndburn	Pendle	Preston
NRF grant	£4,334,824	£3,007,888	£1,273,270	£1,367,309	£1,960,942	£2,500,000
% spent SS	102.94%	70.64%	71.66%	65.79%	49.81%	47.24%
% spent S&C	1.85 %	14.36 %	16.32 %	7.61 %	15.43 %	14.84 %
% spent OP	5.55%	12.37%	17.65%	11.71%	39.81%	19.60%
% spent V&C	1.41%	2.82%	0.00%	13.95%		11.96%
% spent faith	0.00%	0.00%	0.00%	0.00%	5.00%	2.16%
% held back	0.00%	-0.19%	1.72%	0.94%	2.17%	4.20%
Large grant	£1m Highways	£277,500 Blackpool BC	£500,000 Health and Leisure Centre	£142,044 Community Wardens	£249,597 LCC Education	£568,000 Preston PCT
Total spend	111.75%	100.00%	107.35%	100.00%	112.22%	100.00%

Key:
LA = local authority
SS = statutory sector
S&C = schools and colleges
OP = other partnerships
V&C = voluntary and communitysector

Total spent	£14,444,233
Faith sector total spend	£152,144
% spent by faith sector	1.05 %

Notes

- Blackpool LSPs largest grant was to provide partnership support for the VCFS sector from within the Council

- Blackburn with Darwen figures reflect the managing organizations not the delivery agents – information on delivery agents is not available

- Burnley spent under-spend from 2003-2004

- According to the Government website Hyndburn received a £1.294m grant

- In Pendle "other" and VCS could not be separated

- According to the government website Preston received a £2.52m grant

Summary Table: Faith representatives on Lancashire LSPs
2004-2005

© Dale Barton 2006

Borough	Visible spend on cohesion issues	Faith reps on LSP	Faith reps appointed on multi-faith basis	Councilors on LSP	LSP membership posted on website	Financial info on council website
Blackburn and Darwen	-	2	-	9	-	-
Blackpool	-	1	yes	5	-	-
Burnley	-	3	-	6	-	-
Hyndburn	yes	1	-	7	-	-
Pendle	yes	1	yes	8	yes	-
Preston	-	1	yes	7	-	-
TOTAL	2	9	3	42	1	0

In addition to this statistical research relating to a context where some attempt has been made to "represent" the voice of faith or the faith perspective, but where little in the way of funding for faith-led initiatives results, indeed where there is an overwhelming bias against them, there is further evidence, again on the basis of research by The Reverend Dale Barton, to suggest that outside of LSP-like structures, little if any attempt is made to engage faith communities in ventures which quite clearly could or should have a strong faith dimension.

One specific example concerns a project to produce two heritage trails for Blackburn with Darwen. These have brought four voluntary sector "heritage-interest" bodies together to author of the trails. Following a written enquiry as to whether the faith dimension of the Borough would be recognized in the trails – a council officer assuring the enquirer that faith would come in via buildings of "architectural merit" – it became clear that the bid for public funding to underpin the project – from the Countryside Agency – had been put together at the behest of the Borough, who had noticed the funding source, alerted the voluntary bodies it thought would be interested in such a project, and helped them to apply. All of which is of course excellent in itself. The absence in the Borough's thinking, however, of the possibility that a faith community or even the interfaith council, should be part of such a bid[166], and the subsequent resort to a rhetoric sort of "the funding was open to all", when challenged on this – further illustrates the way in which local government can consistently ignore central government advice, which is that faith communities must be included at all levels of decision-making in the

---

166 Not least given the fact that some of the only buildings of architectural merit in heritage terms are faith-based

local context and that their enormous contribution must be celebrated – as, for example, through a heritage trail – as well as being reflected at every level in the policy-thinking and policy-enactment of a local authority or region.

Given the chasm in thinking, at times, between central and local government in this area, it is perhaps worth rehearsing and emphasising the consistent line which central government has taken, all of which is borne out by research which the North West Development Agency has sponsored to encourage local authorities to work much more closely and effectively with faith communities. The research demonstrates convincingly the value of faith communities at every level of society.

7. Faith communities as social and economic capital

Since 1999, which is before the civil disturbances in Bradford, Burnley and Oldham in 2001 – which accelerated the development of a UK central government policy and definition of community cohesion (fully formulated in 2002) – the impact of faith communities in terms of social cohesion was already being emphasized. In 1999, the Home Office stated:

"Strong community-based organizations are a key starting point for any disadvantaged community. In many cases faith groups [...] will be the strongest around and yet their potential may be overlooked by funders and others engaged in programmes of community development. There can be a tendency not to see beyond the "faith" label to the community role of these groups".

In December 2001, following the disturbances in Oldham, the *Oldham Independent Review Panel* report stated:

"Faith leaders play a leading role within their own communities, never more important than now when hard things need to be said about the importance of contact across the communal divide and of bringing down barriers, the disavowal of racist attitudes and the rejection of violence as a means to solve society's ills."

Taken together, these two snap-shots of a developing rhetoric and policy in central governmental terms illustrate both an emerging notion of "social capital" – namely, the degree to which faith communities are forces for unity across societal divides – and an increasing expectation, indeed reliance on faith communities to play-up this aspect of their role.

This was emphasized further in 2003 when David Blunkett, the then Home Secretary, said this:

"Every faith has a "development worker", full or part-time, paid or voluntary. In other words, the priest or pastor, the Vicar or Minister, the teacher, Imam or Rabbi. This is the resource available to all areas of the country, even the most deprived, the least active and the most likely to be disengaged from the political process."

It was emphasized unequivocally in the Home Office document *Working Together: Co-operation between Government and Faith Communities* (February 2004).

Yet, time and again, there is evidence that local authorities are ignoring one of the most important sources of social and economic capital at their disposal. In this sense, the findings of two of the only UK surveys to attempt to quantify the social and economic capital of faith communities[167] are instructive.

Writing in the foreword to the 2003 survey, Bryan Gray, Chairman of the North West Development Agency asserts:

"The findings of this report will hold few surprises for those who already have an appreciation of the range of activities undertaken by faith communities in our region. As a self-funded and often voluntary group, faith communities contribute to our region in many ways, from increased levels of social inclusion to the conservation of our built heritage.

This groundbreaking survey of the faith communities in England's Northwest will, however, surprise a good many both within the "faith sector" and more widely across the public and voluntary sectors. It reveals the sheer scale of faith communities' contribution to regional development and makes it clear that while media headlines may suggest that faith is in decline and minority faith communities are to be viewed with distrust, the truth is very different indeed.

Our region's faith communities are important stakeholders right across our region, from rural to urban, from the deprived to the affluent. They have a part to play in delivering our regional strategy for economic development and, as this survey powerfully shows, **they have to be engaged with as vital partners in our region's future prosperity and quality of life.**" *[Our emphasis]*

Writing two years later, in the foreword to the second survey (2005), designed to amplify the first and clearly concerned that the challenge

---

167 Surveys both of which were conducted for the North West Development Agency [NWDA] – *Faith in England's North West* (November 2003) and *Faith in England's North West: Economic Impact Assessment* (February 2005)

to engagement has not received the response that was hoped, Steven Broomhead states:

"The Home Office document "Working Together" (February 2004) [...] has stressed the value of public authorities working in partnership with faith communities. The Church of England report "Building Faith in our Future" (October 2004) calls for close co-operation with Regional development Agencies, Cultural Consortia and Local Strategic Partnerships. This "Economic Impact assessment" [...] substantiates the claim that faith communities are de facto stakeholders in the life of the region. **It determines once and for all the right of faith communities to be given a seat at the table at regional, local and community level when decisions are taken affecting the community. This document also establishes the entitlement of faith communities to receive public funding for the work they do in the wider community to the same extent as any other public, private or voluntary body.** The NWDA is confident in recommending that this document should be required reading for all those involved in regeneration throughout the Northwest." *[Our emphasis]*

On what had the NWDA based these assertions?

Now is not the place for a detailed analysis of both surveys. Suffice it to say, however, that the following is a précis of the key findings in relation to faith communities.

2003 Survey summary:

• Faith communities are notable for their willingness to be listened to and to play a constructive role in discussion.

• Whilst also represented in the most affluent areas, faith communities are especially concentrated where there is highest social need and are best placed amongst voluntary (or in some cases statutory bodies) to assist the most vulnerable groups, including older citizens and children.

• They are important custodians of built heritage. Almost all faith communities have rooms within their buildings used by other community groups.

• They bring visitors and tourists to the regions. The survey found that not only cathedrals and "greater" churches but many other buildings have untapped potential for "faith tourism" which could play a key economic role in the region.

• They offer social support services (at the time of the survey, 45% of rural churches were involved in responding to the Foot and Mouth crisis).

- They are active delivery agents of care in their local communities. One in ten manage community projects totalling 5,140 projects which address a range of issues, including housing, homelessness, anti-racism, crime prevention, drug and alcohol abuse, employment and training, social enterprise and personal finance. Involvement was apparent in the spheres of health and fitness, art, music and education, and the environment (14% of faith communities are involved in environmental projects).

- They are significant patrons of the arts (choral and instrumental music, dance, drama, art, poetry recitals etc) and of all major sports.

- They stimulate unprecedented levels of volunteering, 45,667 volunteers across the Northwest being involved in community activities outside of worship. They give approximately 6,810 hours a week to these activities.

- They are engaged in significant regeneration projects (e.g., Single Regeneration Budget schemes, Sure Start, Learn Direct, etc.).

- They are not being engaged with by LSPs in a way which concurs with the Government's emphasis on involvement of faith communities. Many are not aware of LSPs or their significance. Very few were aware of the Community Empowerment Fund.

- They are largely self-financing. Only 27% received any form of public funding.

- They reach those parts of society that others cannot reach.

2005 Survey summary:

Using the data from the 2003 survey, and assessing it in terms of the economic value generated by volunteer time, by service to the community in terms of social concern targeted, and social group engaged, the value generated by use of premises associated with faith communities, the economic value of faith tourism and heritage status, the number of Full Time Equivalent jobs (FTE) equivalent to the 8,088,379 volunteer hours employed by faith communities in the Northwest, and the number of FTE jobs supported by day visitor faith tourism expenditure, the survey found that

- 45,667 faith volunteers in the Northwest generate between £60.6m and £64.4m *per annum*.

- Premises made available by faith communities in the Northwest generate between £574,755 and £811,472 *per annum*.

- 697,114 faith visitors and tourists to the Northwest generate around

£8.4m *per annum*.

• Overall, faith communities in the Northwest generate between £90.7m and £94.9m *per annum* to civil society in the region.

8. The Way Forward

Given these statistics – which do not appear to have been contested by the relevant local or regional authorities – and their clear indication of the role that faith communities already play in economic, regenerative and cohesive terms, it is our hope that local authorities may be encouraged to rethink their attitude and relationship to faith communities, so as to avoid the widespread feeling that the voice of faith – which, after all represents the vast majority of the UK's citizens will not continue to be marginalised but utilized for the good of all.

It is hard to be too precise in terms of charting ways forward, not least because Local Government is one of the most rapidly-evolving areas in UK terms. As we write, *Strong and prosperous communities: The Local Government White Paper* (2006) has just been published with a clear, decentralising thrust, not least through the removal of many central Government targets, a desire to see councils much more accountable locally, and thus an attempt to address disparities at the most grass-roots levels between the UK and continental European countries like France and Germany which employ much more devolved and decentralised networks of local governance.

At present, England is governed locally by much more substantial "units". It has in fact only 356 councils with any real power (leaving aside the 8,700 parish and town councils with little if any powers). These consist in 84 all-purpose unitary and metropolitan authorities, 34 shire counties and 238 districts. This compares with France, whose population is a mere 10% bigger than England's, but whose "communes" total a staggering 36,000, or Germany whose 15,000 municipalities serve a population a third bigger than England's. The emerging rhetoric is of returning power to the most grass-roots levels. But we suspect that the issues that we have outlined in relation to the relationship between local government and faith communities will continue to undermine such seemingly reforming radicalism, unless the following areas are urgently addressed.

• Public debate and discourse, in short, a conversation or dialogue between local and regional authorities and faith communities needs to be initiated as to the role of faith in society. This will strengthen the understanding of both, since as well as there being a tendency for local/

regional authorities to shy away from the "faith" component of their communities, the faith communities themselves can sometimes seem unaware of the influence that they have or could have, and the impact that they make or could make in society at large.

- A Royal Commission to look at the relationship of Church and State and of all faith communities to local, regional and national government, and to make recommendations as to how, structurally, to proceed, would, in the UK context, perhaps be the most effective constitutional tool to use. This would however need to have a strongly devolved structure so that it was not London-centric, which is a danger for many such commissions.

- The public debate initiated and the Royal Commission would need to be underpinned by the kind of statistical data of which the North West Development Agency's surveys are an illustration. In this regard, if, as is often contended by local authorities, they perceive the 2001 Census data as being too imprecise to be useful in terms of public policy, then they should a) be encouraged to make representations to Central Government as to improving the data-gathering for the next census and b) they should carry out their own data gathering in collaboration with the faith communities themselves. This sort of audit is very common in other spheres – in relation to poverty indicators, for instance –why should it not become commonplace in the context of the relationship of faith to society?

- Given the time that it would take to set-up a Royal Commission, and the urgent need to rectify the disengagement of local authorities and faith communities, we would recommend the appointment of a "faith Tsar" with an appropriate regional structure and staff, accountable to the Secretary of State for Communities and Local Government whose sole job was to monitor the evolving conversation and relationship in such a way as to ensure that faith did not continue to be subsumed under the umbrella of other categories – culture, race and ethnicity among them. Such an ombudsman or woman would also encourage faith communities to define how they see their role in relation to society in the widest sense. The lack of encouragement to do so at present is, we would contend, one of the factors in the "privatisation" of faith to the point where some are clearly articulating views which are not in the interest of society. An honest and open debate would "flush-out" such thinking for the good of all. The lack of understanding of the faith-culture boundary on the part of many elected politicians and unelected office-holders in this sense contributes to a lack of understanding and negotiation of this boundary within faith communities themselves (the recent debate on the *niqab* in the UK would illustrate this from both perspectives). This post and attendant structure should be time-limited. Such centralisation would only be necessary whilst strong local structures were being grown, as the latter are of course by far the most effective.

- We would wish to see a tightening up of the regulations in terms of the faith representation on Local Strategic Partnerships to ensure that the particular and nuanced distribution of faith communities as faith communities – and not, for instance, as ethnic minorities – is reflected in each locality.

- We would also wish to see each local authority obliged to appoint and fund a faiths officer whose sole responsibility was to support the engagement of local government and the faith communities, and to enable faith communities to gain access to public funding not to support their worshipping lives but to assist with the development of their community work. This could be part of the structure that would emerge from the "faith Tsar".

We would hope that any guidelines which the Council of Europe may wish to draw up would consider these recommendations based on the experience of the UK situation. The gap between central UK governmental wishes in relation to faith communities and the engagement of faith communities by local authorities needs to be narrowed as a matter of urgency since:

- Faith communities uniquely provide a level of stability which elected representatives or appointed officers can never provide in any community.

- Faith communities have long histories of investment in the community and track records which are unmatched. These resources must be used to promote cohesive community-living in the twenty-first century.

- Faith communities must be seen as part of the solution, not the problem. At present, regrettably, they are very much an under-utilised and under-appreciated part. This is a situation which in every sense represents a missed opportunity.

Bibliographical references

Samuel P. Huntington, *The Clash of Civilisations and the Remaking of the World Order* (New York, 1996)

Michel Foucault, *Discipline and Punish: The Birth of the Prison* (Paris, 1975; London 1979)

Amartya Sen, *Identity and Violence: the illusion of destiny* (London, 2006)

Home Office, *Community Cohesion: A Report of the Independent Review Team* (London, 2001)

Home Office, *The end of parallel lives? Final report of the Community Cohesion Panel* (London, 2004)

Ted Cantle, *Community Cohesion: a New Framework for Race and Diversity* (Basingstoke and New York, 2005)

Local Government Association, Office of the Deputy Prime Minister, Home Office, Commission of Racial Equality, *Guidance on Community Cohesion* (London, 2002)

Home Office, *Life in the United Kingdom: a Journey to Citizenship* (London, December 2004 with October 2005 amendments)

George Steiner, *No passions spent, Essays 1978-1995* (London, 1996)

Mohammed Siddique Seddon, Dilwar Hussain and Nadeem Malik, *British Muslims between assimilation and segregation* (Islamic Foundation, Leicester, 2004)

Abraham H. Maslow, *Motivation and Personality* (New York, 1954, revised 1970)

N. T. Wright, *Believing in the Real World: The Challenge of Faith to Secularism and Fundamentalism* (Blackburn, 2006)

Jimmy Carter, *Faith and Freedom: the Christian challenge to the world* (London, 2006)

Blackburn with Darwen Borough Council Information Gateway [website]: *http://www.blackburn.gov.uk*

UK Census 2001 website: *http://www.statistics.gov.uk/census2001*

Home Office, *Working Together: Co-operation between Government and Faith Communities* (London, February 2004)

North West Development Agency, *Faith in England's North West: the contribution made by faith communities to civil society in the region* (Warrington, November 2003)

North West Development Agency, *Faith in England's North West: Economic Impact Assessment* (Warrington, February 2005)

Department for Communities and Local Government, *Strong and prosperous communities: The Local Government White Paper* (London, 2006)

Chapter 7

Interfaith developments in the United Kingdom

Brian Pearce[*]

*   Brian Pearce, "Inter Faith Network", United Kingdom

The initiative launched by the Council of Europe on inter cultural and interreligious dialogue is very much to be welcomed, and as part of this, the focus of the Congress of Regional and Local Authorities in Europe on the contribution which these authorities can make to promoting intercultural and interreligious dialogue.

In recent years, increasing attention has been given by the UK's Government to its relationships with the major faith communities and to encouraging good interfaith relations. This reflects the Government's commitment to creating a society where people of all faiths are active and valued participants in national life. It also reflects a growing recognition that faith communities, as part of the "third" or voluntary sector (albeit a distinct part), have great potential to contribute to civil society.

The religious landscape differs from country to country in Europe. A smaller percentage of the population in the UK than in some other European countries belongs to minority ethnic or minority faith communities. The figures for the UK are roughly 8% and 5% respectively. But there is within the UK a greater diversity than in any other European country in terms of the range of significant communities linked to different faith traditions. In the 2001 Census, 76.8% of people in the UK identified themselves as having a religious faith, including 42 million Christians, 1.6 million Muslims, 560,000 Hindus, 370,000 Sikhs, 270,000 Jews, 150,000 Buddhists and 180,000 who described their faith as "other". Diversity is at its greatest in cities such as Birmingham, Glasgow, Leicester and London. For example, 45% of the ethnic minority population of the UK recorded in the 2001 Census lived in Greater London, where around 30% of the total population came from minority ethnic groups and 17.35% identified themselves as belonging to minority faith groups. The local authority area in Britain with the highest proportion of its population from ethnic minorities was the London Borough of Newham with 60.6%. The London Borough of Harrow was the local authority area in Britain with the highest proportion from minority faiths, with 47.71% identifying themselves as Christian and 34.2% as being of other faiths. In England and Wales, out of 376 local authorities, ethnic minorities constituted 1% or less of the population in 56 of these, and in 62 of them 80% or more of the population identified themselves as Christian.

The Inter Faith Network for the UK[168] was set up in 1987. It does not have individual members but links organisations with an interest in building good inter faith relations in the UK. It currently has 135 member organisations in four categories of membership: national representative bodies of the main faith communities; national and regional interfaith organisations; local

---

168 The work of the organisation is described at http://www.interfaith.org.uk

interfaith organisations; and educational and academic bodies with a particular interest in interfaith relations. Its primary focus is on good relations work but as part of this it has also promoted the engagement of a broad range of faith communities in public life in the UK. This aspect of its work has developed significantly in the last ten years. The faith communities which are directly represented within the Network are the Baha'i, Buddhist, Christian, Hindu, Jain, Jewish, Muslim, Sikh and Zoroastrian communities. However, people from other religious groups may well belong to the interfaith organisations in membership of the Network.

The number of interfaith organisations in the UK has expanded significantly in recent years and the pattern of these is probably more developed than in other European countries. There are currently 23 interfaith organisations operating at UK level or covering Scotland, Wales and Northern Ireland; 12 regional interfaith organisations; and over 220 local interfaith organisations.

National interfaith organisations may focus on particular bilateral or trilateral relationships, such as Christian-Jewish, Jewish-Muslim, Christian-Hindu or Jewish-Christian-Muslim or they may be open to membership from all religious groups, focusing on particular issues. In some cases, they are the UK branches of international interfaith organisations such as Religions for Peace or the United Religions Initiative. In some cases such as the Council of Christians and Jews and the Three Faiths Forum, they have local branches.

However, the majority of local interfaith organisations are multifaith ones drawing participation and membership from a city or town or a more local area. The number of these local interfaith organisations (many of which are in membership of the Network) has more than doubled over the last five years.

A detailed survey of local interfaith structures and activity across the UK was carried out by the Inter Faith Network in 2003. There is no single correct "model" for a framework for the promoting of interfaith relations locally; initiatives need to develop in ways which take account of local circumstances and needs. Local interfaith organisations have varying aims. Some are relatively informal and focus on the promotion of mutual understanding and encounter between people of different faiths and beliefs at a personal level. Others seek engagement with the local authority and other public bodies in their area and have been set up on a more formally representative basis. Some organisations combine both roles. Most local interfaith organisations have been initiated by Churches or other faith groups but some at the initiative of local authorities in order to provide a more structured sounding board for them and other public authorities.

Naturally these local interfaith organisations vary in quality and in the depth of their engagement within local faith communities and in the "public square". While many of them seek to be "representative", issues arise over the range of faith communities to be included within a local interfaith structure and about the way these faith groups are to be represented within in. There is a need to work to extend and deepen the work of local interfaith bodies but they are succeeding in attracting substantial commitment and engagement from different faith communities in their local areas.

Those local interfaith initiatives which have developed most effectively, have the following characteristics:

- A strong degree of commitment from several key figures in the main local faith communities

- One or more sensitive and effective "development workers", whether these individuals are carrying out this work on a paid or voluntary basis

- A good deal of time and effort spent on a continuing basis to build up a pattern of effective local interfaith relations and to ensure that there is mainstream and broad based participation, with active involvement from more recently settled communities

- Resourcing from local government or other sources, even if of relatively modest amounts

- A physical centre as a base for their work in the local area

In 1999 the Inter Faith Network published *The Local Inter Faith Guide: Faith Community Cooperation in Action*[169] in association with the Government's Inner Cities Religious Council; a revised edition of which was published in 2005. In 2000, a conference was held exploring the contribution which local authorities are able to make in promoting and supporting the development of interfaith activity in their areas. This led to the publication, in early 2002, of *Faith and Community: a good practice guide for local authorities*[170]. This was produced by the Local Government Association in partnership with the Inter Faith Network and relevant Government departments. It included guidance on engagement with faith communities including partnership working; guidelines on what funding might appropriately be made available to them and on handling planning issues relating to places of worship; and advice on ways to encourage and support local interfaith activity. It is hoped to embark soon on a review and revision of this guidance to take account of more recent experience. The material in this ground breaking document was subsequently drawn upon for inclusion in more general guidance for local authorities for

---

169 Available at http://www.interfaith.org.uk/publications/index.htm

170 Available at http://www.lga.gov.uk

their work as a whole on community cohesion[171].

Both central and local government have been making important contributions in recent years to the development of interfaith activity in the UK. Faith communities are naturally concerned that they should maintain their independence and integrity in this context, while welcoming the support which they receive from Government and the relationship naturally is more likely to be fruitful when it is based on partnership respecting the roles and concerns of each partner. Over the last two years the Government's Faith Communities Capacity Building Fund, administered by the Community Development Foundation, has made grants to faith community and interfaith organisations in England and Wales to strengthen their work. The Government has also set up a new Faith Communities Consultative Council which has brought together previous streams of consultative work. It has an advisory role to the Department for Communities and Local Government.

Local authorities have been increasing significantly their engagement with faith communities in their areas, in some cases providing support for local interfaith structures. In the past, there had been a tendency on the part of many local authorities to steer clear of engagement with faith communities. However, there is now a recognition that strong and broadly based local interfaith structures in towns and cities have an important role to play as part of the community cohesion agenda. Local authorities have also been prompted to develop an interest in partnerships with faith groups, and interfaith structures because of the statutory requirement for them to develop a community strategy and to consult with all groups in their area in doing so.

In the summer of 2006 the Government set up a Commission on Integration and Cohesion which is due to report in the summer of 2007, making recommendations on ways in which cohesion and integration can be promoted, particularly at local level. The Commission has been collecting examples of good practice in this field and these are likely to include a number of interfaith initiatives.

It has been helpful to have an overall policy framework within which these developments have been promoted and encouraged and the Inter Faith Network has played a continuing role in providing advice and guidance to new local interfaith initiatives and in ensuring that there is a sharing of experience and good practice between local interfaith organisations.

In addition to the Northern Ireland Inter Faith Forum, Scottish Inter Faith

---

171 *Guidance on Community Cohesion* and *Community Cohesion – an action guide: guidance for local authorities* are available at http://www.lga.gov.uk

Council and Inter Faith Council for Wales, which promote interfaith work in those parts of the UK, recent years have seen the emergence within England of regional multifaith forums. All of these bodies are in membership of the Network and engage with governmental institutions and public bodies in their geographical areas. Considerable effort goes into ensuring that there are good working relationships between the different organisations involved in promoting interfaith activity at national, regional and local level.

The development of good interfaith relations is a long term task. It presents challenges but also opportunities for enrichment through the contribution which different faith communities are making to the life of their localities. Interfaith relations can promote a broader perspective and a deeper understanding not only of local concerns, but also national and local issues. For interfaith work to be successful there is a need to develop relationships of mutual respect and trust not only at leadership level but among the members of different faith congregations. It involves some searching questions about the kind of society in which we wish to live.

Chapter 8

The relationship between national and local authorities and religious communities in post-communist Russia

Agnieszka Moniak-Azzopardi[*]

[*] Center of studies for Russian, Soviet and post-Soviet world School of superior studies in social sciences – Paris.

Seven years ago, Julia Kristeva wrote in the pages of the newspaper *Le Monde*[172]: "*The desire for intellectual clarity, with its insistence on questioning and criticism, even to the point of doubting not only the deity but also social bonds, contrasts with the Orthodox exaltation of ineffable religious intimacy and of the ecclesiastic community in which that intimacy flourishes*". This exaltation is described as mysterious and even as endowed with a "power" capable of transforming reality. As a result of their historical, traditional and religious Orthodox inheritance, citizens have an uncritical, affective sense of belonging, and transform this into an omnipresent religious ideology. This process, described by Kristeva, embraces the entire sphere of politics in predominantly Orthodox countries, and even leads to a clear identification with the state and the nation, whose sources of Orthodox faith – the concept of the individual, the concept of God and the concept of power, to mention the three most important – combine to form a common base.

The principal features of the current relationship between politics and religion in Russia are to be found in the depths of religion as it has been shaped by history. God, unknowable and unquestionable, who deifies Man and transcends all through his deifying force[173], appears to render all rational analysis impossible, and even sacrilegious. Ultimately, this is the argument invoked by Russians in answer to persistent questions about the nature of Orthodoxy – the dominant religion of the Russian Federation – and about the relationship between it and politics and society. This argument frequently takes the literary form of the famous adage of Tiuchev: "Russia cannot be understood by reason".

However, since the fall of the USSR, Russia has been aspiring to become a democratic country. A variety of political, religious and intellectual commentators have repeatedly used the terms "democracy", "democratisation", and "period of transition"[174] ; and have continually asked: Where is Russia going? Who are we? Where is Russia now[175]? The relationship between politics and religion at both national and local level is

---

172 "Le poids mystérieux de l'orthodoxie", *Le Monde*, 19th June 1999, p. 6.

173 A theological thesis developed by the Eastern Fathers and then renewed and popularised by Saint Gregory Palamas in the 14th century. What is peculiar about Christian dogmas is their irrationality and incomprehensibility: "*Affirming now one thing, now another when both are true is the feature of every good theologian*". This quotation from Saint Gregory Palamas demonstrates awareness of the theology of different levels of being. Antinomies are therefore not to be excluded but integrated into one transcendent whole. Reality is thus exceeded, and logic becomes meta-logic. This expression of faith was regarded as the most authentic in the Orthodox world by the Synod of Constantinople in 1351. Saint Gregory Palamas was able to synthesise the thinking of Saint Athanasius, the Cappadocians and the Areopagians, in which he upheld the traditional distinction between fundamentally unknowable transcendence and the immanent manifestations of divine energy. On Saint Gregory Palamas see: J. Meyendorff, *Introduction à l'étude de Grégoire Palamas*, Paris, Seuil, 1959 and the same author, *Saint Grégoire Palamas et la mystique orthodoxe*, Paris, Seuil, coll. Maîtres spirituels, 1959.

174 In Russian: demokratia, demokratizatsia, perekhodnyi period.

175 In Russian: Kuda idet Rossia? Kto my? Kuda prishla Rossia?

inherent in these questions and the process of emerging from communism and building a new State.

The dissolution of the USSR in December 1991, marks in fact a religious as well as a political turning point. After years of insistence on the ideological monopoly of communism, in which there was no place for religion, perestroika meant that religion could once again return legitimately to the public arena. In 1988, the authorities granted the Orthodox Church undoubted legitimacy. They permitted celebration of the thousandth anniversary of the Baptism of Russia in 988, they returned to the Patriarchate the monastery of Danilovski in Moscow, its official seat, and shortly before this, they had released the believers and priests still imprisoned in the gulags. Finally, on 29th April 1988, Mikhail Gorbachev received Patriarch Pimen (Izvekov) and the members of the Holy Synod in the Kremlin[176]. On 8th April 1988, the newspaper Izvestia published an interview with Patriarch Pimen. On 6-9th June 1988, the Church convoked the local Assembly, which had not met since August 1917. There is no doubt that the year 1988 marked not only the dissolution of the USSR but also a radical shift in the political and religious landscape in Russia.

The Russian Federation, made up of 89 subject entities[177] and over 28,000 local districts, is a country that is so vast and varied in economic, social, religious and political terms[178], that any attempt to define the relationship between its politics and its religion is a huge challenge that is not comparable with any other case study in Europe. It is largely for this reason that we shall emphasise the enormous changes in the national context that have taken place over the last 15 years in the first part of this report. In our description of interfaith relations and the relationship between politics and religion, we shall use regional examples. Let us look first, therefore, at the religious landscape in present-day Russia.

1. The post-Soviet religious landscape in Russia

At the present time, the Russian Orthodox Church of the Moscow Patriarchate is the principal religious community in the country. Almost 80% of Russians claim to be Orthodox, although the number of people practising

---

176 Internal structure of the Patriarchate, the executive authority of the Church, made up of Patriarch Alexis II, 8 permanent members and 6 temporary members. The Holy Synod meets 6-7 times a year for short sessions lasting one or two days. Among its members, Metropolitan Kyril, head of the Department of External Affairs of the Patriarchate, is the most influential and the most widely known in Russian religious and political circles. The temporary members do not play a large role. They are elected for 6 months only and represent the smaller dioceses.

177 21 republics, 6 territories (krai), 50 regions (oblast), 2 cities with federal status (Moscow and Saint Petersburg) and 10 autonomous districts (okrug)

178 There was some political diversity in the early 2000s. As we shall show, this is becoming less and less the case.

that faith does not exceed 6% and may be as low as 2%[179]. The Muslims, who are largely to be found in the border republics and in the south of the Russian Federation, make up between 10% and 15% of the population, according to the sources. Vladimir Zorin, the former Minister of Nationalities, speaks of more than 14 million Muslims, or 10% of the population, while the principal Imams claim between 15 and 20 million Muslims[180]. The Jews, the third religious community in the country, comprised in 2003 0.2% of the population, or 230,000 people, who were generally concentrated in some hundred districts. The number of Buddhists, the fourth community, is even more difficult to quantify. The Buddhist temples in Moscow and St. Petersburg have between 600 and 800 practising adherents and thousands of sympathisers[181]. Catholics, various branches of Protestantism, Evangelical and charismatic churches, and Orthodox churches under the jurisdiction of other patriarchates, account for between 1 and 2% of the population. 23% of Russians state that they are atheists.

All these figures, dating from the recent past or describing the current situation (the latest figures published by the Ministry of Justice date from 1st January 2004) are rather imprecise, but they indicate the existence of over 1,000 different religious communities in Russia. This lack of precision is due, first, to the religious bodies themselves, which do not produce statistics about their own believers. Secondly, it derives from the procedure for registration with the Ministry of Justice, and more specifically, with the Department for the Affairs of Social and Religious Organisations[182]. This registration records the religion, and the number of parish churches, monasteries, educational establishments, etc., but does not take into account internal changes, the exact numbers of believers, or whether the establishments registered are actually functioning. Thirdly, there are many institutions which operate without registration, either by choice or because it is impossible to register for bureaucratic reasons[183], etc. However, although the figures are imprecise, we

---

179 Several statistical sources confirm these figures. For the World Values Surveys, conducted in Russia since 1991, see for example D. Fourman, K. Kaariainen, *Staryie tserkvi i novyie veruiushchie*, St. Petersburg – Moscow, Letnii Sad, 2000. FOM – Fond obshchestvennogo mnenia – http://www.fom.ru, Levada Centre – http://www.levada.ru and Romir – http://www.romir.ru, regularly carry out surveys on the subject. The last figure, 2% of practising believers, comes from surveys carried out each year on Easter night in Orthodox churches in Russia by the police, who count the numbers in the congregations. This is a practice dating back to the time of the Soviet Union. On this subject see: N. Mitrokhin, *Russkaia pravoslavnaia tserkov*, Neprikosnovennyi zapas, Moscow, 2004, p. 41 et seq.

180 Interfaks, 10th November 2003 or Soviet muftiei Rossii, *Islam i musulmane v Rossii*, Moscow, KDT, 1999, pp. 163-165.

181 V. Porekh, "Russkii buddizm kak eto vozmozhno?", *Religia i obshchestvo. Ocherki religioznoi zhizni sovremennoi Rossii*, St. Petersburg – Moscow, Letnii Sad, 2002, p. 398, text pp. 383 –400.

182 Ministerstvo Iustitsii, Upravlenie po delam obshchestvennykh i religioznykh organizatsii.

183 Studies carried out on the ground, by us and by Russian colleagues, show that there is an Evangelical community and a community of Jehovah's Witnesses in every village of at least 1,000 inhabitants. For example G. Gudim – Levkovich, Religioznaia situatsia i konfessionalnaia politika na Russkom Severe (na primere Arkhangelskoi oblasti), *Preodolevaia goudarstvenno-konfessionalnyie otnoshenia*, collected papers, N. Novgorod, published by the Civil Service Academy of the Volga Region, 2003.

can state with certainty that Orthodoxy dominates and shapes the Russian religious landscape since it determines the relationship between politics and religion on account of its historical dominance[184].

It is nonetheless difficult to show with any rigour how the "religious market" has evolved in the Russian Federation. First, there are few figures for Moscow Patriarchate Orthodoxy in the early 1990s, and we have doubts about the reliability of those figures that are available. Furthermore, this period is marked politically by the break-up of the USSR, the emergence of new states and republics where "Moscow" Orthodoxy was and is widely found, and then the gradual spread of conflicts based on religious allegiance. In Ukraine, for example, in 1991, the Russian Church had 5,031 parishes, as against 3,458 in the Russian Socialist Republic. In 2004, it had 10,384 parishes in Ukraine and 10,767 in the Russian Federation. In Ukraine, in fact, the number of Orthodox parishes is far greater because some of the "Moscow" parishes have passed to the jurisdiction of the Patriarchate of Kiev, which was created in 1994. In 2004, the Patriarchate of Kiev stated that it managed 10,310 parishes. Some of the former Orthodox parishes now belong to the Greek Catholics[185] (3,328 parishes in 2004). Between 1991 and 2004, 1,154 parishes joined the Autocephalic Orthodox Church[186]. It is almost impossible to say today how many parishes have been lost by Moscow and exactly what has happened to their former adherents. When we speak of the Moscow Patriarchate, it must always be remembered that it has establishments not only in Russia but also in the Community of Independent States, in Eastern Europe, in China, the United States, Western Europe and elsewhere. However, let us return to the Russian Federation.

In 1991, the Ministry of Justice gave a single figure – 3,451 – for local Orthodox organisations in Russia. By 2004, there were 82 central Orthodox establishments, 10,767 local establishments, 49 educational establishments, 354 monasteries, and 273 other Orthodox establishments[187]. There was therefore a huge explosion in the number of Orthodox religious establishments in Russia between 1991 and 2004. Since then, these figures

---

184 According to the sociologist Danièle Hérvieu-Léger, every state constructs its own model of a relationship with religion, basing this on the specifics of the relationship with the dominant religion. In the case of France, this is Catholicism. See D. Hérvieu-Léger, "L'objet religieux comme objet sociologique: problèmes théoriques et méthodologiques", in J. Joncheray (ed.) Approches scientifiques du fait religieux, Paris, Beauchesne, 1997, pp. 151-157.

185 Known as the "Uniates". These are the Orthodox believers who accepted union with the Church of Rome at the Union of Brest in 1596. They kept their Byzantine rites but accepted the jurisdiction of Rome, the primacy of the Pope, etc.

186 This last church was set up abroad by the diaspora before it was able to re-establish itself in Ukraine. For the figures see N. Boyko, K. Rousselet, "Les Eglises ukrainiennes. Entre Rome, Moscou et Constantinople", Le Courrier des pays de l'Est, No 1045, September-October 2004, pp. 39-50.

187 Mitrokhin, op. cit., p. 72.

have risen by an average of 5% a year[188]. However, the most recent enquiries, particularly those of Nikolai Mitrokhin, show that government statistics are unreliable[189]. Almost 10% of churches do not really function. When an Orthodox newspaper, Pravilo very, tried to distribute free copies in Moscow in 2000, it was only possible to make contact with 280 Orthodox parishes out of the 450 declared. In the regions, the situation is similar because some parish churches are only open for a few days a year. It should be noted that while government and Church figures differed considerably during the Soviet era, they have been practically identical since 1994. The Russian Church predominates on account of the number of communities registered. However, in some regions of Russia, Protestant and Evangelical communities outnumber Orthodox ones. Currently, those regions are Kalmukia, Karelia, Northern Ossetia, Tuva, Khakassia, the regions of Primor and Khabarovsk, Amur, Irkutsk, Kaliningrad, Sakhalin, and two administrative okrugs, Aginski Buriatia and Taimyr. Of the 89 entities making up the Federation, 46 are "Orthodox" according to the data of the Ministry of Justice. In the others, it is Muslim communities that predominate.

Similar changes have occurred in belief and declared allegiance. In December 1988, a study carried out by the Moscow Institute of Social Studies with the involvement of American sociologists, showed that 10% of Muscovites believed in God, 43% were sure that God did not exist, and 7% believed in life after death[190]. In 2002, 59% of Russians said that they believed in God[191]. Yet in 1991, 1996 and 2002, only 6% of Russians still went to church at least once a month[192] and 48% said that they never went and never prayed. At the same time, 79% of those surveyed said that had been baptised. In 1991 and 1993, 80% of Russians said that they were Orthodox. In 1996, 91% of them said the same thing. In 2006, 76% of Russians said that they were Orthodox, 8% Muslim, and 1% Buddhist, while the other groups did not exceed 1%. 11% of Russians stated that they had no religion[193]. Our own enquiries and interviews carried out at the State University in Tver, in October-November 2003, confirm this trend. Of the 127 students surveyed, 85 were Orthodox, 2 were atheist and 5 belonged to other faiths. The level of practice was as low as that of the population as a whole.

---

188 This is an estimate based on figures supplied by the Patriarchate during the Christmas Readings, an annual meeting bringing together the hierarchy, politicians and others in Moscow, http://www.mospat.ru

189 N. Mitrokhin, Russkaia…, op. cit., p. 69.

190 V. Marinov, "Tri voprosa o religii", Nauka i religia, No 7, 1989, pp. 18-19.

191 Author's interview with D. Fourman, author of the World Values Surveys in Russia, Moscow, 25th October 2002.

192 D. Fourman, K. Kaariainen, op.cit., p. 110.

193 http://www.fom.ru, 11-12th February 2006.

The structure of the Russian Church has also changed greatly now that there is freedom of conscience. The Patriarchate was established first of all after the synodal period[194] in 1917 but abolished by the communists. It was then re-established by Stalin in 1943. The Patriarch "leads" the Autocephalic Church in council with all its members[195]. This refers to the councils which play a prime role in decisions concerning the Church. The way in which it operates has nevertheless been severely criticised recently. Many of those within the hierarchy, and experts on these issues in Russia[196], say that power within the Russian Church is becoming increasingly centralised. Councils are being held less often and take place quickly, without preparation, with no time for discussion, etc. The executive power of the Institution[197], the Patriarch Alexis II Ridiger, the Holy Synod[198], the Directorate of Affairs[199] and the synodal departments take decisions instead of the councils.

During the Soviet era, the Russian Church had 3 synodal departments: external affairs, publishing and science. Since 1991, the Patriarchate has set up the Department of Social Service and Charitable Works, headed by the Metropolitan of Voronezh, Sergei (Fomin), the Department for Relations with the Army and the Organs of Justice, headed by protoerei[200] Dmitri (Smirnov), the Department of Religious Education and Catechesis, headed by Archimandrite[201] Ioann (Ekonomtsev), the Missionary Department headed by the Archbishop of Belgorod, Ioann (Popov), and lastly the Department of Youth Affairs headed by the Archbishop of Kostroma, Alexander (Mogilev). The Holy Synod also has a number of committees which did not exist during the communist era, notably the theological committee, the financial committee, etc.

All these govern the Church, which is divided administratively and geographically into dioceses (eparkhia). Each diocese covers the territory of an oblast. At the head of a diocese is the bishop, who appoints the priests – blagochinnyi, who are responsible for the parish churches. There is no Ecclesiastical Court within the Russian Church, although there is constant discussion of the need to create one.

---

194 Period which began in 1721 with Peter the Great's reforms of the Russian Church, which was subject to the political authorities until 1917.

195 All the Orthodox patriarchs recognise the supremacy of the Ecumenical Patriarch of Constantinople.

196 For example Bishop Veniamin Pushkar of Vladivostok, Father Benjamin Novik of St.Petersburg and Nikolai Mitrokhin, who is quoted here.

197 We use this sociological term to denote the Russian Orthodox Church.

198 Sviashchennyi sinod.

199 Upravlenie delami.

200 A parish priest is a member of the "white" clergy, as distinct from the "black" clergy, who belong to the monasteries.

201 Title of the head of a monastery, second (middle) tier of the ecclesiastical hierarchy, and a title sometimes given to a monk for exceptional or meritorious acts.

Other faiths, listed above, also have specific structures that have evolved since the fall of the communist regime. The Russian Muslims, the majority of whom are Sunni, are divided into a number of communities, the three largest of which are:

- the Central Directorate of Russian Muslims headed by Mufti Talgat Tajuddin – this is the oldest body and existed "quasi" legally during the Soviet era;

- the Spiritual Directorate of Russian Muslims of Ravil Gainutdin, who is also the President of the Council of Russian Muftis, a body set up on 2nd July 1996 (this directorate currently has more than 40 regional directorates);

- and the Co-ordination Centre for the Muslims of the Northern Caucasus, headed by Mufti Ismail Berdiev, who has a high media profile, which should also be mentioned.

The Directorate of Ravil Gainutdin, although younger, covers around 49% of the Muslim communities, compared with 25.2% for Talgat Tajuddin[202].

The Buddhists have had their own Spiritual Directorate since 1922. This changed its name in 1996 and became the Russian Traditional Buddhist Sangha. This organisation is headed by Pandida Khambo Lama-Damba Aiucheev, who represents this community in Russia. In a further schism in 1998, the Central Spiritual Directorate of Buddhists split away from the Russian Traditional Buddhist Sangha.

The Jews, who have been living in Russian territory since the 1st century (according to archaeological research on the Black Sea), were persecuted during the Soviet era. Anti-Semitic campaigns took place just after the 2nd World War, and then in 1960-1961 during Krushchev's anti-religion campaign, when the synagogues were shut down completely and most rabbis were forced to emigrate. It is only the fall of the communist regime that has made it possible for Jewish institutions to be slowly rebuilt. The Jewish community is currently divided into the Congress of Jewish Religious Communities in Russia and the Federation of Jewish Communities in Russia. Adolf Shaevich is the President of the Congress. Berl Lazar is the President of the Federation and the principal rabbi of Russia, elected by the Federation alone in 2000[203].

The Christian denominations present in Russia have also modified their institutions. In February 2002, the Catholic Church set up 4 dioceses in

---

202 O. Nedumov, M. Smirnov, "Oshibka prezidenta ili tonkii raschet", Nezavisimaia Gazeta, 15th January 2003.

203 See A. Moniak-Azzopardi, "Pouvoir religieux et pouvoir politique", Pouvoirs, No. 112, January 2005, pp. 93- 110.

place of the Catholic administrations. Since the early 1990s, the number of these administrations had grown. The Seventh Day Adventist, Baptist and Pentecostalist churches are now registered, which was generally not the case under the Soviet regime. They are currently grouped into the Communities of Christians of the Evangelical Faith, and the Communities of Evangelical-Baptist Churches. The Lutheran and Anglican Churches have their own institutions that are independent of the other Protestants.

It should be stressed that it was the fall of communism that made possible this expansion of religious faith groups, which were legalised when freedom of conscience was introduced. Religious plurality, equality and freedom were thereby established, and they appear to be observed in the Russian Federation. A brief look at interfaith relations and the relationship between the political and religious authorities during the post-Soviet period will reveal the complexity of the issue, however, in which there are many subtle distinctions.

2. Interfaith relations

While interfaith relations were very limited during the Soviet era within the territory of the USSR, it was during that time that the Russian Orthodox Church joined the World Council of Churches, in 1961, and the Conference of European Churches (KEK). Patriarch Alexis II was the President of the latter throughout the 1990s. Since the fall of communism, the hierarchy of the Russian Orthodox Church has increasingly frequently expressed its fears about belonging to ecumenical movements. These primarily concern the possible "dissolution" of Orthodox truths and the weakening of Orthodoxy in the world. These "official" fears hide the internal divisions within Russian Orthodoxy. Powerful conservative currents within the Moscow Partiarchate are opposed to ecumenism.

Within Russia, the issue of interfaith relations is more complex, being governed by a number of parameters. First, there is the legal aspect, and the division of faiths into various categories. Then, there are the relations that the faiths have established with the political authorities (under Yeltsin and now Putin) and with the local authorities. These two factors affect the social perception of religions and thus ultimately the relations between faiths at the national and local level.

According to opinion polls, 70% of Russians thought in 1996 that all religions should have the same rights, and as many as 77% of the inhabitants of Moscow took this position[204], but a year later, the Russian Parliament, the Duma, passed a law on freedom of conscience which posed a threat to this equality. Local authorities in the regions had begun adopting laws against "Western spiritual expansion" well before that date, and by 1997, there were a score of regional laws restricting freedom of conscience. These laws often had no effect, such as the one adopted in May 1995 in the Kostroma Region ("Measures to strengthen control of respect for the law and for religious faiths") which gave the police powers to put a stop to the activities of foreign missionaries. This was never implemented[205].

Since 1993, Russian parliamentarians and religious leaders have been engaged in drafting a new law on freedom of conscience to replace the law passed in 1990 that is said to be "too liberal". The 1997 law, passed on 19th September 1997, divides religious faiths into organisations and groups, and affirms the primacy of Orthodoxy and the traditional religions: Islam, Judaism, Buddhism and Christianity. The last of these is oddly dissociated from Orthodoxy, which is nonetheless part of it. There are a number of reasons for this, seen most clearly in interfaith dialogue. Over the years, the Orthodox hierarchy has played on its closeness to the political authorities, which can be seen in the exchanges of letters and various documents, in meetings, etc., and has forcefully supported the new law[206]. The United States Congress, the Vatican, and most of the organisations defending human rights have protested against the adoption of this law[207]. Criticism has been levelled in particular at the distinction drawn between organisations, which have greater rights, and groups, with the accusation that this is a serious breach of the December 1993 Constitution of the Russian Federation and of international conventions signed by Russia[208]. This law, which is still in force, is not the only factor governing the growth of interfaith relations in Russia. At the official level, the closeness between the Orthodox hierarchy and the national

---

204 K. Kaariainen, *Religion in Russia after the collapse of communism*, The Edwin Mellen Press, New York,1998, p. 143

205 E. Mikhailov, "Religioznaia situatsiia v provintsii. Kostromskaia i Ivanovskaia oblasti", *Russkaia mysl*, 17-23rd September 1998.

206 Many publications report on this. For example: A.Verkhovski (V. Pribilovski, E. Mikhailovskaia), *Politicheskaia ksenofobia*, Panorama, Moscow, 1999, p. 80 et seq; M. Elliott, S. Corrado, "The 1997 Russian Law on Religion: the Impact on Protestants", *Religion, State and Society*, No 1, 1999, p. 109-134; M. Bordeaux, "Religion Reviews in all its Variety: Russia's Regions Today", *Religion, State and Society*, Vol 28, No 1, 2000, p.11 and seq.

207 M. Shevchenko, S. Startsev, "Novyi zakon o svobode sovesti i veroispovedania stanovitsia predmetom politicheskogo tolka. Vatikan i kongres SSCHA, khotia i po raznym prichinam predostregaiut Borisa Eltsina ot ego podpisania", *Nezavisimia Gazeta*, 19th July, 1997, p. 1.

208 This relates more exactly to Articles 19 and 28 of the Constitution on rights relating to the unfettered exercise of religion, to Article 14 which stipulates equality, and Article 35 which guarantees the right to private property, of which religious groups were deprived under the 1997 law. The conflict of legislation also relates to the International Convention on Political and Civil Rights and the European Convention for the Protection of Human Rights and Fundamental Freedoms. The Universal Declaration of Human Rights was only ratified by Russia in 1998.

and local political authorities, to which we shall return, strongly influences dialogue and conflicts between religions. In practice, most politicians claim to be Orthodox, so that they uphold it, at least officially, against other denominations. The Russian Church generally has no hesitation in calling on the support of political leaders when conflicts arise.

2a. Orthodox-Catholic relations

The relationship with the Catholics embodies the full impact of this dependency. From the outset, dialogue was very difficult and principally concerned the question of the Greek Catholics. In 1987, the committee on dialogue between the Orthodox and Catholic Churches, meeting in Bari, decided to set up a special commission to examine the Uniate question. On 21st January 1990, John Paul II sent a delegation to Moscow to discuss the same issue. These meetings, conferences and declarations became more numerous throughout the 1990s and beyond, but without producing answers that were sufficiently definitive or legitimate for the question to be considered resolved.

The declared hostility towards Catholics began in the early 1990s, at all levels of the ecclesiastical hierarchy. In summer 1991, for example, Alexis II criticised the expansion of the Roman Catholic Church in Russia. During his visit to Novosibirsk, he told the press and the members of the regional parliament that there was: "a serious danger that Catholicism may penetrate into the heart of the Orthodox country"[209]. In October of the same year, the Russian Church refused to take part in the Synod of European Bishops. For its part, the Vatican set up a special "Pro Russia" commission in 1930, to deal with Russian questions. Since the early 1990s, this commission has pursued its task actively, putting forward a programme of "General principles and practical rules to co-ordinate evangelism and ecumenical engagement of the Catholic Church in Russia and the countries of the CIS". However, the Russian Patriarch has regularly criticised the fact that "the Catholic Church does not inform the Orthodox Church of the appointment of new priests, monks..."[210]. The Catholic Church has continued to expand its work on the ground with grand projects such as building a cathedral in Novosibirsk. Mgr Werth stressed the importance of this act following the destruction of the Catholic cathedral in that city in the 1960s. The Russian Church does not see the matter in the same way: "Catholic expansion on the canonical territory of the Russian Orthodox Church... All this seems inconsequential at first [...] children are approached under the cover of humanitarian aid,

---

209 *Irénikon*, 1991, p. 423.

210 For example, at the meeting with the Verona delegation in Moscow, on 29th September 1995, *Irénikon*, 1995, pp. 426-427.

then the parents, and then catechisation begins, and that is how the heart of Russia is being converted to Catholicism"[211]. The mutual hostility between Orthodoxy and Catholicism is such that the Patriarch of Russia is the only Orthodox patriarch who has never met the Pope, even though statements about the possibility of such a visit have been repeated constantly. A meeting was to have been held outside Vienna in 1996, but it was cancelled at a few days' notice. Moreover, the Russian heads of state Mikhail Gorbachev, Boris Yeltsin and Vladimir Putin, each in turn repeatedly invited Pope John Paul II to Russia, but without result. Each visit to the countries of the CIS, such as Ukraine in June 2001, has brought to the surface the pro- and anti-Western positions that have been tearing Ukraine apart since the collapse of the USSR. The reactions to the papal visit need to be seen in this geopolitical context. It should be remembered that the Pope was not invited by the Orthodox Church but by President Kuchma. On the Russian side, the visit of the Pope was interpreted as a political gesture aimed directly against Russia. Russian television devoted to it an edition of the programme *The House of Russia*, which is renowned for its conservative stance: viewers saw Alexis II explaining his refusal to meet the Pope and accusing Ukraine and its President of "high treason". The President of the Union of Orthodox Citizens stated that the Catholic Church was trying to worsen relations between Ukraine, Belorussia and Russia: "the Catholics and their collaborators are launching a powerful attack to stamp out Holy Orthodoxy in Kievan Russia so as to completely separate Ukraine, which has the same faith and the same blood, from Russia. If their plans come to fruition, Uniate Ukraine will become a new Croatia and a "Trojan horse" among the Eastern Slavs[212]".

The most recent major crisis between the Russian Church and the Catholic Church broke out on 12th February 2002 following the establishment of dioceses by Pope John Paul II on Russian territory. According to Catholic canon law, the dioceses replaced administrations which were merely temporary. The Vatican informed the Ministry of Justice of the change, but not the Russian Church. The reaction on the Russian side was quite violent. Vladimir Zhirinovski, leader of the Liberal Democratic Party (which is right-wing despite the name), took part in the debate. On 15th February, he put forward in the Duma a proposal that the Ministry of Foreign Affairs should "not grant visas to the representatives of the Vatican because of the worsening of the situation and the actions undertaken without authorisation concerning the change of status of the Catholic bishoprics"[213]. The Duma

---

211 Statement by Alexis II during the annual Assembly of the Moscow Clergy, 21st December 1995, *SOP*, January 1996, *Irénikon*, 1995, pp. 560-562.

212 V.V. Lebedev, "Mirnaia pravoslavnaia intifada", *NG-religii*, 14th June 2001.

213 Duma rekomenduiut MID-u ne davat viz predstaviteliam Vatikana, http://www.polit.ru, 15th February 2002.

adopted this proposal. And in 2002, four Catholic priests and a bishop, Jerzy Mazur, were barred from entering Russia. At the local level, we also found widespread incomprehension and hostility. In December 2003, in Nijnii Novgorod, the local authorities upheld Orthodox objections to the opening of a Catholic nunnery. The mayor of the city, Vadim Bulianov, sent mechanical diggers to prevent the nuns from establishing themselves and threatened to destroy their building. Two other examples come from the city of Moscow. In the early 1990s, the Catholic Community of the Beatitudes (French branch) opened an ecumenical apartment right in the city centre. An Orthodox Russian family lived there with two Catholic nuns. Several times a week, they organised prayer evenings between Christians, Jews and others in the chapel of the apartment. The nuns had to leave in 1998 following threats from neighbours and from the district authorities. The Orthodox couple had already been threatened with expulsion three times for reasons never clearly identified as religious.

Similarly, the Catholics opened a charity centre in Moscow in 1992 for drug-takers and the homeless. In November 2004, when we visited, they told us that following pressure, their bank account had been blocked and their activities virtually brought to a halt. Moreover, the Moscow City Government had accused them of "illegal purchase of premises". The purchase, made in 1992, was regarded as legal at the time[214].

2b. Orthodox-Protestant relations

Relations with the other Christian communities are also very difficult. First, the so-called schismatic Orthodox Churches (Old Believers, Russian Orthodox Church Outside Russia, the Orthodox Churches of the Catacombs) are in conflict with the Moscow Patriarchate. Each of these churches claims to embody Orthodox truth. Dialogue between them continues, but with the exception of the Russian Orthodox Church Outside of Russia, it is not leading to any resolution of the discord.

Relations between Orthodoxy and other Christians should ideally be a relationship of dialogue, given the closeness of their faiths. Not so – while the Russian Church tolerates the Lutheran and Anglican communities, basing its attitude on the link between ethnic and religious allegiance, it is very hostile to Evangelical Churches and new religious movements. The campaign inspired by Protestants known as the "Volga Mission 1992" was intended to bring together the Russian Orthodox Church, which initially agreed, and Western missionaries. The Russian Church then withdrew on 10th December 1992, and Metropolitan Kyril received Pastor Markku Happonen, Director of Mission

---

214 Our discussions with the sisters of the House of Mary, author's archive.

Volga, to stress the failure of the enterprise. He referred to the "ambiguous consequences of Mission Volga for the internal life of our Church and for the different faiths in Russia", apparent from the placards put in Kazan – "Protestant colonists go home", "You're a thousand years too late", "Our faith is the only true faith"[215].

Meetings between the Orthodox hierarchy and Protestant bodies on Russian soil almost always produce the same communiqués on the part of the Orthodox, who say that relations are deteriorating because of the arrival of huge numbers not only of Protestant organisations but also of pseudo-religious, Evangelical and even sectarian bodies[216]. However, in the early 1990s, the Russian state signed agreements with the Evangelical Churches and their missions, which were even allowed freely into state schools before a stop was put to the trend by the Orthodox Church's powerful influence.

Russian Orthodoxy constantly complains that they are "not traditional" in Russia and use proselytising methods. This is said, for example, by Father Vladimir Fedorov of the Theological Academy of Saint Petersburg, who has worked with these "other" forms of Christianity[217]. Such collaboration takes place almost exclusively in the area of charity: the Orthodox hierarchy is not opposed to financial aid from Evangelical Churches.

The climate in which Protestant and Evangelical denominations operate in Russia is such that they are looking to acquire some "Russian identity". This may appear paradoxical, but a considerable number of religious organisations claim an Orthodox tradition. For example, the Evangelical Christian Mission of Krasnodar includes Saint Sergei of Radonezh and Father Alexander Men in its community's history. The Russian Evangelical Church, headed by Yevgeni Nedzelski in Saint Petersburg, uses Orthodox elements of the liturgy such as icons, chants and candles. The "Slovo" Christian bookshop in St. Petersburg, although functioning thanks to Protestant funds, arranges meetings for Orthodox believers on "Orthodox" topics[218]. At the same time, Evangelical religious organisations are becoming increasingly centralised. In February 2002, the Russian Union of Christians of Pentecostalist Evangelical Faith, the Russian Union of Evangelical Baptist Christians and the Western Russian Union of the Church of Seventh Day Adventists set up a Consultative Council of the leaders of the Protestant Churches in Russia.

---

215 *Irénikon*, 1993, p. 126.

216 See for example, the meeting between Alexis II and the heads of the Union of Baptist Evangelical Christians, 3rd November 1992, *Irénikon*, 1993, pp. 124-125.

217 L. Chipkova, "Une vie consacrée à l'unité des chrétiens", *Unité des chrétiens*, No 117, January 2000, pp. 22-23.

218 The examples are drawn from: M. Bourdeaux, S. Filatov, Sovremennaia…, op. cit., p. 155; K. Rousselet, "La nébuleuse évangélique en Russie", *Critique internationale*, No 22, 01, 2004, pp. 125-138; author's archives and interviews, St. Petersburg, June 2002 and November 2003.

Cases of persecution of denominations with a Protestant background are quite frequent, and regular complaints are made by the Sova Centre in Russia and the Keston Institute abroad. These attacks take the form of speeches, refusals of registration, deliberately misleading items in the press and even arbitrary arrests and criminal prosecution. This happened, for example, to a small Baptist community in the Siberian region of Khanty-Mansiysk. The local police, an Orthodox priest and the teachers in the state school decided arbitrarily to forbid the activities of the community. A Baptist missionary in the Ugut region, Dmitri Mannikov, was summoned to the police station a number of times for interrogation without being told the reason and without charge[219]. A similar affair occurred in the town of Talitsa in the district of Sverdlovsk, where newspapers such as Pravoslavnaia Gazeta accused the Baptists of missionary activity at their place of work, in schools and elsewhere. The Ekaterinburg telephone directory lists all Baptist places of worship under the heading "pseudo-Evangelical sects", and this same description is also used on several websites[220].

2c. Orthodox-Muslim relations

The best interfaith relations in Russia have been established between Moscow Orthodoxy and so-called "traditional" Islam. The first half of the 1990s was characterised by the establishment of good relations between the Russian Orthodox Church and the Muslims. The Orthodox hierarchy recognised the "specific" place of Islam and did not criticise it openly. The situation became far more complicated when the first Chechen war broke out and then after the terrorist attacks and the second war in Chechnya. However, we need to realise that this relationship between Orthodoxy and Islam is complex and not homogeneous. As in the case of the Jews and the Catholics, relations with the Muslim communities are dominated by a certain geopolitical vision that is shared by both religious leaders and politicians. The Sunni clergy are the ideal partners for the Orthodox Church. They agree over the division of their "spheres of influence" and over the absence of missionary activity among "their" respective peoples. In the regions of the Russian Federation where the majority of the inhabitants are Orthodox, the hierarchy of the Russian Church finds it difficult to accept the existence of Muslims. Officially, all is well, and Islam is recognised as the second religion of Russia, but Orthodox bishops often take the initiative in this field. This is what happened in Yaroslav, Vologda and Petrozavodsk. In February 2003, Mufti Ravil Gainutdin told the newspaper Nezavisimaia Gazeta religii that the authorities in Stavropol had refused to restore to the Muslims the mosque

219 http://www.keston.org, News Service, 2nd April 2002.

220 G. Fagan, "Court Agrees that Baptist Church Breaks Up Families", 15th March 2002, http://www.keston.org,

built before the Revolution. In towns near Moscow, Muslims are not allowed to build mosques because of protests from Orthodox bishops[221]. Such occurrences have become increasingly frequent since Putin came to power and, we believe, demonstrate the tight control exercised by the State over the activities of religious communities: while it may be Orthodox bishops who protest, it is the regional authorities that take the decisions. The first war in Chechnya was condemned by all religious leaders equally. Until 1999, when Putin began the second war, the Orthodox Church was engaged in charitable relief for refugees living in the camps in Ingushetia and Dagestan. The attacks of August and September 1999, 11th September in New York and then the taking of hostages at the Dubrovka in Moscow and in Beslan produced deep anti-Islamist resentment, however, and helped to create the view that " Muslims are extremists". If we are to believe the Russian media, the official view of the Church is that the Islam represented by the Chechen separatists is not true Islam but a sectarian movement that poses a particular danger to Russia and the world in general. The Patriarch himself has said: "I am completely opposed to the use of the term "Islamic extremism", because that is akin to saying "Orthodox" or "Christian extremism"[222]. Other religious figures are less circumspect. The newspaper *Izvestia* published an article by Deacon Andrei Kuraev a few days after the hostage-taking at the Dubrovka[223]. The article argues that the ethnic element is far more important than the religious, and that it is this ethnic element that makes certain nations into terrorists, who need to be fought because there is no alternative. It is the Chechens who are obviously meant. Such opinions are becoming increasingly widespread in both political and religious circles. On 10th September 2004, just after the hostage-taking in Beslan, the Interfaith Council of the CIS[224], which brings together various religious leaders in its ranks, called the physical liquidation of all Chechen terrorists "a just action not forbidden by traditional religions"[225]. The Russian Orthodox Church has made no protest against such simplistic urgings since the hostage-taking at the Dubrovka in Moscow. Even the Orthodox hierarchy seems not to take any exception to an ethnic view of religious allegiance.

Orthodox leaders are distancing themselves from dialogue even at the highest level. Metropolitan Kyril has said openly: "We must forget the term "multifaith country": Russia is an Orthodox country with national and

---

221 O. Nedumov, "Musulmane spasaiut imidj strany" interview with R. Gainutdin, *NG-religii*, 19th February 2003.

222 "Katolicheskaia ekspansia v Rossii", interview with Alexis II, *Radonezh*, 1999, #19-20.

223 "Kak borotszha s terrorizmom bez spetsnaza", *Izvestiia*, 14th November 2002.

224 Organisation founded in 2001. It did not meet until 10th September 2004. This "latest" meeting was convened by Putin.

225 http://www.religion.sova-center.ru/events/13B74CE/14C8529/41D9B54?print=on

religious minorities"[226]. Relations with the Jews are also marked by evidence of hostility and mutual misunderstanding. Many priests told us that there can be no understanding between the Orthodox and the Jews[227]. Patriarch Alexis II began his work at the head of the Russian Church by putting forward the opposite view in December 1991 in New York, where he declared: "Your prophets are our prophets. For the richness of Christianity includes within it both Judaism and the richness of Judaism – that is Christianity". Reactions were immediate. One group of priests sent the Patriarch an open letter in which they said: "You do not know how many misfortunes the "heresy of the Judaicists" has brought upon Russia"[228]. Accusations continued to be levelled against the Patriarch until 1996. Since making that statement, Alexis II has said nothing more about the Jews.

3. Political and religious authorities: some features of how they operate

3a. Searching for an organisational model

We have already seen, in the context of interfaith relations, that local and regional State authorities influence the religious authorities, and that these in turn, especially Russian Orthodoxy, influence the actions of the State.

Each State institution has its own committee or commission responsible for religious affairs. During the Soviet period, the Patriarchate of the Russian Church was subject to the Council for the Affairs of the Russian Orthodox Church (*Sovet po delam russkoi pravoslavnoi tserkvi*), which reported to the Council of Ministers of the USSR. In 1966, the Council was replaced by the Council for Religious Affairs (*Sovet po delam religii*), which is responsible for all religions. In December 1993, the Russian Parliament, the Duma, set up a Committee for Religious Associations and Organisations for the first time[229]. The committee established a Council of Experts composed of representatives of the traditional religions. The committee is chaired by Sergei Popov, of the Edinaia Rossia Party, and his deputy for most of the last 10 years has been Alexander Tchuiev, the leader of the Russian Christian Democratic Party, which is currently a member of the Rodina Patriotic Bloc. The Government has

---

226 "Rossia pravoslavnaia a ne mnogokonfessionalnaia strana", *Radonezh*, No 8, 2002.

227 For example, Father Alexander Chistiakov of the parish of Bogoroditsy vsekh skorbiashchikh radost, Shpalernaia Street 35, in St. Petersburg.

228 http://www.russian-orthodox-church.org.ru

229 Komitet po delam oshchestvennykh obedineni i religioznykh organizatsii.

its own commission working on issues relating to religious organisations[230]. This was set up by a decree dated 5th May 1994, and brings together representatives of the main ministries, the Presidential Administration and the faith communities. It is chaired by First Deputy Prime Minister Dmitri Medvedev[231]. Branches of the commission operate in each constituent part of the Federation (regions, districts, etc.). In February 2006, the Council of the Federation put a single commission in charge of national policy and relations between the State and religious organisations[232]. Religious leaders were invited to the commission's meetings. The President of the Russian Federation also has a council working on relations with religious organisations. This is chaired by Dmitri Medvedev, who is head of the Presidential Administration, and it is made up of religious leaders. The Orthodox Church is widely represented. The Jews, for example, have a single representative, Berl Lazar, Rabbi Adolf Shaevich having been stripped of his seat on the council just a few months after Putin came to power. The Baptists are not represented either, despite their large numbers. This council was set up by decree under Yeltsin on 24th April 1995[233]. There is also a Council for Interfaith Dialogue in the CIS, the Community of Independent States.

The upper chamber of the Russian Parliament, made up of governors and heads of regions between 1993 and 2002, used to defend the interests of the Church directly at the regional level. In February 2002, the Vice President of the Missionary Department of the Church, Higumen Filip Simonov, became adviser to the Vice President of the Federation, Valerii Goregliad[234]. Goregliad several times roundly criticised the presence of other faiths in Russia, especially the Catholics. A number of businesspeople, such as S. Pugachev in the Tuva region, belong to the council and stress their closeness to the Moscow Patriarchate. However, the role of the Council of the Federation is constantly weakening, and this chamber of Parliament now has practically no power.

Since the fall of the communist regime, city governments have set up their own expert committees or councils on religious affairs. In Ekaterinburg, for example, there is a municipal department comprising five staff, while in Novgorod just one person at the Ministry of Justice takes care of the registration of communities.

---

230 Komissia povoprosam religioznykh obedinenii.

231 http://religion.sova-center.ru/events/13B7354/1431015/74B0A5B – the exact list of current members.

232 Kommissia po natsionalnoi politike i otnosheniam mezhdu gosudarstvom i religioznymi obedineniami.

233 On this topic, A. Ignatev, "S kem sovetuetsa Poutin", *Nezavisimaia Gazeta*, 18th February 2004, http://religion.ng.ru/facts/2004-02-18/2_putin.html

234 D. Shchipkov, "My ne begaem s krestom ni v mechet ni v sinagogu", *Nezavisimaia gazeta*, 17th July 2002.

Since the 1997 law was passed, the closeness between the Orthodox hierarchy and the national and local political authorities in Russia has created a situation that makes it easier for the former to interfere in the legislative process, to the detriment of other faiths. From the start of Putin's first term of office, A.Chuiev, Vice-President of the Parliamentary Committee for Religious Affairs, and various other members of the Putin administration have been pushing the idea of revising the 1997 law, which they regard as still too liberal. They are supported by the Orthodox hierarchy. Simultaneously, defenders of human rights, notably Oleg Mironov, the Russian Federation officer responsible for this field, have launched another campaign against the 1997 law. Talk of "security" appears to be the common factor among the first group. The notion of security and of the spiritual security of Russia have played an important role in Russia since 1996. In 1997, Yeltsin signed a national security plan in which the term spiritual and Orthodox security appeared. However, although Putin signed a document in January 2000 which read: "it is necessary to resist the negative influence of religious organisations and foreign missionaries", the national security plan passed by Parliament a few months later did not contain any such assertion.

Nevertheless, politicians are continually looking for a doctrine that they think can govern relations between the State and religion in Russia. This quest takes different forms, but above all it demonstrates the lack of policy on religion in the Russian Federation. This is true not only in dialogue between politics and religion, but also in specific contexts such as public education, teaching the "Foundations of Orthodox Culture"[235], and rebuilding and funding churches.

On 5th June 2001, the main section of the Ministry of Justice of the Russian Federation published a proposed doctrine[236] setting out the background to State policy in the sphere of religion. The authors of this proposal, Vladimir Zhbankov and Igor Ponkin, suggested introducing strict regulation of religions and giving full legitimacy to "traditional" religions defined by three criteria: the number of adherents, the part played historically in the development of the country, and current activities. Three days after this was published, another proposal was published by the Russian Civil Service Academy (Akademia gosudarstvennoi sluzhby) on the same website. Nikolai Trofimchuk[237], its principal author, suggested introducing a new law to govern the status of traditional religions. Since 2001, a multitude of other proposals of this type have been published. To our knowledge, three have been published by

---

235 A teaching subject that the Russian Orthodox Church is trying to introduce into State schools. We shall come back to this.

236 http://www.state-religion.ru, No 1270 htm.

237 Died 10th April 2002.

Member of the Duma A. Chuiev alone. Reading all these proposals gives an impression of general confusion. In practice, although Russia recognises the supremacy of international legislation over its own laws, it cannot find suitable models for the relationship between State and Church. Nor does the Russian Constitution go into this issue in any detail. It merely provides guarantees about freedom of conscience, equality and separation between religion and politics. It is therefore not inappropriate in this context to wonder whether exploring the very notion of Church-State relations on Russian soil is purposeful, necessary or relevant. Is it evidence of Russian peculiarities in this field, or does it reflect other phenomena, other shortcomings that are glimpsed indirectly? Might it not be preferable, as is done in other democratic countries, to base this kind of relationship on legislation common to all non-profit organisations and associations in order to avoid the risk of government favouritism or denominationalism? These are open questions, to which we cannot provide answers because these processes are still ongoing.

We note, however, that all these proposals tend to impose by force a traditional, correct religion – Orthodoxy – and a system of traditional values that is nonetheless not spelt out. This follows the argument put forward in the 1997 legislation while considerably strengthening the Orthodox angle. The proposals also contain a few practical resolutions relating to a system of legal supervision of the rightness of beliefs and faith. The desire to create a federal body to oversee all religious affairs is clearly expressed in them.

3b. Central place of Orthodoxy

At the same time, political leaders in Russia maintain direct and quite close contact with the religious hierarchy. First, the two meet twice a year at the World Assembly of the Russian People[238] and at the Christmas Readings[239]. Some of these meetings bring together the President of the Federation, government ministers, party leaders, the hierarchy and the patriarch, and each legislative and presidential campaign has been marked by the closeness between the two authorities, their meetings and their pronouncements. Orthodoxy is manifestly the "favourite" in these arrangements. President Putin frequently makes statements in its favour. On 6th January 2002, for example, Christmas Eve: "Orthodoxy, which has occupied a special place in the history of Russia, continues to play an important role in maintaining the moral foundations of public life... The Orthodox Church, in close co-operation with the representatives of other traditional religions and faiths, is making considerable efforts to strengthen the spiritual health of our citizens by

---

238 Vsemirnyi russki narodnyi sobor, an organisation set up by the leaders of political parties of all persuasions, including the Democrats, who joined in 2000. It has been chaired by Patriarch Alexis II since 1995.

239 Rozhdestvennye chtenia, always in mid-December, otherwise knows as the Annual Assembly of the Moscow Clergy.

teaching patriotism... this activity deserves the greatest respect and support on the part of the state"[240]. On 20th September 2003, at the conference of his party "Edinaia Rossia", Putin called on members to "remember that 90% of Russians are Orthodox". Putin's religiosity has aroused much interest ever since the start of his presidency. Patriarch Alexis II said in 2002: "Vladimir Putin is a very good person, a profoundly honest man. He has no problem with his religious convictions because he was baptised as a child. His wife, Ludmila, is a true believer and their two daughters likewise. Theirs is a fine Christian family! ..."[241]. Alexis II was present, as the only religious representative, when the television cameras showed the hand-over of power from Boris Yeltsin to Vladimir Putin on 31st December 1999. The presidential campaign of 2000 gave prominence to the Orthodox hierarchy, especially Metropolitan Kyril, who worked closely with German Gref, the mastermind of the presidential campaign and current Minister of Finance. A similar scenario was played out in March 2004. Putin remains, however, very diplomatic. When opening the World Assembly of the Russian People in December 2001 he stated: "Russia has always been a country of a multitude of independent national cultures and beliefs. Russia has united and unites the nations of Europe and Asia, Orthodoxy and Islam, Buddhism and Judaism"[242]. Similarly, at the end of May 2004, the President said when greeting Muslims on the day of the centenary of the Moscow mosque: "I should like to assure you that we, the representatives of the state, being answerable to religious bodies – Muslims, Christians and representatives of other faiths – are going to support you in every way possible"[243]. Noticeably, however, that support has been extremely circumscribed.

Russia does not have many political parties that could be described as "Christian". The celebrations to mark the millennium of the Baptism of Russia saw formation of the first Christian party in Russia – the "Christian Democrat Assembly of Russia"[244] – led by Valerii Borshchev, Alexander Ogorodnikov and Alexander Chuiev. This party fell apart quite quickly. Chuiev left the Assembly in 1990 and founded the Russian Christian Democratic Party[245], which still exists but as a component of the Rodina Bloc, which won 9% of the parliamentary seats in the 2003 election. Its leader, Dmitri Rogozin, emerged from the obscurity of Orthodox movements. Since this victory, the issue of Orthodoxy has been increasingly raised in the Russian Parliament,

---

240 *Mir Religii*, 6th January 2002.

241 Interview with Alexis II, in *Komsomolskaya Pravda*, 24th December 2002.

242 http://www.russian-orthodox-church.org.ru, accessed on 10th January 2002.

243 http://www.strana.ru/print/216416.html, 26th May 2004.

244 Khristiansko-demokraticheskii soiuz Rossii.

245 Khristiansko-demokratitheskaia partia Rossii.

particularly through the voice of Sergei Glazev, former Minister of Economic Affairs, who argues for Orthodox values. In February 2004, at the annual meeting of the World Assembly of the Russian People, Glazev put forward a charter of moral principles and economic rules. This stigmatises corruption and economic criminals under the same heading as privatisation, which it calls "the way of the lie" and "unsuited to the foundations of Orthodox economics"[246]. The Charter was signed by Gennadi Ziuganov, Georgi Poltavchenko (the plenipotentiary representative of the President in the okrug of Central Russia), former Minister of Foreign Affairs Igor Ivanov and Metropolitan Kyril, with whom Ivanov seems to have close links.

The third Duma (1999–2003) witnessed the emergence of a parliamentary grouping of Duma members called "For the maintenance of traditional spiritual and moral values". The grouping comprised 45 members and was led by V. Galchenko from Dmitrovski Okrug (in the Sergev Posad region). The grouping was instigated by the Interfaith Council of Russia. Its aim was to defend the interests of the four traditional religions[247]. The chair of the group, V. Galchenko, who had previously been allied with the National Party (*Narodnaia partia*), chiefly defended Orthodox interests, taking legal action against NGOs which dared to criticise A. Borodina's textbook *Foundations of Orthodox Culture* and the teaching of that culture in state schools.

The most spectacular shift in this area has taken place in the Communist Party. As early as 1996, the Communist leader, Gennadi Ziuganov, who was standing for the presidency, attempted to reach out to the Orthodox electorate. In 1999, he "orthodoxised" certain communist doctrines, particularly through his booklet *Faith and fidelity*. Russian Orthodoxy and the question of the renaissance of Russia, which he distributed in the eparchies before the parliamentary election. In similar vein he published another booklet in 2003, before the next parliamentary election, *Holy Russia and the eternal empire. Foundations of the Russian spiritual renaissance*[248], in which he stressed the need to draw closer to Orthodoxy.

Certain Russian government ministries in particular work quite closely with the Orthodox Church. These are principally the Ministries of the Interior, Defence, Extreme Situations (shtrezvychainykh situatsii) and Justice. The Ministries of Health, Employment, Education and Culture oscillate between a pro-Orthodox position and a refusal to take account of Church opinion. However, since Putin's first term of office, we can see a number of trends in the direction desired by the hierarchy. The Ministry of Culture is increasingly

246 A. Makarkin, "Vsemirnyi russkii narodnyi sobor: tserkov, vlast i biznes", http://www.politcom.ru/20040211/print

247 V. Lukashina, "Odno lobbi na chetyre konfessii", http://www.gazeta.ru, 6th June 2003.

248 Sviataia Rus i koshcheevo tsarstvo. Osnovy russkogo dukhovnogo vozrozhdenia, Rezerv, Moscow, 2003.

working with the Church on problems concerned with the return and rebuilding of Church assets. The Ministry of Education has shown itself to be in favour of the introduction of an optional teaching subject entitled "The foundations of Orthodox culture".

The Ministry of Foreign Affairs also expresses its friendship towards the patriarchate. Former minister Ivanov is a very close friend of Metropolitan Kyril. His administration responded positively in 2002 and 2003 to overtures from the Church not to issue visas to "Vatican spies". In addition, at least 84 people were expelled from Russia at the end of 2003 for religious reasons: 54 Protestants, 15 Muslims, seven Catholics, three Buddhists, three Mormons and two Jehovah's Witnesses[249]. Since May 2003, the Ministry and the Church have been co-operating through a working group.

Within the Ministry of Justice, the Department for the Affairs of Social and Religious Organisations records and monitors all religious activity in Russia. This department has regional branches, which manage matters locally. The Ministry of Justice also has a Council of Religious Expertise (Ekspertnyi Sovet po provedeniiuo religiovedchenskoi ekspertizy) headed by the philosophy professor M. Mchedlov. This council has 34 regional branches.

3c. Challenges of teaching religions

The closeness between the political authorities and the Orthodox hierarchy also extends to education. The other so-called "traditional" religions are once again pushed to the margin. Since the mid-1990s, the Russian Church has wanted to introduce faculties of theology into secular institutes, and a subject called "Foundations of Orthodox culture" (Osnovy pravoslavnoi kultury) into state schools. It also wishes to obtain state funding for its education projects[250].

Priests arrived in schools right at the start of the 1990s, and began wherever possible to teach Zakon Bozhii – a catechism according to rules and textbooks dating from before the 1917 Revolution. In 1994, the Ministry of Education published a decree forbidding this practice as contrary to the Constitution. Since 1997, contrary to the 1994 decision, some regions have been funding courses of Orthodox catechism in secondary schools: Foundations and values of Orthodoxy in Novosibirsk and Smolensk, and History of the Church in Voronezh[251]. In 1999, the patriarch himself asked priests in the provinces to

249 L. Uzzell, "O politike Putina po otnosheniu k religioznym organizatsiam", http://www.religion-sova-center. ru/discussions/18BAA14/18FA5E9/389E1E2?print=on

250 Father Petr Yeremeev, "Gosudarstvennyie teologicheskie obrazovatelnyie standarty i tradytsii dukhovnogo obrazovania", http://www.russian-orthodox-church.org.ru, 20th April 2002.

251 Interview with N. Mitrokhin, 22nd October 2004, Moscow.

introduce teaching of the foundations of Orthodoxy in all regions of Russia. This decision was not discussed or co-ordinated with the central or local authorities. It appears to be a Church initiative alone. One year later, 35 regions have signed agreements on this teaching. It is only now that the patriarch has spoken officially about this education to the federal authorities. On 1st July 1999, a Co-ordination Council was set up between the Ministry of Education and the patriarchate. On the Church side, it is headed by Metropolitan Sergei (Fomin) of Solnechnogorsk. On 4th July 1999, the Ministry agreed to open the doors of schools to religious organisations for optional teaching. In 2002, the Church celebrated a major success in the field of education – the introduction of a national higher curriculum in "Theology".

The tenth conference on the "Education system of Russian Schools" held in Moscow from 25th to 29th March 2003[252], issued statements that Orthodox education was the patriotic education best suited to resolving the difficult issue of post-communist identity. A few months before the conference, in October 2002, the Minister of Education, V. Filipov, sent all regional education departments a circular on methods of introducing the teaching of the Foundations, causing the Muslims (the Russian Council of Muftis) to send letters of protest to the Ministry. The authorities in the former Republic of Tatarstan responded to this initiative by a provocative statement that they were introducing courses in Islam and Judaism[253]. Despite these protests, further agreements between the Orthodox hierarchy and the authorities were signed in the regions. The Foundations began to be introduced more widely[254]. Each local authority resolved the problem in its own best interests. Some regions have, for instance, introduced courses in theology rather than the Foundations, while others have made them compulsory.

At the same time, it is true, school heads and parents have protested against the Foundations of Orthodox Culture. This happened in Moscow and Saint Petersburg, where only one of the 703 schools in the city was in favour of Orthodox teaching[255]. The complexity of the situation eventually obliged President Putin to launch a national debate on 9th February 2004. This is still continuing, against a background of the issuing of refusals to Muslims, who have, for example, been applying since 2002 to build a Muslim university in Moscow[256]. According to what we were told by a city official, the City of Moscow has no need of such a university for a variety of reasons, but the

---

252 Russkaia shkola kak sistema obrazovania i vospitania, http://www.newsru.com. 26th March 2003

253 http://www.rosbalt.ru, 21st February 2003.

254 Particularly in Ekaterinburg, *Pravoslavnaia Gazeta*, 16th September 2003; http://www.newlife.kz, 5th February 2003 on the situation in Samara, Interfaks of 26th March 2003, etc.

255 http://www.rosbalt.ru, 18th September 2003.

256 Information available at http://www.state-religion.ru, accessed on 6th June 2002.

principal arguments are the "Russianness" of the city, and the danger of interfaith conflicts and the propagation of Islamist ideas in the capital[257].

In 2000, 7% of Russians thought that it was important to bring up children to believe in God; in 2006, the figure was 12%[258].

4. Local and regional dimension of religious conflicts

The field of co-operation between the state and religion in thus quite extensive in present-day Russia. These contacts and relationships of dependency, described in general terms here, play a particularly important role in the situations to which we shall now allude. Taking into consideration the scale of the topic, we shall concentrate on the registration difficulties experienced by religious communities, on supervision of them, on problems relating to the building and rebuilding of religious premises, and on "religious" education in state schools.

4a. Ban on registration

In Tiumen Region, the Commission for Religious Affairs decided in February 2004 to strengthen supervision of all religious organisations. The Governor, Sergei Sarychev, declared that he would take personal charge of this process. The region's representative of the Ministry of Justice upheld the registration of 214 religious organisations. At the same time, she stated that nine others were to be dissolved. We still do not know which were in fact dissolved, or why. This demonstrates the power of the authorities and the control that they exert in matters of this kind. We can only suppose that the organisations were those "persecuted" elsewhere: the Salvation Army, Jehovah's Witnesses, the Pentecostalists, etc.

In Novgorod, the representatives of the Ministry of Justice have set about dissolving the Salvation Army, which is recognised as a religious organisation in Russia. In April 2005, officials began regularly inspecting the premises and the activities of the organisation, noting irregularities on every visit. On 25th April 2005, they noted that there was no board in the organisation's main room setting out the name of the organisation in full. On 29th September 2005, the Novgorod Region public prosecutor's office requested complete lists of the members of the organisation. On 19th October 2005, the organisation

257   These arguments are general but are repeated by the Ministries concerned with education, justice and the interior. May be consulted at http://www.state-religion.ru, accessed on 29th August 2002.

258   http://www.levada.ru/press/2006070301.html

was accused of infringing point 5 of the 1997 law relating to participation by children in religious activities. According to members of the organisation, these were their own children, whose parents consented to their religious activities. This was not taken into account. The representatives of the registration service asked for a change in the organisation's statutes on 16ᵗʰ November to bring them into line with the statutes of non-profit organisations. The Salvation Army complied and, in accordance with procedure, submitted the new statutes for re-registration. Registration was refused three times in a row. The state authorities then asked the courts to dissolve the organisation[259]. The proceedings for dissolving the Salvation Army in Novgorod have been under way since 9ᵗʰ June 2006.

The Salvation Army has also been under attack since 1999 in Moscow. The approach has been the same. Following complaints from officials about its statutes, the organisation changed them and, from 2000, unsuccessfully made further attempts to register. The deadline for registration, the end of January 2001, passed. On each occasion, the courts of the City of Moscow refused registration. Currently, the organisation is attempting to defend its rights in the Court of Human Rights in Strasbourg.

In the okrug of Khanty-Mansiysk, north of Tiumen, the authorities do not wish to register the Greek Catholic communities. In this region there are many Ukrainian immigrants, who have been trying to establish a religious life for themselves since 1998. This is the Russian region with the second highest number of Greek Catholics, after Kemerovo. Administratively, they belong to the Catholic diocese of Western Siberia. In Surguts, and in Nizhnevartovsk, it has been impossible to register these communities, attempts having met with dozens of refusals, officially for "lack of documents". However, neither the officials nor the religious leaders know what the list of documents is. In the municipality of Surguts, Tamara Gurenkova is a Greek Catholic and an adviser on religious questions. Protoerei Georgii Beznurtov, who is responsible for the parishes in the Nizhnevartovsk Region on behalf of the Moscow patriarchate, is particularly active with the authorities in preventing the registration of the Greek Catholics. He follows the official policy of the patriarchate, which regularly accuses the Catholics of proselytising. One of the representatives of the government of the City of Surguts has publicly stated that the presence of the Uniates is undesirable and will lead to conflicts between the local authorities and Orthodox and other Christians. This has already happened to the Pentecostalists in this region[260]. Paradoxically, it is the Pentecostalists who have opened their house of worship to the Greek Catholics.

---

259 http://religion.sova-center.ru/events/13B742E/14349FC/766BE44

260 R.Lukin, http://www.portal-credo.ru, http://portal-credo.ru/site/print.php?act=news&id=39036.

Registration problems are the visible tip of the difficulties faced by local authorities in managing the different religious communities. Frequently, since 2004-2005, we have witnessed deliberate attacks on religious leaders and communities seen as a nuisance. During the celebration of Easter in April 2006, for example, more than 300 Pentecostalists who had gathered for a service in the village of Spass Tashtagolskii in Kemerovo Region, in a room in a cultural centre rented from the municipality, were beaten up by a gang of 20 to 25-year-olds. The police were called, came and examined the damage, but did not arrest anyone. The local court did not pursue the complaint lodged by the Pentecostalists. They therefore approached the public prosecutor's office for Kemerovo Region and also appealed to the Governor, Aman Tuleev. During a hearing, the Orthodox specialist, Alexander Dvorkin[261], gave expert testimony that the Pentecostalists did not comprise a Church, but were a sect[262]. The matter was not followed up.

The struggle against "sects" very often unites the authorities and the Orthodox hierarchy. A conference held in Siberia on 10-13rd January 1999, with close co-operation from the Orthodox Church, stressed the need for urgent State aid in combating sects. The participants stated that they were insulted by attempts by the Krishna Society to conduct a dialogue with the Church as if between equals. The best solution seemed, to the conference participants, to be the creation of an interfaith commission of experts, without whose support it should be impossible to register any group. The final document was signed not only by religious representatives but also by members of the government administration in Altaiskii Krai, and by representatives of the FSB and the MVD (the Ministry of the Interior) in the region. This practice once again confirms the interdependence of political and religious bodies.

4b. Economic and financial interests

This also applies in the financial sphere. The Russian Orthodox Church is highly dependent on the national and local authorities in this area. The other faiths cannot count on any help of this nature. However, data on Church finances are generally kept secret[263]. The patriarch merely provides information at councils of archbishops on the overall position of the Church without giving exact figures. The large-scale rebuilding of churches almost everywhere in Russia makes such calculations even more complex. These

---

261 Author of a number of publications about sects in Russia, and textbooks on Sektovvedenie – an introduction to sects. Professor of Church history at the Orthodox University and the Theological Institute of St. Tikhon.

262 http://www.portal-credo.ru/site/print.php?act=authority&id=508

263 See on this topic the publications by N. Mitrokhin, "Ekonomika Russkoi Pravoslavnoi Tserkvi", *Otechestvennyie zapiski*, No 1, 2001, pp. 144-155; "Tserkovnyie myshi, ikh zakroma i kryshi", *Ogonek*, No 24, 2000, pp. 20-23, "Korporatsia Tserkov", *Moskovskie Novosti*, No 25, 2000, pp. 10-11, etc.

are major investments, which are seen as having priority over every other obligation. There are huge disparities between parishes and dioceses. The current finances of the Church are part of a peculiar economic landscape typified by illegal dealings, corruption and large amounts of liquid capital[264]. During the communist era, the Church "owned" three industrial enterprises. The best known, Sofrino, produced a whole range of goods needed by the Church for Church services, while the other two, in Irkutsk and Tashkent, exclusively produced candles. At the present time, there are numerous Church enterprises in practically every diocese.

Orthodox production and the economic activities of parishes and the Patriarchate raise acute questions about Church taxation. The tax system in Russia as a whole is not yet stabilised[265]. The Church says that these activities are a special case of a socio-economic relationship[266] and that it should therefore not pay taxes. In practice, throughout the 1990s, the Church paid no tax in respect of its religious activities. It should have done so in respect of any activity classified as non-religious. The new version of the Tax Code, which took effect on 1st January 2002, introduced tax at a rate of 24% on all the profits of every corporate body. The religious organisations have succeeded in avoiding this obligation[267]. Discussions on the Tax Code and the Real Property Code (Zemelnyi Kodeks, to take effect from 1st January 2005) have centred on the question of the taxation of Church assets. The patriarch has again been able to avoid all tax. However, the new code allows entrepreneurs to lease premises "belonging" to the Church but not so far bought by it. This is possible even at sites where historic monuments are located. Thus, if the Church declines to pay the lease at the official tariff or to buy "its" land, it can be deprived of "its property"[268]. The Church hierarchy took fright at this and started negotiating with the authorities with the aim of postponing introduction of the code until 1st January 2006. On that date, full implementation of the code was again postponed. In addition, the Church does not pay for any local services such as water or electricity, or in some cases receives large rebates.

At the same time, the Church was embroiled throughout the 1990s in a

---

264 K. Yacheistov, "Rossiiskuiu glubinku nanesut na plastikovuiu kartu", *Kommersant*, 4th March 2004, p. 20; L. Koval, B. Safonov, "5 milliardov $ iz-pod matrasov vytashchili Rossiianie v proshlom godu", *Vedomosti*, 12th March 2004, p. A 6 and the World Bank reports, Gallup International reports, etc.

265 Author's interview with the authors of the current taxation programme, Mr Vladimir Frolov, manager of the Severnaia Kazna Bank, 28th October 2004, Ekaterinburg.

266 *Osnovy sotsialnoi kontseptsii RPC*, Sbornik dokumentov i materialov Iubileinogo Arkhiereiskogo Sobora Russkoi Pravoslavnoi Tserkvi, Moscow, 13-16th August 2000, p. 204.

267 "Vopros nalogooblozheniia religioznykh organizatsii rassmotren Gosudarstvennoi Dumoi, http://www. russian-orthodox-church.org.ru, 21st April 2002.

268 Prava religioznykh organizatsii na zemliu: voprosy i otvety, *Radonezh*, No 4, 2003.

significant number of financial scandals. Under the cover of Sofrino, and even synodal and patriarchal bodies, the Church imports alcohol, tobacco, a range of other goods and even smuggled gold[269]. It has also exported oil, up to 8% of Russian oil exports. It has taken part in the export of Iraqi oil. Some senior churchmen, such as the influential Metropolitan Kyril, have earned money from the export of rare fish from the seas of northern Russia.

The rebuilding of churches is one of the financial problems of the Russian Orthodox Church. It is probable (we cannot obtain reliable data) that no Orthodox church has been rebuilt using funds collected or earned by the parish. Instead, every rebuilding attracts a number of "benefactors". Most of the time, these are local authorities such as the Penza oblast, where the Governor in person, V. Bochkarev, helped with the rebuilding of the church in the village of Iva[270]. Obviously, the rebuilding that has received the greatest media coverage is that of the Cathedral of Christ the Saviour in Moscow[271]. The Moscow City Government and a number of businesspeople played a part in this. In 1994, with the support of the patriarch and President Yeltsin, Mayor Yuri Luzhkov took the decision to rebuild it[272]. The work was completed in 2000, and the official opening took place in October. By virtue of its location, form and "national" symbolic value, the cathedral is physical testimony to Orthodoxy's presence in public life[273]. The cost of rebuilding, and the procedure itself, have given rise to much argument. The budget for the reconstruction was put at 250 million, and then at 500 million dollars. We do not know what the final total really is[274]. At all events, the figures are huge. They exceed the annual cost of running schools and hospitals[275]. There is talk of large sums coming from private connections of the Mayor of Moscow. Luzhkov is said to have offered companies contributing to the rebuilding major investment opportunities and markets in the capital. The Stolichnyi Bank offered 50 kg of gold for the cupola, thereby attracting all the bank accounts of the patriarchate. The Russian Government for its part spent almost 12 million dollars buying the icons that are currently in the Cathedral. This gift by Viktor Chernomyrdin remained secret for a long time, until the Duma asked for clarification of public spending. It became apparent that the

---

269 N. Mitrokhin, *Russkaia...*, op. cit., p. 164.

270 Filaret, Bishop of Penza and Kuznetsk, "Bez vozrozhdeniia vnutrennei zhizni cheloveka nelzia govorit ob obustroistve Rossii", Interfaks, 10th November 2003.

271 Built in 1883 under Nicholas I and blown up by Stalin in 1931.

272 The rebuilding project was submitted in 1993, covering around a hundred Moscow churches. Nearly 70 billion rubles were allocated to the project. I. Frolova, "Moscow churches will be restored", *Moscow News*, 24th January 1994, p.12.

273 E. Tsivileva, "Vostanovlenie sviatyni zaversheno", *Nezavisimaia gazeta*, 6th October 2000, p.2.

274 D. N. Jensen, "The Boss: How Yuri Luzhkov Runs Moscow", *Demokratizatsiya*, January 2000, vol 8.

275 Opinion of the Vice President of the State Property Committee, Alfred Kokh, quoted by K. Frilend, "Khram Khrista Spasitelia stanovitsia simvolom rossiskogo kapitalizma", *Finansovyie izvestia*, 29th August 1995, p. 8.

patriarchate did not have up to date accounts, that the money came from a variety of sources, and that funds could not be identified. The symbol of the renaissance of Russian Orthodoxy has thus become the symbol of dishonest, opaque dealings, and above all the symbol of the power of Luzhkov and the patriarchate[276].

The role of Russian businesspeople in the rebuilding of churches and monasteries is gradually becoming known. We naturally have very few documents on this matter, only what journalists have succeeded in uncovering. However, we were ourselves able to interview the Managing Director of UMMC Holding, Vladimir Beloglazov, in Verkhnia Pyshna, near Ekaterinburg. He told us that 15% of group profits went to the local Orthodox Church. Thanks to this money, the diocese of Ekaterinburg has been able to rebuild around 10 churches, to fund an Orthodox cultural centre, and to finance the rebuilding of monasteries in the region, notably the Monastery of Gonninaia Yama, the place where the last Tsar and his family are buried in the Forest of Ekaterinburg. The symbolic importance of this site, and therefore of UMMC Holding, needs little emphasis. Since the reconstruction, the principal politicians in the country have been there, accompanied by the local Orthodox bishop and the directors of the holding company.

The other faiths have much greater difficulties. The Muslims have been refused building permits for mosques in the capital and other cities, notably Sergiev Posad. Metropolitan Kyril appears to regard these decisions by the authorities as legitimate by stressing "the real problem of branches of non-traditional Islam in Russia, which clearly aims at a violent change in the historical destiny of the country"[277]. The same problem is faced by the Buddhists, who were not allowed to start building their temple in Moscow until 2000. This unfinished building project has been greeted with protests from Orthodox quarters, and it has been surrounded by scandals and disputes between the different Buddhist communities.

Conclusion

A conference on the theme of religious freedom in the context of Church-State relations was held in Strasbourg on 10-11th December 2001, chaired by the European Commissioner for Human Rights, Alvaro Gil Robles. It was

---

276 M. Ivanov, "1931: Razed and 2000: Raised", *Russian Life*, No 43, April 2000, p. 18; L. McGann, "The Russian Orthodox Church under Patriarch Alexis II and the Russian State: An Unholy Alliance?", *Demokratizatsiya*, vol 7, January 1999.

277 Interview in the Macedonian newspaper *Premin*, No 5, September-October 2001; "Pravoslavie pered litsom stikhi mira", some arguments are taken up again in the interview "Tserkov i vneshnii mir", *Trud*, 20th November 2001.

attended by politicians and religious leaders from fourteen countries, among them Nikolas Balashov, Secretary of the Department of External Affairs of the patriarchate of Moscow. According to the Russian delegate, the declared secularity of the State and the separation between politics and religion in no way prevented preferential links or support for socially significant initiatives to support one Church in particular. Balashov cited a number of criteria giving legitimacy to this state of affairs. He also said that he was in favour of religious education, and of the material support that the state needed to give the Church. The head of the Department of Social Relations and Humanitarian Policy in the Presidential Administration, Andrei Protopopov, emphasised at this meeting the closeness of view between the Russian Orthodox Church and the State.

The examples that we have given in this study testify in fact to the special nature of the relationship between politics and religion in present-day Russia. It is evident that Moscow Orthodoxy is given preferential treatment at national and local level. However, we would argue that the processes linking it with the authorities reveal dangerous trends, which are hidden beneath claims of a special case. They can best be summed up in the result of a survey. In August 2006, 54%[278] of Russians agreed in a survey by the Levada Centre that Russia should only be for Russians. Given the growing rapprochement between ethnicity, politics and religion, we regard this figure as significant.

---

278 http://www.levada.ru/press/2006082500.html, survey of 1,600 people at 128 study points across Russia. Margin of error not exceeding 3%.

Conclusion

Twelve Principles of Intercultural and Interreligious Dialogue for the Local authorities

Draft prepared by the Secretariat on the basis of contributions presented at Montchanin Conference

The importance of the principles which must govern the conduct of intercultural and interfaith dialogue is commensurate with the implications of growing cultural and religious pluralism at international, national and local levels.

These principles espouse, as a basis for discussion and action, the approach proposed by the Council of Europe in the consultation process for the White Paper on Intercultural Dialogue:

"Intercultural dialogue is an open and respectful exchange of views between individuals and groups belonging to different cultures that leads to a deeper understanding of the other's global perception."

Local authorities are invited to adopt the Council of Europe's fundamental principles in an important area with a major impact on **social cohesion**:

- cultural diversity is an economic, social and political asset that needs to be taken into account and whose potential must be exploited if it is to bear full fruit;

- intercultural dialogue is based on respect for human rights, democracy and the rule of law. It reflects the most ancient and most fundamental form of democratic exchange. It is an antidote to rejection and violence.

Dialogue is a means of securing joint action, but it is also, and above all, a value in itself. It is synonymous with the sharing of truths, conciliation and **reconciliation**, and its participants are taking part in an active peace process. Because it represents an opening up to others, based on their shared humanity, it makes it possible to put forward new ideas based on solidarity and collective action.

Interfaith dialogue has become a central element of this intercultural dialogue. The social manifestations of belief and the impact of religious organisations extend beyond the purely private sphere and are becoming increasingly visible aspects of the public domain.

Political authorities must therefore pay close attention to their links with religious organisations and to the relationships, including conflicts, between different confessions themselves. Dialogue is a **practical means** of condemning intolerance and discrimination, particularly those based on ethnic origin and religion, and is in itself a tool for managing diversity.

Local communities are a particularly suitable focus for political representatives to initiate and develop intercultural and interfaith dialogue, as a means of defining what is in that community's general interest and securing agreement on what its members have in common and their shared hopes for the future. **Local authorities** are invited to develop their activities in four related areas:

- Knowledge and understanding of the local religious situation;
- Promoting understanding between participants in the dialogue;
- Establishing partnerships;
- Evaluation.

Knowledge and understanding of the local religious situation

1 - Local authorities are invited to note the growing role that religion is now playing in **the construction of individual and collective identities**, and its impact on socialisation and the formation of social representations, and on many of their citizens' view of the world. Religion is the expression and result of a system of beliefs passed down from generation to generation and of loyalty to a tradition. It helps to mould people's way of thinking and establishes values and rules of conduct.

2 - These authorities must have a good **knowledge** of the relative size of local religious groups and how they are organised. They must be seen to be aware that through their teaching and training and the services they offer, the activities of local religious organisations are of real benefit to the public. They offer their members a sense of meaning and help to create social relationships, and as such are fully fledged participants in local society. Awareness of the place and role of ethnic and/or religious minorities might usefully be accompanied by an equal awareness of the latent authority exercised by the **majority**, who generally has a quasi-monopoly of local levers of power. Such an approach will help to prevent minorities being pushed, against their better judgment, into defensive postures. Particular attention will be paid to the role of families, and especially of mothers, who help to transmit their cultural values to the next generation, in an attitude of openness to society.

3 - Religious organisations should be considered not as homogeneous entities but as organisations that are themselves the subject of sometimes **conflicting views**. Local authorities' decision as to which interlocutors will be open to dialogue while at the same in a position to influence their own community is therefore critical, for both the present and future.

Promoting understanding between participants in the dialogue

4 - Local authorities must contribute to the process of **discovering other cultures**, by observing cultural similarities **and** differences, understanding those whose outlook is different and at variance with local custom and practice and disseminating and sharing this information. They can do so by encouraging the teaching of the full range of religious knowledge, with a view to developing cultural knowledge and not religious practices. Such education, provided both at school and through civic religious study centres, will be a key factor in fostering greater openness and a quest for knowledge. Openness to others may also awaken a desire for a better understanding of one's own faith or one's own personal and social values, thus helping through greater cultural awareness to reduce the risk of radicalisation. This action will be guided by a desire to create conditions for equality between women and men and to ensure that these come into play.

5 - Local authorities must identify **opportune moments** for developing mutual knowledge and person to person contacts and for reducing feelings of mistrust, and even fear. The aim should be a steady progression from ignorance to knowledge, from knowledge to understanding and from understanding to confidence. Relevant activities might include visits to different places of worship or the establishment of an annual intercultural or interfaith forum or festival. This could be accompanied by the institution of a council for intercultural and interfaith relations, as a focus for multilateral exchanges of view.

Establishing partnerships

6 - Local authorities are in the **front line** and their active presence on the ground, their familiarity with all those concerned and their capacity for innovation gives them a leading and fully **legitimate** role in relation to religious activities. Their discussions and activities must be guided by a concern for openness, innovation and experimentation.

7 - Local authorities' role in promoting dialogue and establishing partnerships will be more effective and valid in the long term if certain **conditions are met from the outset**:

• respect for legality;

• promotion of equality between women and men;

• religious neutrality and non-discrimination;

• transparency in all their activities.

8 - Local authorities should not become directly involved in the conduct of interfaith dialogue. The principles of subsidiarity and religious autonomy should be bars to official sponsorship or organisation of such dialogue. The official stance should be one of **non-indifference** and **non-interference**. Local authorities' role is essentially that of facilitators, mediators or, if necessary, regulators, on the basis of clearly defined and negotiated objectives. From their standpoint, namely that of studied neutrality, interfaith dialogue is in fact based on reason rather than faith, knowledge rather than belief.

9 - By emphasising the notions of recognition and confidence, local authorities can ensure that religions are seen not as a problem but as a **resource**, through the adoption of a positive attitude to the democratic management of pluralism. Their activities should be geared to two objectives: establishing a more **coherent organisational** structure for local religious confessions and strengthening **social cohesion**. The bodies and partners involved in the dialogue should not step outside their own specific roles, and should treat the dialogue first and foremost as a shared asset that needs to be encouraged.

10 - Activities such as building or managing places of worship should be designed to promote balance and harmony and should encourage greater openness and not ghettoisation. This means that an **interfaith approach** must gradually take precedence over a multifaith one. Local authority activities should be guided by a concern to promote a shared belief in a God with many faces.

11 - Local authorities' concern with religious diversity and interfaith dialogue needs to be reflected in concrete terms in local social, sports, education, town planning and cultural policies and in their relations with local associations, thus giving it a **transversal dimension**. As such it must influence and inform all fields of activity rather than constituting a specific area. If all those concerned are willing to listen to each other, it will be possible to achieve what the Canadians call a "**reasonable accommodation**", which means offering confessions the maximum opportunity to express their religious beliefs, so long as this does not conflict with other fundamental rights.

Evaluation

12 – In consultation with local religious organisations, local authorities should determine in advance, what <u>criteria and indicators</u> they should use to assess the effectiveness of their intercultural and interfaith dialogue. These might include the development of their own expertise and the establishment of networks for exchanges between faiths or of training and information centres. They should also enter into contact with representatives of other local authorities to compare and contrast their different arrangements in order to develop their own particular approach.

Sales agents for publications of the Council of Europe

BELGIUM/BELGIQUE
La Librairie Européenne -
The European Bookshop
Rue de l'Orme, 1
B-1040 BRUXELLES
Tel.: +32 (0)2 231 04 35
Fax: +32 (0)2 735 08 60
E-mail: order@libeurop.be
http://www.libeurop.be

Jean De Lannoy
Avenue du Roi 202 Koningslaan
B-1190 BRUXELLES
Tel.: +32 (0)2 538 43 08
Fax: +32 (0)2 538 08 41
E-mail: jean.de.lannoy@dl-servi.com
http://www.jean-de-lannoy.be

CANADA
Renouf Publishing Co. Ltd.
1-5369 Canotek Road
OTTAWA, Ontario K1J 9J3, Canada
Tel.: +1 613 745 2665
Fax: +1 613 745 7660
Toll-Free Tel.: (866) 767-6766
E-mail: order.dept@renoufbooks.com
http://www.renoufbooks.com

CZECH REPUBLIC/
RÉPUBLIQUE TCHÈQUE
Suweco CZ, s.r.o.
Klecakova 347
CZ-180 21 PRAHA 9
Tel.: +420 2 424 59 204
Fax: +420 2 848 21 646
E-mail: import@suweco.cz
http://www.suweco.cz

DENMARK/DANEMARK
GAD
Vimmelskaftet 32
DK-1161 KØBENHAVN K
Tel.: +45 77 66 60 00
Fax: +45 77 66 60 01
E-mail: gad@gad.dk
http://www.gad.dk

FINLAND/FINLANDE
Akateeminen Kirjakauppa
PO Box 128
Keskuskatu 1
FIN-00100 HELSINKI
Tel.: +358 (0)9 121 4430
Fax: +358 (0)9 121 4242
E-mail: akatilaus@akateeminen.com
http://www.akateeminen.com

FRANCE
La Documentation française
(diffusion/distribution France entière)
124, rue Henri Barbusse
F-93308 AUBERVILLIERS CEDEX
Tél.: +33 (0)1 40 15 70 00
Fax: +33 (0)1 40 15 68 00
E-mail: commande@ladocumentationfrancaise.fr
http://www.ladocumentationfrancaise.fr

Librairie Kléber
1 rue des Francs Bourgeois
F-67000 STRASBOURG
Tel.: +33 (0)3 88 15 78 88
Fax: +33 (0)3 88 15 78 80
E-mail: francois.wolfermann@librairie-kleber.fr
http://www.librairie-kleber.com

GERMANY/ALLEMAGNE
AUSTRIA/AUTRICHE
UNO Verlag GmbH
August-Bebel-Allee 6
D-53175 BONN
Tel.: +49 (0)228 94 90 20
Fax: +49 (0)228 94 90 222
E-mail: bestellung@uno-verlag.de
http://www.uno-verlag.de

GREECE/GRÈCE
Librairie Kauffmann s.a.
Stadiou 28
GR-105 64 ATHINAI
Tel.: +30 210 32 55 321
Fax.: +30 210 32 30 320
E-mail: ord@otenet.gr
http://www.kauffmann.gr

HUNGARY/HONGRIE
Euro Info Service kft.
1137 Bp. Szent István krt. 12.
H-1137 BUDAPEST
Tel.: +36 (06)1 329 2170
Fax: +36 (06)1 349 2053
E-mail: euroinfo@euroinfo.hu
http://www.euroinfo.hu

ITALY/ITALIE
Licosa SpA
Via Duca di Calabria, 1/1
I-50125 FIRENZE
Tel.: +39 0556 483215
Fax: +39 0556 41257
E-mail: licosa@licosa.com
http://www.licosa.com

MEXICO/MEXIQUE
Mundi-Prensa México, S.A. De C.V.
Río Pánuco, 141 Delegacíon Cuauhtémoc
06500 MÉXICO, D.F.
Tel.: +52 (01)55 55 33 56 58
Fax: +52 (01)55 55 14 67 99
E-mail: mundiprensa@mundiprensa.com.mx
http://www.mundiprensa.com.mx

NETHERLANDS/PAYS-BAS
De Lindeboom Internationale Publicaties b.v.
M.A. de Ruyterstraat 20 A
NL-7482 BZ HAAKSBERGEN
Tel.: +31 (0)53 5740004
Fax: +31 (0)53 5729296
E-mail: books@delindeboom.com
http://www.delindeboom.com

NORWAY/NORVÈGE
Akademika
Postboks 84 Blindern
N-0314 OSLO
Tel.: +47 2 218 8100
Fax: +47 2 218 8103
E-mail: support@akademika.no
http://www.akademika.no

POLAND/POLOGNE
Ars Polona JSC
25 Obroncow Street
PL-03-933 WARSZAWA
Tel.: +48 (0)22 509 86 00
Fax: +48 (0)22 509 86 10
E-mail: arspolona@arspolona.com.pl
http://www.arspolona.com.pl

PORTUGAL
Livraria Portugal
(Dias & Andrade, Lda.)
Rua do Carmo, 70
P-1200-094 LISBOA
Tel.: +351 21 347 42 82 / 85
Fax: +351 21 347 02 64
E-mail: info@livrariaportugal.pt
http://www.livrariaportugal.pt

RUSSIAN FEDERATION/
FÉDÉRATION DE RUSSIE
Ves Mir
9a, Kolpacnhyi per.
RU-101000 MOSCOW
Tel.: +7 (8)495 623 6839
Fax: +7 (8)495 625 4269
E-mail: orders@vesmirbooks.ru
http://www.vesmirbooks.ru

SPAIN/ESPAGNE
Mundi-Prensa Libros, s.a.
Castelló, 37
E-28001 MADRID
Tel.: +34 914 36 37 00
Fax: +34 915 75 39 98
E-mail: libreria@mundiprensa.es
http://www.mundiprensa.com

SWITZERLAND/SUISSE
Van Diermen Editions – ADECO
Chemin du Lacuez 41
CH-1807 BLONAY
Tel.: +41 (0)21 943 26 73
Fax: +41 (0)21 943 36 05
E-mail: info@adeco.org
http://www.adeco.org

UNITED KINGDOM/ROYAUME-UNI
The Stationery Office Ltd
PO Box 29
GB-NORWICH NR3 1GN
Tel.: +44 (0)870 600 5522
Fax: +44 (0)870 600 5533
E-mail: book.enquiries@tso.co.uk
http://www.tsoshop.co.uk

UNITED STATES and CANADA/
ÉTATS-UNIS et CANADA
Manhattan Publishing Company
468 Albany Post Road
CROTTON-ON-HUDSON, NY 10520, USA
Tel.: +1 914 271 5194
Fax: +1 914 271 5856
E-mail: Info@manhattanpublishing.com
http://www.manhattanpublishing.com

Council of Europe Publishing/Editions du Conseil de l'Europe
F-67075 Strasbourg Cedex
Tel.: +33 (0)3 88 41 25 81 – Fax: +33 (0)3 88 41 39 10 – E-mail: publishing@coe.int – Website: http://book.coe.int